DIBELS

Dynamic Indicators of Basic Early Literacy Skills

THE

PRACTICAL

MANUAL

Answers to Questions About
Administering, Scoring, and
Interpreting DIBELS

Linda Farrell, MBA

Carrie Hancock, PhD

Susan Smartt, PhD

foreword by Dr. Louisa Cook Moats

SOPRIS WEST EDUCATIONAL SERVICES
A CAMBIUM LEARNING COMPANY

BOSTON, MA • NEW YORK, NY • LONGMONT, CO

ISBN 1-59318-496-4

DIBELS is a registered trademark of Sopris West Educational Services

Printed in the United States of America

Published and Distributed by

SOPRIS
WEST™
EDUCATIONAL SERVICES
A Cambium Learning™ Company

4093 Specialty Place • Longmont, Colorado 80504
(303) 651-2829 • www.sopriswest.com

262PRACGD/8-05

To my mother, who encourages me in every way to pursue my passions.
—Linda Farrell

*To my professors, mentors, and colleagues (past and present) at the
University of Oregon, who continue to provide me with professional
guidance, support, and inspiration.*
—Carrie Hancock

To my husband, who is my best friend.
—Susan Smartt

ABOUT THE AUTHORS

Linda Farrell developed the Scoring and Administration Workshop used by Sopris West DIBELS trainers and many other DIBELS trainers around the country. She also offers three DIBELS-related workshops, *Understanding DIBELS Scores, Grouping Children,* and *Planning and Delivering Intervention Lessons and Informal Assessment to Supplement DIBELS,* which she presents nationally. Linda obtained her practical classroom experience as an English teacher and a middle school reading teacher, positions that sometimes frustrated her because she didn't know how to teach her students who were struggling readers. She left teaching and worked as a bank executive and investment banker for 20 years. Linda finally learned to teach struggling readers when she volunteered to teach adults to read. Although she cherishes her time spent with the scores of adults she tutored during her 12 years as a volunteer with the Washington Literacy Council, Linda's fervent wish is to eliminate the need for adult literacy organizations by ensuring that all children learn to read in early elementary school. Linda is the founder and director of Accent on Reading, LLC, based in Alexandria, Virginia. Accent on Reading offers workshops for early literacy skills, conducts a summer reading program in the Washington, D.C., area, and develops and markets multisensory materials for reading instruction. Linda is both a DIBELS trainer and a national LETRS trainer for Sopris West. She consults with many schools, districts, and states on literacy issues. She has written phonological awareness, phonics, and spelling curricula for private corporations and state departments of education.

Carrie Hancock, Ph.D., is Education Program Director for the Arizona Department of Education. Carrie is a 2002 graduate of the University of Oregon School Psychology program, in which she worked closely with Drs. Roland Good and Ruth Kaminski in training education professionals to use DIBELS. While a student at the University of Oregon, she also assisted in the development and revision of DIBELS measures. Carrie has conducted training sessions in numerous states focused on implementing DIBELS within a data-based decision-making model. She was a school psychologist for the Kyrene School District in Tempe, Arizona, from 2002 to 2003, during which time she coordinated and implemented a schoolwide DIBELS benchmark assessment and progress monitoring program for students in grades K–5. Currently, she is the director of K–3 reading assessment for the state of Arizona. One of Carrie's responsibilities is to develop and deliver statewide DIBELS training sessions. These sessions include overviews and address administration and scoring, report interpretation and use, and data-based decision making at all levels (state, district, school, teacher, and student). Carrie has considerable experience training state employees, regional reading specialists, district administrators, principals, and K–8 teachers.

Susan M. Smartt, Ph.D., served as a member of the U.S. Department of Education Reading First Review Panel. She has worked as a classroom teacher, reading specialist and tutor, school psychologist, teacher trainer, and consultant to numerous state departments of education and local education agencies. She worked on the professional staff of the Child Study Center of the John F. Kennedy Center at Vanderbilt University's Peabody College. Dr. Smartt was principal and later director of education at the Vanderbilt Child and Adolescent Psychiatric Hospital at the Vanderbilt University Medical Center. She has coauthored articles in national professional publications that focus on early literacy intervention. For the past 18 years, she has co-owned and directed a reading clinic, Smartt, Johnson and Associates, concentrating primarily on dyslexia, speech and language disorders, and related learning difficulties. Dr. Smartt is past president of the Tennessee Branch of the International Dyslexia Association. She is a nationally certified LETRS and DIBELS trainer and provides workshops throughout the country.

ACKNOWLEDGMENTS

Dr. Roland Good and Dr. Ruth Kaminski developed DIBELS. By doing so, they gave educators an efficient, useful, research-based early reading assessment that identifies those students who need extra instruction in order to be proficient readers. These pioneers have provided us with a vital step toward ensuring that every child receives appropriate reading instruction. We are in great debt to them for carefully reviewing drafts of this book and providing us with insight and comments.

Dr. Louisa Cook Moats has been relentless in her efforts to inform educators about the importance of reading instruction that includes methods based on scientific research. Many teachers, reading coaches, administrators, reading experts, and curriculum designers have been influenced by her workshops and her writings.

Dr. Reid Lyon has expended herculean efforts conducting and encouraging research that shows us the most effective ways to assess reading skills and teach children to read. His efforts also encompass countless speeches, dinners, and meetings at which he spreads the word about scientifically based ways to teach reading.

Dr. Susan Long Hall has worked tirelessly with schools, districts, and states to help them organize DIBELS screening for all children with the DIBELS program and understand what the DIBELS data mean.

Many talented and energetic teachers have attended our workshops and let us into their classrooms. They gave us the benefit of their experience with DIBELS, including administering assessments and using the data to plan intervention lessons. We thank the committed teachers from all over the country who are using DIBELS as the first step toward achieving the goal of every child reading.

CONTENTS

LIST OF ILLUSTRATIONS & TABLES

15 Retell Fluency (RTF)

16 Word Use Fluency (WUF)

FOREWORD

As I travel the country, I work with many enthusiastic users of DIBELS who are excited about the power of this innovative assessment from the University of Oregon. With DIBELS, educators can focus resources on prevention and early intervention of reading problems more easily than ever before. Many educators, however, have persistent questions about administering and scoring DIBELS and about interpreting DIBELS scores. Until the publication of this book, there was no authoritative, comprehensive source that provided answers to their questions.

Linda Farrell, Carrie Hancock, and Susan Smartt bring to this book a level of expertise about DIBELS and early reading instruction that embraces both the academic and the practical. They first intended to write a simple guide for examiners who are learning to administer and score DIBELS, but the manual became a treasure trove of details about the ins and outs of DIBELS assessment. The book includes simplified scoring rules and procedures but also answers many questions these experts hear in their workshops across the country. I am delighted that the book has grown beyond its modest beginnings.

In addition to scoring and administration guidance, the book includes instructional implications for the seven DIBELS measures. Chapter 3 provides information about all the uses for DIBELS scores to those who think of it as only a screening device. The purpose and use of progress monitoring are fully explained in Chapter 4. Chapter 5 is a guide to interpreting and understanding DIBELS scores. The school or district struggling with how to organize the enormous task of administering DIBELS to all its children will benefit from the ideas in Chapters 6 and 7. Excellent advice is given in Chapter 8 for training examiners so that the integrity of the scores is maintained. In Chapter 9, those unfamiliar with DIBELS reports can learn about some of the more popular ones available from the DIBELS Data System, including their most common usage. The most popular and often-used parts of the book may be the "frequently asked questions" sections at the ends of many chapters.

It will be the rare reader who finds a question about administering and scoring DIBELS unanswered in this thorough guide to using DIBELS.

Dr. Louisa Cook Moats

PREFACE

Overview of the Manual

DIBELS[1] is an assessment tool used primarily to identify children who are at risk for reading failure. Over the past few years, DIBELS has become increasingly popular as school systems seek effective and efficient ways to identify children who are not on track to be good readers. Teachers use DIBELS scores to group students for intervention, to monitor student progress, to identify skill gaps that may affect future reading, and to better understand the characteristics of specific difficulties struggling readers have. School systems use DIBELS scores for a myriad of purposes, including determining the effectiveness of reading instruction in states, districts, schools, and classrooms.

As educators use DIBELS, they naturally have questions about its use and utility. Some of the answers to technical questions may be found in the *DIBELS Administration and Scoring Guide* (Good & Kaminski, 2003), available from Sopris West and at http://dibels.uoregon.edu. However, teachers ask many questions and raise a number of issues that are not answered in that publication. The primary purpose of this manual is to provide a single source for the many technical and practical questions posed by teachers as they learn to administer DIBELS and try to better understand the measures. This manual is intended to complement the *DIBELS Administration and Scoring Guide*, and we recommend that examiners and others who need to understand DIBELS read both publications.

In addition to answering many questions teachers have as they use DIBELS, this manual is a practical guide that explains scoring and administration, offers tools to help when giving the assessments, and answers questions about the general use of DIBELS as a screening tool. It also provides information about how schools can efficiently administer DIBELS, how to train teachers to administer DIBELS accurately, and how to interpret certain reports available from the DIBELS Web site.

This manual focuses on scoring and administration issues related to DIBELS. It does not explain how to use DIBELS scores, how to group children using DIBELS scores, or how to structure intervention lessons around information obtained from DIBELS scores. It also is not intended to be a primer on effective techniques for basic reading instruction. These topics are the basis for the forthcoming *I've DIBEL'd: Now What?* by Susan Hall (2006).

To prepare this manual, we have relied heavily on our own experience administering and scoring DIBELS, information from the *DIBELS Administration and Scoring Guide*, articles published about DIBELS, discussions with other DIBELS trainers, our experience working with examiners who routinely administer DIBELS benchmark and progress monitoring assessments, and our attendance at workshops conducted by Drs. Roland Good and Ruth Kaminski, two of the

---

[1] DIBELS is pronounced with a short *i* in the first syllable, to rhyme with "nibbles."

primary creators of DIBELS. Drs. Good and Kaminski also reviewed this book and gave many insightful comments.

Importance of Attending a Workshop

Anyone who administers DIBELS or uses DIBELS scores in any way can benefit from this manual. This includes, but is not limited to, administrators, teachers, reading coaches, paraprofessionals, speech–language pathologists, school psychologists, and other school personnel who administer, score, and interpret DIBELS in their schools. However, the best understanding of the information in this manual will come after the reader attends an interactive workshop that includes substantial practice scoring of each of the seven DIBELS measures. DIBELS scoring can be confusing, and practice is necessary to master the scoring intricacies of each measure.

We recommend that everyone using DIBELS in any way take a Scoring and Administration Workshop prior to administering the assessment. This is because scoring integrity is maintained only if the examiner knows how to score the student assessments properly. An interactive workshop is the best way for examiners to learn proper scoring. Workshops also offer an opportunity to understand the logic and rationale for the DIBELS assessment. Regular and train-the-trainer workshops are available through Sopris West at http://www.dibelsassessment.com/training.htm, or trainers can be found on the DIBELS Web site at http://dibels.uoregon.edu. The authors of this book also offer both regular and train-the-trainer workshops. Their e-mail addresses are: Linda Farrell, lindadibels@earthlink.net; Carrie Hancock, drcarriehancock@cox.net; Susan Smartt, susandibels@comcast.net.

> We recommend that everyone using DIBELS in any way take a Scoring and Administration Workshop.

DIBELS Acronyms and Initialisms

The thousands of teachers, administrators, trainers, and researchers who regularly work with DIBELS quickly tire of using the long names assigned to the seven DIBELS measures. "DIBELSers" commonly use acronyms and initials for each of the measures. Throughout this guide, the following are often used in place of the official names for each of the seven measures:

- LNF—Letter Naming Fluency
- ISF—Initial Sound Fluency
- PSF—Phoneme Segmentation Fluency
- NWF—Nonsense Word Fluency
- ORF—Oral Reading Fluency (ORF is often pronounced as a word, "ORF." In some academic circles, this measure is referred to as "DORF," which stands for DIBELS Oral Reading Fluency. However, ORF is more commonly used in schools.)
- RTF—Retell Fluency
- WUF—Word Use Fluency (WUF is sometimes pronounced "woof.")

DIBELS "Extras": Grades 4–6; Spanish Language Version; Wireless Administration

DIBELS was originally developed for use in grades K–3 and until recently was always scored by hand. In the past few years, DIBELS researchers have developed a Spanish language version (*IDEL*) for grades K–3.[2] In addition, DIBELS measures are now available for both benchmark assessments and progress monitoring for grades 4–6.[3] Another relatively recent development is that Wireless Generation, Inc. (http://www.wirelessgeneration.com) now offers software (*mCLASS:DIBELS*) enabling DIBELS to be scored using a handheld computer. Although this manual primarily discusses the pencil-and-paper version of DIBELS in English for grades K–3, the information presented is generally applicable to all versions of DIBELS.

Organization of Manual

Each chapter in this manual is intended to stand alone, which requires that some information is presented more than once.

Chapter 1 is an overview of DIBELS, including a brief history and description of the assessment.

Chapter 2 describes the Spanish language version of DIBELS, DIBELS assessments available for grades 4–6, and the Wireless Generation option for scoring DIBELS with a handheld computer.

Chapter 3 discusses the difference between formal and informal assessment in relation to DIBELS. This chapter also includes a definition of the four types of assessment related to reading instruction—screening, diagnostic, progress monitoring, and outcome—and how DIBELS relates to each.

Chapter 4 provides information about implementing DIBELS progress monitoring.

Chapter 5 describes terminology related to benchmark assessments, discusses general scoring and administration rules, lists the materials needed to administer assessments, summarizes allowable accommodations, and provides answers to frequently asked questions about administering benchmark assessments.

Chapter 6 describes how a district or school can plan for and administer DIBELS assessments three times a year and discusses the various responsibilities when DIBELS is implemented on a widespread basis.

Chapter 7 helps schools and districts understand how to plan for and organize the administration of DIBELS.

Chapter 8 discusses examiner qualifications and options for providing examiners and other DIBELS users with training.

Chapter 9 is an overview of the most frequently used reports available from the DIBELS Data System.

Chapters 10–16 give detailed information about each of the seven DIBELS measures, including the following: marking and scoring rules, progress monitoring,

---

[2] The Spanish language version of DIBELS is discussed in Chapter 2.

[3] DIBELS for grades 4–6 is discussed in Chapter 2.

how to help children prepare for the measure, interpreting DIBELS scores, common mistakes, and answers to frequently asked questions.

Chapter 17 explains that obtaining DIBELS scores is only the first step in helping all children learn to read at grade level in the elementary grades. This chapter recommends resources to help teachers find effective reading programs and instructional strategies.

DIBELS Overview

BRIEF HISTORY

DIBELS is a scientifically validated assessment instrument used to assess early reading skills. DIBELS was first developed as a tool that would help identify children as early as possible who were not likely to read at grade level by the end of third grade (as measured by high-stakes test of reading comprehension[1,2]). As DIBELS was developed, the researchers considered it important to correlate DIBELS scores to other state-mandated high-stakes reading tests. In the more than 15 years of research conducted with DIBELS, the instrument has been found to be highly correlated with a wide range of measures of reading readiness and achievement. DIBELS has also been found to be predictive of success on high-stakes reading tests in many states (Barger, 2003; Buck & Torgesen, 2003; DIBELS Web site, 2004; Good et al., 2001; Shaw & Shaw, 2002).

DIBELS' widest uses are as screening, outcome, and progress monitoring assessments for Grades K–3. However, DIBELS recently added benchmark assessments and progress monitoring assessments for Grades 4–6 and benchmark assessments in a Spanish language version for Grades K–3. Wireless Generation, Inc., has worked with the DIBELS team to offer the ability to administer and score DIBELS using a handheld computer. These DIBELS "extras" are discussed in more detail in Chapter 2.

DIBELS was developed by a team of professors and graduate students at the University of Oregon. Drs. Roland Good and Ruth Kaminski, who lead the team of DIBELS researchers, supported their research with several grants from the U.S. Department of Education. One grant, titled Early Childhood Research Institute (ECRI), was awarded to three universities whose investigators were charged with identifying and developing Individual Growth and Development Indicators (IGDIs[3]) for children from birth to age 8. The IGDIs were intended to address language and literacy development, social and emotional skill development, and motor development. DIBELS resulted from the University of Oregon's study on developing IGDIs for children in Grades K–3. Two other universities are developing IGDIs for children from birth to age 3 and from age 3 until they enter

---

[1] DIBELS ORF is based on a program of research and development of Curriculum-Based Measurements of Reading (CBM-R), which was developed by Stan Deno and colleagues at the University of Minnesota (Deno et al., 1982).

[2] The importance of developing a valid early reading assessment was based on numerous longitudinal research studies that found third grade reading outcomes to be strongly related to middle and high school reading achievement.

[3] Pronounced "ig'–dees."

kindergarten. The University of Kansas developed a set of measures designed and validated for use by practitioners and interventionists for children from birth to age 3. The Web site is http://www.lsi.ku.edu/jgprojects/igdi. The University of Minnesota has assessments for children age 3 until they enter kindergarten that are called Get It, Got It, Go on its Web site: http://ggg.umn.edu/. The studies these researchers conducted and continue to conduct are adding to the growing body of research detailing the importance of early literacy and language skills in achieving later reading outcomes.

SUMMARY DESCRIPTION

> All DIBELS measures emphasize both accuracy and fluency.

DIBELS includes seven measures, six of which correspond to one of the five essential components of reading[4] as established by the National Reading Panel (National Institute of Child Health and Human Development, 2000). The DIBELS assessments all have been approved by the National Reading First Assessment Committee, as described in the committee's report, which is available at http://idea.uoregon.edu/assessment/index.html. Within that review, Word Use Fluency and Retell Fluency are not addressed. However, since the initial publishing of the review, the committee has approved Word Use Fluency and Retell Fluency for assessing vocabulary and comprehension, respectively.

DIBELS benchmark assessments and progress monitoring assessments are given individually to each student. DIBELS benchmark assessments are given three times a year: at the beginning, middle, and end of the school year.[5] The set of measures given varies from grade to grade, and the set of measures also varies within every grade except third grade, which has the same measures for all three benchmarks. All seven DIBELS measures emphasize both accuracy and fluency and are powerful indicators of the early skills that predict reading success. Each of the measures is described briefly in *Table 1–1* and in detail in Chapters 10–16.

DIBELS is an acronym for Dynamic Indicators of Basic Early Literacy Skills. Each word is a partial description of the assessment. The **D** stands for *Dynamic*, which describes three aspects of DIBELS. First, *dynamic* means that the assessments are sensitive to small changes in early literacy skills, and they show how students are changing, not just where they stand at a specific point in time. Second, *dynamic* means that specific measures given at benchmark assessment periods change over time, depending on their utility for predicting reading outcomes. Third, *dynamic* means that DIBELS scores provide information about how students are changing, not just where they are at a certain point in time.

---

[4] The five essential components are phonemic awareness, the alphabetic principle (phonics), fluency, vocabulary, and comprehension. Each is described in the Glossary.

[5] There are a few exceptions, notably Florida, that have elected to give DIBELS assessments to all children four times each school year. For those schools, the middle-year set of benchmark assessments is repeated. Benchmark and target scores for four assessment periods in a school year are available on the DIBELS Web site.

Description of Seven DIBELS Measures `Table 1-1`

DIBELS Measure	Essential Component of Reading Measured	Description
Initial Sound Fluency (ISF)	Phonemic awareness	Students identify pictures with a target initial sound and they articulate the first sound or sounds in a word.
Phoneme Segmentation Fluency (PSF)	Phonemic awareness	Students break words with two to five sounds into parts, with the highest score for each word being the number of phonemes in the word.
Nonsense Word Fluency (NWF)	Alphabetic principle (phonics)	Students read nonsense words spelled with two and three letters. All nonsense words are spelled with a consonant–vowel–consonant (CVC) or vowel–consonant (VC) pattern.
Oral Reading Fluency (ORF)	Fluency	Students orally read a grade-level passage.
Retell Fluency (RTF)	Comprehension	Students retell the passage they read in Oral Reading Fluency.
Word Use Fluency (WUF)	Vocabulary	Students give an oral response using a target word in a sentence, definition, or description.
Letter Naming Fluency (LNF)	None—contributes as a risk factor (LNF as a risk factor is explained later in this chapter and in Chapter 10).	Students name uppercase and lowercase letters presented in random order.

The **I** in DIBELS stands for *Indicators*, which means that the measures don't tell us everything about a child's early literacy skills. Rather, the few specific measures given at each benchmark period have been shown through research to be highly predictive of skills that lead to early reading success, and they are strong indicators of current emerging literacy skills. Students who score below benchmark scores[6] may need further focused diagnostic assessment to determine which specific skills they are missing and, therefore, how intervention instruction should be designed.

The letters **B**, **E**, **L**, and **S** in DIBELS stand for *Basic Early Literacy Skills*. This means that DIBELS measures a small, selected set of the student's emerging and early reading skills chosen specifically to predict later reading achievement at the end of third grade. Phonemic awareness, decoding, fluency, vocabulary, and comprehension are measured by DIBELS. However, these skills are predictive of early literacy development only. Sophisticated vocabulary knowledge and higher-order thinking skills, such as prediction and inference, are not measured by DIBELS.

All DIBELS benchmark assessments are standardized assessments. That means that directions are given exactly as written and that the measures are scored consistently for all assessments in order for the comparative scores to be valid.

OPTIONAL MEASURES: RTF AND ORF

Two of the measures, Retell Fluency and Word Use Fluency, are labeled as "optional." WUF is optional because this is a newer measure and DIBELS researchers have yet to identify nationally normed benchmarks and risk categories

---

[6] See Chapter 5 for an explanation of the term "benchmark scores."

for WUF. However, indications are that Word Use Fluency is a good predictor of vocabulary knowledge. When Word Use Fluency scores are submitted to the University of Oregon data system, local norms are provided on the reports from the DIBELS Data System. Districts and schools that elect to use Word Use Fluency as part of the benchmark assessment measures and do not use the DIBELS Data System determine their own risk categories. (See Chapter 16 for how to develop risk categories for Word Use Fluency.)

Retell Fluency is the other optional DIBELS measure. RTF used in conjunction with ORF is a stronger predictor of comprehension skills than the ORF score without RTF. For most children, the ORF score alone will give a good indication of whether or not the student comprehends what he or she reads. However, occasionally a student reads text accurately and fluently but does not retain or understand the content. In that case, the ORF score alone may not indicate comprehension difficulties. An RTF score in the At Risk range will identify this student. For this reason, administering ORF and RTF is especially important to identify children who may decode well but have difficulty with comprehension. (Students with an ORF score of 40 or higher and an RTF score lower than 25% of their ORF score are considered to be at risk for comprehension difficulties. Unlike other measures, there is no Some Risk category for RTF scores.) The schedule for giving the measures for benchmark assessments is shown in *Table 1-2*.

Table 1-2	Schedule of Individual Measures Administered at Each Assessment Period											
	Kindergarten			First Grade			Second Grade			Third Grade		
DIBELS Measure	B	M	E	B	M	E	B	M	E	B	M	E
Initial Sound Fluency	x	x										
Letter Naming Fluency	x	x	x	x								
Phoneme Segmentation Fluency		x	x	x	x	x						
Nonsense Word Fluency		x	x	x	x	x	x					
Oral Reading Fluency					x	x	x	x	x	x	x	x

Optional Measures:

Retell Fluency					x	x	x	x	x	x	x	x
Word Use Fluency	x	x	x	x	x	x	x	x	x	x	x	x

Note: The letters **B**, **M**, and **E** stand for beginning, middle, and end of the school year.

TIME REQUIRED TO ADMINISTER DIBELS BENCHMARK ASSESSMENTS

The time it takes to give DIBELS benchmark assessments varies because the combination of measures given is different, depending on the grade and time of year. The time to administer DIBELS at each benchmark assessment period will be shorter for schools that elect not to give the two optional measures: Retell Fluency and Word Use Fluency. Time also is dependent on the efficiency with which the examiners can administer DIBELS, and such efficiency is largely based on how often they give the assessment, how long it has been since they last gave DIBELS, and the time allocated to "chatting" with the student. (Examiners quickly learn that minimizing chat time—without losing rapport with the student—can greatly decrease the time it takes to administer DIBELS to a class!)

Table 1–3 shows approximate times for administering DIBELS benchmark assessments at the beginning, middle, and end of each school year. The table shows times for administering DIBELS to 1 student at each benchmark period and for a team of five examiners to administer DIBELS to a classroom of 25 students at each benchmark period. The times are based on averages for examiners who have given DIBELS at several benchmark assessments. The times shown in *Table 1–3* include the following assumptions: (1) 30 seconds between students; (2) minimal chat time of 30 seconds for the examiner to greet each student and to conclude the student's assessment session; (3) 90 seconds for the examiner to calculate the score for each measure and record the score on the Summary of Scores Page; and (4) time to administer and score each measure given during the specific benchmark the assessment is based on. (*Table 6–3* in Chapter 6 shows in detail the time it takes to administer and score each measure.)

Time for One Examiner to Administer and Score Benchmark Assessments for an Individual Student and for Five Examiners to Administer DIBELS to a Classroom of 25 Students | **Table 1-3**

DIBELS Measure	Kindergarten			First Grade			Second Grade			Third Grade		
	B	M	E	B	M	E	B	M	E	B	M	E
Including Retell and Word Use Fluency												
Individual Student (time in minutes, rounded up to nearest minute)	8.5	13	10	10	15.25	15.25	13.25	10.75	10.75	10.75	10.75	10.75
Classroom of 25 Students With Five Examiners (time in minutes, rounded up to nearest five minutes)	45	65	50	50	80	80	70	55	55	55	55	55
Without Retell and Word Use Fluency												
Individual Student (time in minutes)	7	11.5	8.5	8.5	11.75	11.75	9.75	7.25	7.25	7.25	7.25	7.25
Classroom of 25 Students With Five Examiners (time in minutes, rounded up to nearest five minutes)	35	60	45	45	60	60	50	40	40	40	40	40

For schools that give all seven measures, *Table 1–3* shows that the shortest amount of time needed to administer DIBELS to an individual student is 8.5 minutes per student at the beginning of kindergarten, and the longest time is 15.25 minutes per student at the middle and end of first grade. The table also shows that the shortest time for five examiners to administer all benchmark assessments to a classroom of 25 students is 45 minutes at the beginning of kindergarten. The longest time is 80 minutes at the middle and end of first grade.

If schools or districts elect not to give the two optional measures, the shortest time it takes is 7 minutes per student in second and third grades and the longest time is 11.75 minutes at the middle of kindergarten. The shortest time for five examiners to administer the benchmark assessment to a classroom with 25 students is approximately 35 minutes at the beginning of kindergarten, and the longest time is 60 minutes at the middle of kindergarten and at the middle and end of first grade.

SUMMARY DESCRIPTION OF PRINT MATERIALS

DIBELS print materials consist of the following, all of which can be purchased from Sopris West (http://www.sopriswest.com) or downloaded from the DIBELS Web site (http://dibels.uoregon.edu).

- This manual (available only from Sopris West)
- *DIBELS Administration and Scoring Guide*
- Benchmark Assessment Student Materials (the larger booklets)
- Benchmark Assessment Scoring Booklets (the smaller booklets, about half the size of the Student Materials Booklets)
- Progress Monitoring Student Materials (the larger booklets)
- Progress Monitoring Scoring Booklets (the smaller booklets, about half the size of the Student Materials)

Administration and Scoring Guide

Student Materials Benchmark Assessment

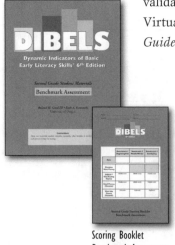

Scoring Booklet Benchmark Assessment

DIBELS Administration and Scoring Guide

The guide contains technical, administration, and scoring information about DIBELS. The guide also includes a list of Approved Accommodations available for use with individual students and technical reports that explain some of the validation research and how DIBELS determines instructional recommendations. Virtually all of the information contained in the *DIBELS Administration and Scoring Guide* is discussed in this manual, with the exception of the technical reports.

Benchmark Assessment Materials

Benchmark assessment materials are different for each grade. They include all of the print materials necessary to administer the benchmark assessments three times a year. These materials consist of Scoring Booklets and Student Materials for each measure

Scoring Booklets—One Benchmark Assessment Scoring Booklet is needed for each student. Examiners use the Scoring Booklets to mark student responses and record the scores for each measure. The scoring pages for all the benchmark assessments for an entire year are included in the

Scoring Booklet. Most schools put labels on the front page of the Scoring Booklets that have the student name, teacher, school, and other identifying information such as the student number.

The first page of the Scoring Booklet is called the Summary of Scores Page in this manual (*see Figure 1-1*). The examiner records the scores for each measure given during the benchmark assessment. This is also where the examiner would note whether an Approved Accommodation was used for any measure and would provide other comments. When this page is completed, it offers a summary of the student's benchmark assessment scores. The Summary of Scores Page makes data input easy and allows the teacher a one-page overview of the student's scores, including how the scores change as the year progresses.

Summary of Scores Pages, Kindergarten–Grade 3   **Figure 1-1**

Kindergarten

Name: _____   Teacher: _____
School: _____   District: _____

	Benchmark 1 Beginning/Fall	Benchmark 2 Middle/Winter	Benchmark 3 End/Spring
Date			
Initial Sound Fluency			
Letter Naming Fluency			
Phoneme Segmentation Fluency			
Nonsense Word Fluency			
Word Use Fluency (Optional)	(Optional)	(Optional)	(Optional)

First Grade

Name: _____   Teacher: _____
School: _____   District: _____

	Benchmark 1 Beginning/Fall	Benchmark 2 Middle/Winter	Benchmark 3 End/Spring
Date			
Letter Naming Fluency			
Phoneme Segmentation Fluency			
Nonsense Word Fluency			
DIBELS Oral Reading Fluency		(Middle score)	(Middle score)
Retell Fluency (Optional)		(Middle score)	(Middle score)
Word Use Fluency (Optional)	(Optional)	(Optional)	(Optional)

Second Grade

Name: _____   Teacher: _____
School: _____   District: _____

	Benchmark 1 Beginning/Fall	Benchmark 2 Middle/Winter	Benchmark 3 End/Spring
Date			
Nonsense Word Fluency			
DIBELS Oral Reading Fluency	(Middle score)	(Middle score)	(Middle score)
Retell Fluency (Optional)	(Middle score)	(Middle score)	(Middle score)
Word Use Fluency (Optional)	(Optional)	(Optional)	(Optional)

Third Grade

Name: _____   Teacher: _____
School: _____   District: _____

	Benchmark 1 Beginning/Fall	Benchmark 2 Middle/Winter	Benchmark 3 End/Spring
Date			
DIBELS Oral Reading Fluency	(Middle score)	(Middle score)	(Middle score)
Retell Fluency (Optional)	(Middle score)	(Middle score)	(Middle score)
Word Use Fluency (Optional)	(Optional)	(Optional)	(Optional)

Student Materials - NWF

Scoring Booklet - NWF

Student Materials Progress Monitoring

Scoring Booklet Progress Monitoring

Student Materials—Each examiner needs one set of Student Materials for each grade being assessed. The Student Materials contain all the pages with pictures, letters, nonsense words, and passages that students need to look at or read during the benchmark assessments. Student Materials booklets are larger than Scoring Booklets and contain all of the materials students read or look at during each benchmark assessment. (There are no pages in the Student Materials booklets for PSF, RTF, and WUF because these measures are oral and do not require the student to look at anything.)

With the exception of the look of the cover page, the Sopris West and downloaded versions of the Student Materials booklets are identical if the downloaded ISF pictures are printed in color. (Although it is acceptable to print the ISF booklets in black and white, our informal observation is that students respond better to color pictures. Therefore, we recommend printing the ISF pictures in color, if at all possible.)

Progress Monitoring Materials

Materials used for DIBELS progress monitoring differ from those used for benchmark assessments because they are organized to include materials for only one measure. Progress monitoring materials for ISF, PSF, NWF, ORF, and WUF are available from Sopris West and in downloadable form on the DIBELS Web site.

Sopris West and the DIBELS Web site do not offer progress monitoring materials for LNF. This is because the creators of DIBELS view letter naming as a skill that is not one the five essential components of reading. Therefore, they believe letter naming practice should not be a focus of intervention lessons. (See Chapter 10 for more discussion of the purpose of the DIBELS LNF measure.)

RTF is another measure for which there are no progress monitoring materials. Teachers who want to track a student's progress in RTF can write the number of words and the RTF–ORF percentage on the page with the progress monitoring chart for ORF. Some teachers make their own charts for progress monitoring RTF and staple them to the ORF booklet.

Progress monitoring materials include a Scoring Booklet for each measure listed above and Student Materials books for ORF, NWF, and ISF. There are no Student Materials for PSF, RTF, or WUF progress monitoring because students do not look at anything during these assessments.

All Progress Monitoring Materials contain 20 or more different forms of the same measure. Intervention teachers use the first page of the Progress Monitoring Scoring Booklet to draw a goal line and plot the student's scores over time. (This procedure is described in greater detail in Chapter 4.) Completed progress monitoring charts are available for each student electronically through the DIBELS Data System after the progress monitoring scores are entered.

The DIBELS creators decided to label the PSF progress monitoring materials as "Kindergarten" because it is in kindergarten when children are expected to reach the PSF benchmark score to be on track for reading success. Similarly, NWF progress monitoring materials are labeled as "First Grade" because children are expected to reach the NWF benchmark score in first grade. The grade-level label for these materials is somewhat misleading because both PSF and NWF progress monitoring materials can be used with students in *any* grade, regardless of the stated grade designation on the cover page. (Many teachers cover the grade-level designations on PSF and NWF progress monitoring materials so that older students are not offended by working with materials that appear to be for students below their grade level.)

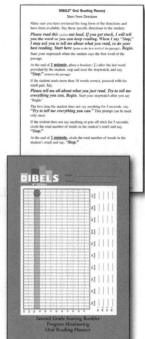

USES FOR DIBELS SCORES

The use of DIBELS as a K–3 early reading skills assessment has greatly expanded since it was first developed at the University of Oregon. Because of the increased emphasis on effective early reading instruction, DIBELS is now used in thousands of schools nationwide. Schools use DIBELS for three primary purposes: a screening instrument, a progress monitoring instrument, and an outcome assessment tool. The use of DIBELS for each assessment purpose is briefly described below and discussed in more detail in Chapter 3.

> Schools use DIBELS for three primary purposes: a screening instrument, a progress monitoring instrument, and an outcome assessment tool.

Early Literacy Screening Instrument

When DIBELS is used as a screening instrument, all children in Grades K–3 are given DIBELS benchmark assessments three times a year.[7] No children are omitted from the screening, even if they had very high DIBELS scores previously or have been tested with other assessments that show high reading scores.

The purpose of screening is to identify any children who have not met established and scientifically validated benchmarks for early literacy skills. Children who do not reach benchmark scores for certain measures are identified as at risk for experiencing reading difficulties. These children may need additional instructional support (above and beyond the time devoted to core reading program instruction) focused on the skill or skills they are missing if they are to meet future early literacy benchmarks.

When a student meets early successive literacy benchmarks measured by DIBELS, there is assurance the student will read at or above grade level by the end of third grade.

---

[7] DIBELS can also be used to screen students in Grades 4–6, as discussed in Chapter 2.

Progress Monitoring Instrument

Progress monitoring scores demonstrate student progress on one skill over time. The progress monitoring charts help teachers and reading assessment teams determine whether the student is "on track" to meet the benchmark score by a specified time. DIBELS progress monitoring assessments are given only to students who are at risk for reading difficulties, and they are generally given every one to four weeks, depending on how low the student's skills are and on the intensity of the intervention. DIBELS progress monitoring assessments serve as frequent checkups on whether students are making enough progress with intervention instruction to meet the end-of-year benchmark score for the skill or skills that need to be improved.

Some schools cannot provide intervention instruction to all students who score below benchmark scores. In these cases, schools may decide to monitor the progress of students who are not receiving intervention but have scores below benchmark. This allows the school to keep track of how these students are doing and to provide them with intervention if they fall further behind. For example, one school decided it had resources to provide intervention only to children with At Risk and Deficit scores. They gave progress monitoring every four weeks to children with Some Risk and Emerging scores. If the scores for any of these children fell into a predefined At Risk or Deficit category, those children were moved into intervention.

In general, intervention students are given the DIBELS progress monitoring assessment for the skill that is the primary focus of intervention group instruction. However, some schools give progress monitoring for higher-level skills that are not the primary focus of instruction because those skills, too, must be mastered. Still, they would give progress monitoring for the higher-level skills less often, perhaps once every month instead of once every one or two weeks, for the skill that is the primary focus. An example of this would be a student in the middle of first grade who has Deficit PSF, Deficit NWF, and At Risk ORF scores. The lesson plan for this student's intervention group may focus on phonemic awareness for a portion of the lesson and phonics for a portion of the lesson. Progress monitoring may be given weekly for PSF and NWF because phonemic awareness and phonics are the primary focus of intervention instruction. Monthly progress monitoring may be given for ORF to determine whether intervention instruction is transferring to the higher-level skills measured by ORF, which has a benchmark score that needs to be achieved by the end of the year.

Outcome Measurement Instrument

Outcome assessments are given for two purposes: (1) to determine whether individual students or groups of students have learned important early literacy skills predictive of later reading success; and (2) to evaluate the overall effectiveness of a reading program for all children. DIBELS end-of-year benchmark measures are used for outcome measurement. The scores show not only whether each student but also whether a class or school or district as a whole has met critical early literacy goals at the end of the school year.

DIBELS scores can be used to measure whether children in kindergarten to Grade 3 are learning the skills that lead to becoming successful readers by the end of third grade. The students' aggregate scores will indicate whether the reading curriculum provides instruction that effectively teaches students the skills necessary to become good readers. If DIBELS scores are consistently low across a school system, the decision can be made to change the reading curriculum, to give the teachers additional professional development, to supplement the curriculum with additional materials and instruction, or to provide some combination of the three changes.

DIBELS RISK CATEGORIES

DIBELS research has established levels of performance for each measure that predict success for the subsequent level of performance.

Benchmark scores are the minimum scores that indicate the student has the ability to apply a basic reading skill. In the DIBELS Benchmark Scores Table in the Appendix, benchmark scores are any scores that are equal to or higher than the cut points for the risk levels labeled Established or Low Risk.

Risk levels are labeled Established, Emerging, and Deficit for some measures at certain benchmark periods, and they are labeled Low Risk, Some Risk, and At Risk at other benchmark periods. For example, in *Table 1–4*, (next page), the scores for ISF are labeled Low Risk, Some Risk, and At Risk at the beginning of the year and Established, Emerging, and Deficit at the middle of the year.

Once scores and cut points are labeled Established, Emerging, and Deficit, they never change. That is because the score to achieve the Established level is the score that shows a student of any age has mastered the skill being measured. These scores are 35 for PSF and 50 for NWF. The established score for PSF is always 35 after it is first on the DIBELS Benchmark Scores Table at the end of kindergarten. The established score for NWF is always 50 after it is first on the same table at the middle of first grade.

The first time the risk categories Established, Emerging, and Deficit appear on the DIBELS Benchmark Scores Table is the time when students are expected to have facility with the skill being measured. For example, students should be able to blend and segment phonemes in one-syllable words (i.e., have phonemic awareness) by the end of kindergarten, which is when the risk categories Established, Emerging, and Deficit first appear for PSF. Similarly, students should be able to demonstrate knowledge of the alphabetic principle (phonics) by the middle of first grade, which is when the categories Established, Emerging, and Deficit first appear for NWF. Meeting the PSF and NWF scores by the time they should be established puts students on track to be successful readers at the end of first grade.

Risk categories Low Risk, Some Risk, and At Risk are used before students are expected to have mastered the skill measured by DIBELS, and the cut points for these scores change from one benchmark period to another because they are provided as steps toward reaching an Established benchmark score.

Table 1-4   **Benchmark and Target Scores for Kindergarten and First Grade**

	Beginning of Year		Middle of Year		End of Year	
	Score	Status	Score	Status	Score	Status
Kindergarten						
Initial Sound Fluency	0–3	At Risk	0–9	Deficit		
	4–7	Some Risk	10–24	Emerging		
	8+	Low Risk	25+	Established		
Letter Naming Fluency	0–1	At Risk	0–14	At Risk	0–28	At Risk
	2–7	Some Risk	15–26	Some Risk	29–39	Some Risk
	8+	Low Risk	27+	Low Risk	40+	Low Risk
Phoneme Segmentation Fluency			0–6	At Risk	0–9	Deficit
			7–17	Some Risk	10–34	Emerging
			18+	Low Risk	35+	Established
Nonsense Word Fluency			0–4	At Risk	0–14	At Risk
			5–12	Some Risk	15–24	Some Risk
			13+	Low Risk	25+	Low Risk
First Grade						
Letter Naming Fluency	0–24	At Risk				
	25–36	Some Risk				
	37+	Low Risk				
Phoneme Segmentation Fluency	0–9	Deficit	0–9	Deficit	0–9	Deficit
	10–34	Emerging	10–34	Emerging	10–34	Emerging
	35+	Established	35+	Established	35+	Established
Nonsense Word Fluency	0–12	At Risk	0–29	Deficit	0–29	Deficit
	13–23	Some Risk	30–49	Emerging	30–49	Emerging
	24+	Low Risk	50+	Established	50+	Established
Oral Reading Fluency			0–7	At Risk	0–19	At Risk
			8–19	Some Risk	20–39	Some Risk
			20+	Low Risk	40+	Low Risk

Reaching a Low Risk score for a DIBELS measure indicates a high probability (approximately 80% or higher) of reaching the next score for that measure if the student has appropriate reading instruction. For example, reaching the ISF Low Risk score of 8 at the beginning of kindergarten indicates a high probability of reaching the ISF Established score of 25 by the middle of kindergarten (with appropriate reading instruction). Reaching an Established score indicates a high probability (approximately 80% or higher) of reaching the next Established score for a different measure, with continued reading instruction (Good & Kaminski, 2003). For example, reaching the PSF Established score of 35 at the end of kindergarten indicates a high probability of reaching the NWF Established score of 50 in the middle of first grade (with appropriate instruction).

In essence, when a student achieves a score in the Low Risk or Established category, he or she demonstrates a facility with a foundational reading skill that is expected for students who are on target to become proficient readers by third grade. Scores below the Some Risk or Emerging categories indicate the student is less likely to achieve reading proficiency with existing instruction. Scores in the At Risk or Deficit categories indicate a child is highly unlikely to become a proficient reader without significant additional reading instruction targeted toward areas of weakness in early reading skills.

> DIBELS benchmark scores indicate the minimum acceptable scores and should not be used as the goal for any student. Goals should be higher than the minimum acceptable score.

DIBELS MILEPOST SCORES

Figure 1–2 shows the major mileposts for DIBELS for kindergarten through third grade.

Major Mileposts in DIBELS   **Figure 1-2**

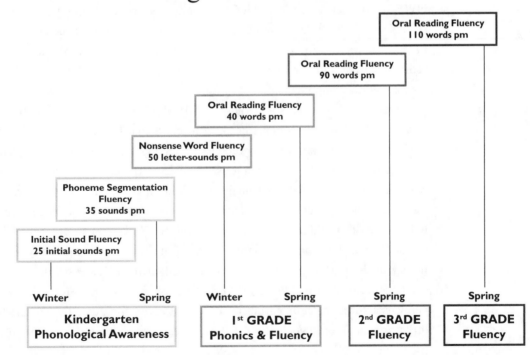

DIBELS Measures:
Learning-to-Read Continuum

ISF, PSF, and NWF scores are benchmark scores. All ORF scores are target scores.

Used with permission from Susan L. Hall. From *I've DIBEL'd, Now What?: Designing Interventions With DIBELS Data* (2006).

The exhibit shows the progression of skills students must make to become proficient readers. Meeting the benchmark score of 25 for ISF by the middle of kindergarten is the first major milepost in developing solid early literacy skills. Students who achieve this score are demonstrating solid early phonemic awareness skills by accurately and fluently identifying initial sounds in words. Students who meet this early phonemic awareness milepost are well on their way to meeting the next major milepost, which is demonstrating full phonemic awareness, evidenced by a score of 35 on PSF by the end of kindergarten. The next major milepost is a score of 50 on NWF by the middle of first grade, which demonstrates mastery of early phonics skill. Finally, the major mileposts become ORF benchmark scores at the end of first, second, and third grades. When students meet the ORF mileposts, they are demonstrating grade-appropriate early reading skills that will enable them to become proficient readers by the end of third grade.

Strong reading skills don't just happen overnight. Rather, a solid foundation is laid as students gain the basic skills and build a solid foundation for reading. *Figure 1–2* makes clear that meeting the benchmark score for each measure at each benchmark assessment period will help to predict and ensure successful reading outcomes.

Achievement of each milepost is based on achieving a prior milepost. Achieving the benchmark score for a milepost provides a probability of approximately 80% or higher that the student will achieve the next benchmark score for the next milepost. For example, the student who achieves the ORF milepost score of 40 by the end of first grade, assuming he or she met benchmark scores for PSF and NWF, is on track to achieve the ORF milepost score in second grade. Once the second grade ORF milepost score is met, the student is on track to achieve the ORF milepost score in third grade. Students achieving the end of third grade milepost score for ORF would be likely to score at or above grade level on a standardized test of reading comprehension at that time.

It is critical to understand that the DIBELS benchmark scores indicate the *minimum* level of skill students need for teachers to achieve confidence that their students are on track to read at grade level. Schools establishing fluency goals for core reading materials often do not use DIBELS ORF benchmark scores for three reasons. First, DIBELS fluency goals are minimum acceptable fluency levels, and they should never be considered "goals" because the goal would be for each student to be above the minimum level. Second, DIBELS ORF benchmark scores are based on the DIBELS ORF passages, which all have an end of grade readability level and not a readability level based on the time of the benchmark assessment. Therefore, even beginning and middle-of-year minimums would not transfer to easier text being used for instruction earlier in the school year. Third, core reading programs often provide fluency goals that the teacher can use for material related to those programs.

OBTAINING DIBELS REPORTS

The University of Oregon offers a variety of reports over the Internet. The reports display DIBELS scores in a number of ways on virtually any level, including individual students, classrooms, schools, districts, and states. To access these reports, DIBELS users establish an account with the DIBELS Data System by paying an annual fee of $1 per student (price at the time of this publication). After DIBELS scores are submitted via the Internet, reports generally are immediately available. The annual fee of $1 per student covers all reporting for all students, including screening (benchmark assessments) and progress monitoring, and all aggregate reports for students in the database for one year.

FREQUENTLY ASKED QUESTIONS ABOUT DIBELS AS AN ASSESSMENT TOOL

1. **Can I use DIBELS with children who have speech or language impairments that delay oral responses? For example, can I use DIBELS with a child who stutters?**

   DIBELS can be used to measure reading accuracy for a child who stutters or has another language impairment that delays oral responses. However, because the child's language impairment is likely to affect his fluency, the established risk categories would not be valid for this student. If a child who has this type of language impairment has DIBELS scores below benchmark, consult with a speech and language expert to determine other means to identify the child's stage of reading development.

2. **Is it permissible to laminate the Student Materials pages and put them in a binder so that I can "flip" the pages as I show them to the students?**

   Yes. Many examiners laminate the Student Materials and put them in a binder as a practical way to make the materials last longer and to help make administering DIBELS more efficient.

3. **How were words, passages, pictures, etc., selected for DIBELS?**

   Lists of words were selected from materials commonly used in typical K–3 materials, as found in *The Educator's Word Frequency Guide* (Zeno, 1995), which was used to identify words for some DIBELS measures (Good & Kaminski, 2002). Over the more than 15 years that DIBELS has been researched, the words have been validated with regard to their predictive value for foundational reading skills. The words determined to be most predictive were put into a database, and then words were randomly selected for each of the measures. For example, the words used in ISF are from typical first and second grade reading materials.

The ORF passages have a grade-level difficulty determined by various reading formulas. The passages for any grade level are selected to represent readability for the end of the grade. (The exception is First Grade ORF, which has readability levels at the beginning of Second Grade.) This means ORF passages have the same difficulty level throughout the year. The passage difficulty may vary only *slightly*, according to the readability formulas. When the passages do show slight variations in difficulty, the first passage is the easiest, the second passage has the middle level of difficulty, and the third passage is the most difficult, based on the readability formulas.

Pictures for ISF are selected from early literacy materials to match the words generated from the database. In other words, first the words were generated. After the word lists were compiled, a picture was chosen to represent each word.

4. Do the stories, words, etc., get progressively more difficult from grade to grade?

It depends on the measure. ORF passages within a grade level are of almost equal difficulty throughout each grade, and they represent end-of-grade reading expectations. Each ISF, LNF, PSF, and NWF probe is of equal difficulty. (For example, no PSF probe contains significantly more difficult words than any other PSF probe.) WUF, however, changes in difficulty. WUF lists used in kindergarten and first grade are of equal difficulty, whereas those used in second and third grades contain more difficult words than K–1 lists but are consistent within lists for Grades 2–3.

5. How can reading words or passages for only one minute give a good indication of the child's true reading abilities?

When ORF was originally developed in the late 1970s and initially researched in the 1980s, researchers administered oral reading assessments for different periods of time, including times longer than one minute. These researchers found that the information gained in one minute was just as reliable, valid, and indicative of student skill as information obtained in multi-minute samples. The reliability of ORF is increased when three passages are administered instead of just one.

6. DIBELS scoring seems to assume that accurate word reading predicts comprehension. Is this an accurate statement?

Accurate reading and fluency are important in ORF. Comprehension is obviously impeded when students read words inaccurately. When students are fluent, they are able to read words automatically without conscious attention to decoding the word, thereby minimizing their attention to decoding and maximizing their attention to comprehending what they are reading.

ORF measures both accuracy and fluency. The RTF score also adds to the predictive power of ORF for comprehension.

7. Can teachers practice the directions for DIBELS benchmark assessments with their students, since the directions are so difficult for so many children to understand?

The creators of DIBELS spent many years developing, testing, and revising directions. They are confident that the existing standardized directions work for most children. Roland Good and Ruth Kaminski told the authors that their "research as well as experience suggests that 95%–98% of children do fine with current directions administered by a trained, skilled examiner. If an examiner feels that a child's performance is not valid because the child did not understand what he or she was supposed to do, the option is available to reassess any measure" (personal communication, fall, 2004).

In a very few cases, an examiner or teacher may determine that a student performed poorly on any DIBELS assessment or on DIBELS in general because the student did not understand the directions. In that case, it may be appropriate to retest the student. Before giving the retest, the teacher or examiner could explain to the student how the test works and teach that student explicitly how to follow DIBELS directions. For students who seem to have difficulty with the skills and the directions, the teacher should design lesson plans that include activities to build the missing skills and to follow the DIBELS directions. This can be done using directions similar to those for the DIBELS measure. *However, in no case should teachers intentionally provide instruction on the specific content, questions, words, or pictures included in any DIBELS measure.* For example, practicing actual DIBELS passages in class or sending them home would be irresponsible because the benchmark assessment or progress monitoring assessment materials given would have been read before, invalidating the DIBELS score. Additionally, posting charts full of DIBELS or other nonsense words would also be irresponsible because this could encourage students to memorize make-believe words instead of teaching them letter sounds and sound-blending skills they can generalize to connected text. An important part of the validity of DIBELS scoring is that the student responds to word lists and passages that he or she is seeing for the first time. This is true for both benchmark assessment materials and progress monitoring materials.

8. Why aren't the benchmarks shown on the scoring booklet so we can know how well the student did immediately as we record scores on the Summary of Scores Page?

Benchmarks and risk levels change from time to time. Therefore, the developers of DIBELS decided not to include risk-level cut points on the Scoring Booklets. Some schools that download materials for copying put the benchmarks and risk levels on the first page of the student booklets before making copies. This helps examiners and teachers to immediately and easily see how well the student performed. Examiners and teachers also can use the

DIBELS Benchmark Scores table from the Appendix to immediately analyze DIBELS scores if they have it handy when administering the assessments.

9. Are DIBELS benchmarks normed?

Yes. DIBELS benchmark raw scores are norm referenced, in that percentiles are given on reports from the DIBELS Data System. The cut points that separate the DIBELS risk categories are criterion referenced. The criterion-referenced cut points are more valuable and are emphasized because they are scientifically valid predictors of reading competence at the end of third grade regardless of the student's percentile ranking. The cut points were established to predict reading success or failure by identifying the risk associated with others in the normative group who scored the same, not by establishing the percentile ranking of the student's score. (See Chapter 3 for a more detailed discussion of the difference between a norm-referenced assessment and one that uses scientifically validated criterion-referenced benchmarks.) Norm-referenced student rankings are provided on the Class List Report, but these are provided for information only and are not the basis for establishing risk categories. The criterion-referenced cut points that define risk levels are the basis for DIBELS intervention recommendations, not the norm-referenced student rankings.

10. Can DIBELS be used as a diagnostic tool?

DIBELS is not considered to be a formal diagnostic tool; however, it can provide some diagnostic information because teachers can look for error patterns in DIBELS Scoring Booklets to guide further assessment. Teachers can also use DIBELS scores and error patterns from the Scoring Booklet to group students for intervention and to identify areas of weakness that will be the focus of intervention instruction for a group. (Teachers should not expect information gained from the DIBELS Scoring Booklets to be exhaustive.)

11. Why isn't DIBELS called a diagnostic tool?

DIBELS does not meet the National Reading First Assessment Committee's guidelines for qualification as a diagnostic tool, partly because DIBELS does not measure multiple skills within any of the five essential components of reading (phonemic awareness, phonics, fluency, vocabulary, and comprehension). DIBELS measures are indicators, and they don't measure multiple subskills within an essential component as most diagnostic assessments do.

12. How long has DIBELS been in use?

At the time this manual was published, DIBELS had been used as an assessment tool in schools for more than 15 years. Oral Reading Fluency (ORF) has been in use for over 25 years. Over those years, the measures have been changed and refined in response to research findings. From school year 1992–1993 to school year 2001–2002, the DIBELS assessment included five measures. Retell Fluency and Word Use Fluency were added as optional measures in school year 2002–2003.

13. Does the annual fee of $1 per student cover only screening (benchmark assessment) reports or both screening and progress monitoring reports?

The annual fee of $1 per student covers all reporting for that student, including screening and progress monitoring. All other available reports, some of which are described in Chapter 9, are also available when a school or district uses the DIBELS Data System.

14. Why don't the DIBELS materials purchased from Sopris West always match the DIBELS materials downloaded from the Internet?

DIBELS materials are changed from time to time. The changes are often reflected first in the materials available to be downloaded from the DIBELS Web site. Because Sopris West materials are printed in advance, changes are not reflected until a new printing of the materials occurs, and printings are often months apart.

Some schools have found that when they download student booklets from the Internet, the student booklets do not match the Student Materials they purchased from Sopris West or downloaded from the Internet at an earlier date. Unfortunately, these schools sometimes discover the mismatch only when examiners begin giving the benchmark assessments. To avoid this problem, we recommend that schools either: (1) download Student Materials and Scoring Booklets at the same time; or (2) check to make sure that student booklets downloaded from the Internet or purchased from Sopris West match the scoring materials in hand.

2

DIBELS Extras: Grades 4–6, Spanish Version, and Scoring on a Handheld Computer

DIBELS was originally developed as an assessment to be given in English with pencil and paper to students in kindergarten to Grade 3. Recently, new innovations have added to DIBELS' usefulness and ease of assessment. Benchmark and progress monitoring assessments are available for Grades 4–6. DIBELS benchmark assessments are available in Spanish for kindergarten to Grade 3. Examiners can now administer and score DIBELS benchmark and progress monitoring assessments using a handheld computer, eliminating the need for pencil and paper and making data input much easier and faster.

DIBELS FOR GRADES 4–6

Description of Materials

Benchmark assessments and progress monitoring materials for Grades 4–6 are available in preprinted versions from Sopris West and on the DIBELS Web site. Oral Reading Fluency and Retell Fluency are the only measures given for screening students in Grades 4–6. These measures are scored the same way that the DIBELS K–3 version is scored. Students read three passages for the benchmark assessment. The median (middle) scores for ORF and RTF are recorded for each student. (Middle scores may be from different passages for ORF and RTF.)

The DIBELS Benchmark Scores Table in the Appendix shows estimated ORF benchmark scores and risk levels for benchmark assessments in Grades 4–6. According to the DIBELS Web site, these estimated benchmark scores and risk levels are based on two well-known fluency studies.

The DIBELS Web site states that a reasonable approximation of risk level for ORF scores in Grades 4–6 can be derived from the local norms. Scores in the 40th percentile and above, based on local norms, can be considered Low Risk. Scores between the 20th and 40th percentiles can be considered Some Risk. Scores lower than the 20th percentile can be considered At Risk. The DIBELS Data System provides local percentage rankings for ORF scores for Grades 4–6.

The formula for calculating the risk levels for RTF for Grades 4–6 is the same as that for Grades 1–3. Students considered At Risk are those whose ratio of *words used for RTF to words read in ORF* (based on the median of three scores for each measure) is lower than 25%. (The Some Risk level does not exist for RTF.)

<table>
<tr><td>

Most students in Grades 3–5 who do not achieve the benchmark score for ORF need further assessment to determine whether they have an underlying weakness in phonemic awareness or phonics.

</td></tr>
</table>

Interpretation of Scores in Grades 4–6

ORF and RTF are the measures used for benchmark assessments in Grades 4–6. The ORF score provides information about whether or not students are reading as accurately and fluently as expected. RTF provides information about whether the student is retaining information concerning what he or she reads, as opposed to reading with reasonable fluency but without obtaining meaning.

Because only ORF and RTF are given to students in Grades 4–6, many teachers are misled and think fluency and comprehension are the only skills that should be taught at these grades—even in intervention. Generally, a substantial portion of students scoring below ORF benchmark scores need more than simply fluency instruction, comprehension instruction, or a combination of both during their intervention lessons. Typically, older students with low ORF scores have weaknesses in their phonological awareness skills or their understanding of phonics, and intervention begins by focusing on these skills.

Students who need intervention that focuses on fluently reading connected text are those who score below the benchmark score on benchmark assessments while reading more than 95% of the words accurately. These students demonstrate the ability to decode on an independent reading level, but they are not fast enough at decoding to be efficient readers. The student with this profile will benefit from fluency instruction.

Students who need extra comprehension instruction and practice during intervention lessons typically have RTF scores that are lower than 25% of their ORF scores. Students with RTF scores between 25% and 50% of their ORF scores often raise their comprehension scores as their accuracy and fluency improve. However, it is important to monitor comprehension for these students by administering RTF after ORF during progress monitoring.

It is very important for teachers in Grades 4–6 to understand that ORF scores alone do not give an indication of the specific skill or skills whose weaknesses may be the cause of a student in Grades 4–6 scoring below benchmark on ORF. Further analysis of the specific reason for the low ORF score is needed before effective intervention can be designed. For a student who has an ORF score lower than benchmark, it is imperative to establish that the student has phonemic awareness and phonics skills, because it is often a lack of these fundamental reading skills that impedes the student's reading abilities, no matter the student's age.

SPANISH LANGUAGE VERSION OF DIBELS

Description of Materials

The Spanish Language version of DIBELS is called IDEL (*Indicadores **D**inámicos del **É**xito en la **L**ectura*). Progress Monitoring Materials and Benchmark Assessment Materials with directions, passages, and words written in Spanish are available for kindergarten to Grade 3 from Sopris West and on the DIBELS Web site.

The letters and words in IDEL reflect the specifics of the Spanish language. Letter Naming Fluency includes the letter *ñ* but omits the letter combination *ll*. Phoneme Segmentation Fluency includes both one- and two-syllable words with two to five phonemes. Nonsense words in Nonsense Word Fluency are either one or two open syllables (open syllables end in one vowel) with the pattern CV or CVCV. (These are the most common letter patterns in Spanish words.)

Scoring and Administration Rules for Spanish Language Version

Scoring and administration rules for IDEL are essentially the same as those used for the English version of DIBELS. Vowels and consonants are articulated according to Spanish conventions, and dialects must be considered when scoring.

Benchmark Scores for Spanish Language Version

Benchmark scores were not available for IDEL at time of printing. Until the IDEL benchmarks are available, local norms can be used.

Reasons to Use Spanish Language Version

Educators choose IDEL for two primary reasons. First, they use IDEL to measure beginning reading skills for native Spanish–speaking children who speak very little or no English. Second, they use IDEL to determine the level of basic reading skills for students who have moderate speaking skills in English but have had little or no exposure to written English.

Studies show that if a person can read accurately and fluently in one alphabetic language,[1] those reading skills can transfer to another alphabetic language once the student masters the sound–symbol relationships in the new language (Gillon, 2004). Students who have weak phonemic awareness, phonics, or fluency in their native language are likely to have similar weaknesses in any new language they learn. Therefore, a student's phonemic awareness, phonics, fluency, vocabulary, and comprehension skills can be measured by having him read in his native language, even if he cannot speak or read English well. By using IDEL, we can still measure whether Spanish-speaking children who speak English poorly and do not understand the English language sound–symbol relationships are mastering the early literacy skills necessary for them to read well in any alphabetic language. Having this knowledge allows us to provide intervention for those weak in specific skills as early as possible, rather than waiting until the student knows English well enough to measure the skills using the English language version of DIBELS.

Qualifications for Spanish Language Version Examiners

Examiners who give the Spanish version of DIBELS need to know the rules for scoring and administering DIBELS in both English and Spanish. Generally,

---

[1] Both English and Spanish are alphabetic languages, meaning that the written languages use alphabets to represent sounds.

attending a workshop in how to score DIBELS in English will suffice for scoring in Spanish because the scoring and administration rules for both versions are the same.

Examiners who give the Spanish version must be able to pronounce words and phonemes in Spanish well enough so that the children will be able to understand the examiner. Examiners also must have phonemic awareness in Spanish so that they can recognize correct and incorrect articulation of Spanish phonemes. Finally, examiners must be fluent in Spanish, with much more than a rudimentary understanding of the language, so that they can accurately and quickly determine whether a student's phonemes (ISF, PSF, and NWF); nonsense words (NWF); real words (ORF, RTF, and WUF); and sentences, phrases, words, and definitions (WUF) are accurate or not.

ADMINISTERING DIBELS WITH A HANDHELD COMPUTER USING SOFTWARE FROM WIRELESS GENERATION

Product Description

An exciting development for DIBELS users is the ability to administer and score all benchmark and progress monitoring assessments on a handheld computer using *mCLASS™:DIBELS®* software from Wireless Generation, Inc. A Spanish version, *mCLASS™:IDEL™* software, is available for benchmark assessments. During the 2004–2005 school year, approximately 30,000 teachers used *mCLASS* software to administer DIBELS. Information about Wireless Generation's *mCLASS:DIBELS* software is available online at http://www.wirelessgeneration.com, by calling Wireless Generation toll free at 1-866-212-8688, or by e-mailing info@wgen.net.

Examiners score DIBELS directly on the handheld computer, eliminating the need for pencil, Scoring Booklets, and stopwatches. The only paper materials the examiner needs are Student Materials booklets that contain the pages students look at or read for a measure. Instructions, prompts, timing, and scoring materials are all integrated into the *mCLASS:DIBELS* software on the handheld computer. Each student's score and risk category are immediately available on the handheld computer after the student's assessment has been administered.

Administering Benchmark Assessments With a Handheld Computer

After a school or district subscribes to use *mCLASS:DIBELS* software, all students are entered into a secure database by Wireless Generation. Each examiner is assigned a password, giving access to those students whom he or she is assigned to examine.

When an examiner administers DIBELS, the handheld computer highlights the applicable measures for each benchmark assessment based on the student's grade and the time of year. To begin the assessment, the examiner taps to select a probe or measure to administer and then places the Student Materials booklet in front of the student. All instructions and prompts are provided for the examiner on the handheld computer. The examiner taps the screen to record student responses. A stopwatch is unnecessary because the software automates timing for each measure.

When a benchmark assessment is completed, the *mCLASS:DIBELS* software immediately delivers a student's score and risk level. After each measure is administered, the examiner can add notes and observations on student response patterns and motivation. Upon request, *mCLASS:DIBELS* software instantaneously provides details on the handheld computer about which answers were correct and which were incorrect for all items and questions on all measures. It also provides the student's risk assessment for each measure. (This information is also available from the Web on a desktop or laptop computer after scores have been submitted, as explained below.) On the handheld computer, *mCLASS:DIBELS* has also incorporated recommendations and guidance from leading reading experts about translating DIBELS scores into appropriate instruction.

Data Transfer and Reports

Examiners transfer all scores directly from the handheld computer to Wireless Generation's secure Web site by placing the handheld computer in a cradle and touching the "sync" button. Reports at state, district, school, classroom, and individual student levels are immediately available from *mCLASS:DIBELS* on the Web site after scores are submitted. The reports are printable and can be viewed on a desktop or laptop computer. Reading First reporting is also easily and immediately available via the Web using *mCLASS:DIBELS* software. (Users of *mCLASS:DIBELS* are assigned a password that allows access to certain student reports. The level of access for each examiner is determined by the school or district administrators.) In addition, Wireless Generation can transfer scores to the DIBELS Data System at no extra charge, giving examiners access to additional reports offered by the DIBELS Data System as well as to the additional reports offered through *mCLASS:DIBELS* software.

Cost and Equipment Requirements

Wireless Generation prices *mCLASS:DIBELS* software on an annual, per-student basis. The two pieces of equipment that schools need to use *mCLASS: DIBELS* software are a Palm OS® handheld computer and a standard Internet-connected computer for syncing the data from the handheld computer to Wireless Generation's Web site. (Most versions of the Palm handheld computer can be used with *mCLASS:DIBELS* software. Wireless Generation provides specific information about Palm handheld computers that are compatible with its software.) Wireless Generation will include the handheld computers in its cost, or the school can purchase handheld computers from another source. To obtain specific information about the cost for using *mCLASS:DIBELS* software, contact Wireless Generation at http://www.wirelessgeneration.com, by calling toll free 1-866-212-8688, or by e-mailing info@wgen.net.

Training for Administering DIBELS With mCLASS:DIBELS Software

Wireless Generation offers training for *mCLASS:DIBELS* software. All examiners should start with a traditional DIBELS Administration and Scoring Workshop and then attend a workshop in which they learn to use the handheld computer to administer DIBELS. (For many examiners, the Wireless Generation training may be their first introduction to using a handheld computer, and this is considered in Wireless Generation training.)

Attending the traditional Scoring and Administration Workshop allows examiners who have not previously administered DIBELS to learn the administration and scoring rules, and they are able to get a visual picture of what the *mCLASS:DIBELS* software accomplishes as the examiners tap the answers into the handheld computers. After examiners who are new to DIBELS finish a traditional scoring and administration workshop, it is ideal if they administer at least five practice benchmark assessments to students with pencil and paper so that they better understand how DIBELS is scored before they take the Wireless Generation training. This accomplishes two purposes. They will better understand DIBELS scoring after they use pencil and paper. They will also appreciate the ease of the *mCLASS:DIBELS* software when they learn to use it.

ADVANTAGES AND DISADVANTAGES OF mCLASS:DIBELS SOFTWARE

The advantages to using *mCLASS:DIBELS* software are obvious. First, using *mCLASS:DIBELS* software is less cumbersome than traditional pencil and paper scoring, and it takes less time because examiners do not have to gather and prepare student Scoring Booklets. The only materials used for benchmark administration and progress monitoring are the handheld computer and the Student Materials booklet. Examiners do not need a stopwatch, a pen or pencil, Scoring Booklets, or a calculator. Second, transferring the scores over the Web is done by the examiner with a push of the sync button on the handheld computer. With pencil and paper administration, all scores have to be manually entered. Data transfer with *mCLASS:DIBELS* software is easier, takes virtually no time, does not require personnel to input scores, and eliminates errors made during data entry.

The primary disadvantage to using *mCLASS:DIBELS* is that the initial investment is more than it is for pencil and paper, because of the significant investment in handheld computers. The annual cost per student is also higher than the $1 per student fee charged by the University of Oregon for the DIBELS data management system. Using *mCLASS:DIBELS* software, however, drastically reduces material expense because only Student Materials are needed, and these are included at no charge with the software. Using *mCLASS:DIBELS* software also saves all the time and expense it takes to manually input the scores into the DIBELS Data System or to otherwise aggregate scores for analysis.

Examiners who use pencil and paper are able to record not only which items are incorrect, but also the particular mistakes the child makes—information that can be useful when planning instruction. The handheld software does not provide for recording these details during an assessment, although it does provide a way for the scoring of each answer to be observed after the assessment is completed.

Another potential disadvantage is that technological "glitches" can cause loss of data. For example, although a rare occurrence, batteries on handhelds run out and scores that haven't been sent to the *mCLASS* data management system before the battery dies may be lost. However, pencil and paper scoring booklets can be misplaced or damaged before data entry, which also results in the loss of data. Neither the pencil and paper nor the handheld computer system is completely immune to data loss.

3

Types of Reading Assessments Related to DIBELS

Educational assessments can be formal or informal, and they can be used for many purposes. The No Child Left Behind Act of 2001 (NCLB; U.S. Department of Education, 2002) requires four kinds of reading assessments: screening, progress monitoring, diagnostic, and outcome. This chapter explains the difference between formal and informal assessment, and it explains DIBELS' relationship to the four types of reading assessments. Perhaps the most important fact for those administering DIBELS in this chapter is that DIBELS benchmark assessments are standardized, which means the directions must be read exactly as written, scoring must conform to DIBELS conventions, and examiners may not help or coach students during DIBELS assessments.

FORMAL AND INFORMAL ASSESSMENTS

Virtually all reading assessments can be categorized as formal or informal. In general, teachers differentiate formal and informal assessments by the way they give the directions.

- *Formal assessments* use standardized directions that must be given to the student the same way every time. In addition, they use standardized data collection procedures (the term "data" here and throughout this manual refers to the scores) and standardized scoring conventions.
- When giving *informal assessments*, teachers generally may give directions in their own words, data are not collected in any specified way, and set scoring rules are not mandated.

Additional characteristics of formal and informal assessment are explained below.

Formal Assessment

Formal assessments ensure that all students have the same opportunity to demonstrate what they know. Formal assessments have been given to a great number of children (often in a wide variety of geographic locations), always using the same directions, questions, scoring procedures, and types of assessment group (individuals, small groups, or whole groups). The large group whose participants are used to establish comparative scores is called the "normative" group. Normative groups are used to establish the standards for both norm-referenced and criterion-referenced assessments. Even though DIBELS emphasizes the criterion-referenced cut points for screening, progress monitoring, and outcome assessment purposes, DIBELS scores are norm referenced because percentile rankings are available from the DIBELS data management system. Therefore, DIBELS is both a norm-referenced and criterion-referenced assessment.

Norm-referenced assessments. Formal, norm-referenced assessments use scores from the normative group as the standard for establishing the individual's standing against the normative group. The question answered by norm-referenced assessment is, "How does the student compare with other students who have taken the same assessment?" The results of norm-referenced assessments are often presented by showing a percentile for the student's standing compared with that for the normative group. For example, if Billy's reading comprehension scores are in the 37th percentile, it means that Billy scored as well as or higher than 37% of the students in the normative group and lower than 63% of the students in the normative group. When using norm-referenced assessments, school districts generally have guidelines as to what percentile represents acceptable performance, and these guidelines may vary from district to district. (DIBELS scores are norm referenced, although the most important information on DIBELS is the criterion-referenced cut points that define risk levels.)

Criterion-referenced assessments. Formal criterion-referenced assessments also use data gathered from a normative group, or the criteria are developed from a standard defined by an expert or experts. With DIBELS, the data are used to establish criterion-referenced standards of performance, also referred to as "goals" by DIBELS. The results of criterion-referenced assessments are presented by showing how the student performed in relation to an established goal or benchmark. Questions answered by criterion-referenced assessments might be: "What percentage of students in a classroom, school, district, or state met the instructional goals for specific early reading skills?"; "Which children are at risk for reading below grade level by the end of a certain grade?"; and "Has our instructional program taught children the skills they need to become good readers by the end of a certain grade?" (ISF, LNF, PSF, NWR, ORF, and RTF are formal criterion-referenced assessments that can be used to answer all of the questions above. DIBELS researchers have not established formal, criterion-referenced or norm-referenced benchmark scores for WUF.)

Description of DIBELS as a Criterion-Referenced Assessment. As discussed above, DIBELS provides formal, criterion-referenced assessment information. Typically, criterion-referenced assessments are used to compare a student's score or scores against an established target or benchmark. DIBELS scores are used to compare a student's scores against "risk levels," as shown in the DIBELS Benchmark Scores Table in the Appendix. The next paragraph is a simple description of the very complex task that researchers performed in order to determine the range for risk levels in the DIBELS Benchmark Scores Table.

Researchers used the data (scores) from the reference groups to establish the early reading skills that children acquired at various points between kindergarten and third grade. Published measures of reading achievement, as well as end-of-third-grade high-stakes reading assessments in Oregon, Alaska, Illinois, and Florida, were used to categorize children into two categories at the end of third grade: (1) those who scored at or above grade level; and (2) those who scored below grade level. DIBELS scores for students in each of these two groups were analyzed at various points between kindergarten and third grade. The analysis was used to determine the DIBELS scores that define risk categories for each measure (Good et al., 2002).

Informal Assessment

Informal assessments are used almost daily in the classroom. Common examples include basic classroom tests, checklists, classroom observation, and any oral reading for which the teacher counts or notes errors. Informal assessments do not require standardized directions, standardized data collection efforts, or standardized scoring rules. Common commercial informal assessments are informal reading inventories (referred to as "IRIs") such as the Qualitative Reading Inventory (Leslie & Caldwell, 2001) or the Jerry Johns Basic Reading Inventory (Johns, 2001). Other informal assessments are those tied to reading programs. Running records are another widely used form of informal assessment.

Informal assessments can be and are useful to provide information to guide instruction. However, the data from informal assessments should not be used to compare scores across classrooms, schools, districts, states, etc., because these measures have not been scientifically validated. It is impossible to reliably compare scores on informal assessments even when teachers give the same assessments within a grade level. This is because their administration, scoring, and interpretation may vary.

When scores from informal assessments are compared, it is often the case that, instead of comparing apples with apples, apples are compared with oranges. For example, Teacher A's scoring rule for a sight-word assessment may be that the student is given three seconds to identify the word correctly, while Teacher B allows the student to sound out the word and take a few guesses. In this situation, Teacher A and Teacher B may have vastly different scores for the same student. The information gathered by either teacher could be useful for instructional purposes, but comparing scores under these circumstances would give no reasonable basis for making assumptions about one student's performance compared with another's. (Standardized procedures developed and implemented through formal assessments are vital to professional conversations and comparisons with regard to student achievement, especially if scores are to be compared over time and across classrooms, schools, districts, etc.)

DIBELS' RELATIONSHIP TO THE FOUR TYPES OF READING ASSESSMENTS

The NCLB Act of 2001 requires schools to use four types of assessments to measure student progress in reading:

- Outcome assessment
- Screening assessment
- Diagnostic assessment
- Progress monitoring assessment.

DIBELS has been validated by the National Reading First Assessment Committee (NRFAC) as a formal assessment for purposes of outcome, screening, and progress monitoring. However, DIBELS can also provide diagnostic information to help guide instruction. Using information from DIBELS Scoring Booklets for informal diagnosis is described in depth in *I've DIBEL'd, Now What?* by Susan Hall (Hall, 2006).

Outcome Assessment

Outcome assessments are generally given at the end of the year, and they are almost always formal assessments.[1] Outcome assessments help teachers, principals, and administrators evaluate the overall effectiveness of the educational program, including reading, for all children. (These are often called "high-stakes assessments" in Grades 3–12.) Outcome assessments provide a snapshot of students' skills and are used to determine whether the instruction given has been successful. Questions that DIBELS and other outcome assessments help answer may include:

1. Is the reading curriculum for this school or district working for most students?

2. How do this year's students compare with last year's students in the same grade?

3. What percentage of students met the end-of-grade goal?

4. What percentage of students is on track to meet the standard for a specific grade on the high-stakes reading comprehension test?

Outcome assessments are most useful for system and school-level administrators. Their utility at the classroom level is generally limited to determining classroom profiles and grouping students for instruction. Some of the reports described in Chapter 9 can be used for purposes of outcome assessment.

Screening Assessment

Screening assessments give the teacher information about an individual student's skills with regard to reading instruction. Typically, screening assessments have been administered at the beginning of the school year, and they may be used to group students for instruction. Screening assessments have taken the form of

---

[1] Outcome assessments are required by Reading First so that schools and districts can evaluate their progress toward the goal of "every child reading at grade level" by third grade. Schools are required to show regular progress toward this goal in order to continue receiving funds from Reading First grants.

teacher-made assessments, assessments provided by the local educational agency or district, or a commercial product such as an informal reading inventory. These informal assessments are not normed or formally criterion referenced, and they are subject to teacher interpretation or to informally established goals that may or may not lead children to be good readers.

Recently, schools have been increasingly aware of the benefit of using formal screening assessments, such as DIBELS, so that they can obtain reliable and valid information about all students. Formal screening instruments tell us with reasonable certainty whether a student is prepared for grade-level instruction. They also provide a "first alert" warning that a child is behind in skills that are essential to becoming a good reader. In this way, formal screening assessments allow the teacher the luxury of not having to wait until the student fails with regular classroom instruction before learning that the student needs extra help.

When a student is not prepared for grade-level instruction, formal screening instruments also provide information about the skill areas in which the student is weak. For example, DIBELS benchmark assessments address all five components of reading instruction, as defined by the National Reading Panel: phonemic awareness, phonics, fluency, vocabulary, and comprehension (National Institute of Child Health and Human Development, 2000).

No screening assessments are intended to be exhaustive assessments of individual early literacy skills. For example, DIBELS doesn't measure every skill within phonological awareness, but measures only whether a student can identify and produce the initial phoneme or phonemes in a word (ISF) and whether a student can segment a word into parts (PSF). DIBELS has selected specific measures that indicate a student's current reading skills and predict later reading success or failure.

After the formal screening tool is administered, the screening results are used to determine which students may need additional instructional support in addition to core reading instruction. In some cases, screening scores are used as a springboard for performing a more in-depth analysis of the specific skills that are missing in order to plan intervention instruction. The further analysis is a diagnostic assessment and is described in the next section.

Diagnostic Assessment

Diagnostic assessments provide more in-depth information than the screening assessment about students' strengths and weaknesses in critical early literacy skills. Diagnostic assessments also help teachers plan instruction.

Formal Diagnostic Assessment

A number of formal diagnostic instruments for early reading skills are norm referenced, meaning that the scores show the student's standing relative to the normative group. These include, but are not limited to, the Test of Phonological Awareness (TOPA) (Torgesen & Bryant, 2004), Comprehensive Test of Phonological Processing (C-TOPP) (Wagner & Torgesen, 1999), Woodcock

Johnson III (Woodcock et al., 2001), and Gray Oral Reading Test (GORT) (Wiederholt & Bryant, 2001). These assessments are student specific and should be given strategically when informal diagnostic methods have not provided enough information to adequately guide instruction. Formal diagnostic instruments typically are also used for purposes such as making the decision about whether to place a student in special education and to identify a specific learning difficulty the student may have.

Informal Diagnostic Assessment

Informal diagnosis for planning instruction can take place every time a student makes an error when reading or learning an early literacy skill such as phonological awareness, letter names, letter sounds, tracking words while the teacher reads, etc. Informal diagnosis requires only that the teacher notice an error pattern and decide to incorporate that error pattern into lesson planning.

DIBELS Scoring Booklets are used by many teachers and reading specialists for informal diagnostic purposes. This occurs when the teacher examines the Scoring Booklet to find specific error patterns made by the student. Intervention instruction can initially be aimed at the error patterns observed in the Scoring Booklet and adjusted as instruction widens to include other error patterns observed during intervention lessons.

An example of using DIBELS for informal diagnosis might occur when examining NWF answers. If the student consistently gets the first and last sounds correct but reads words with the vowels *e* and *i* incorrectly, it is reasonable to begin instruction with a focus on mastering articulation of the short e and i sounds and reading words with the short vowel pronunciations for *e* and *i*. If the teacher finds out during instruction that the student has difficulty with any other letter–sound relationships, those can be incorporated into the instruction. (See *I've DIBEL'd, Now What?* by Susan Hall [2006] for in-depth information about how to analyze Student Booklets for all measures.)

Progress Monitoring

Progress monitoring is an important part of the intervention process because it gives teachers information about the effectiveness of intervention instruction on a frequent basis. Most importantly, it helps intervention to be more effective by giving data about whether students are progressing and whether they are making enough progress. When progress is not satisfactory, intervention is adjusted.

First, benchmark assessment scores provide information about students who are at risk for reading failure and need intervention instruction. The next step is to use the benchmark assessment scores and error patterns observed in the Scoring Booklets and from other sources to form small groups with similar instructional needs. After that, informal diagnostic assessment is used to form an instructional support plan for the group. Then, small-group intervention instruction begins. Progress monitoring is administered to measure the effectiveness of instruction. DIBELS progress monitoring is explained further in Chapter 4.

4

Progress Monitoring

OVERVIEW

Within a short period of time after intervention instruction begins, teachers need to ensure that the instructional support they are providing to students is effective. Progress monitoring is the tool used to measure whether intervention instruction is effective enough for the student to meet or exceed the next benchmark score by the date established. DIBELS progress monitoring assessments are ongoing, meaning they can be administered every one to four weeks (in a few cases, every six weeks). Progress monitoring scores are used to determine whether students are making adequate progress toward end-of-year benchmark scores, which in turn predict whether a student is on track to becoming a competent reader. (DIBELS progress monitoring can be used to evaluate the effectiveness of intervention instruction even when another screening instrument is used to identify and place children in intervention groups.)

At this point, it is important to explain that progress monitoring has two separate but related meanings. Within the context of No Child Left Behind (NCLB) and Reading First, progress monitoring means that children are screened more than once a year to ensure that their reading skills are progressing adequately. Under the NCLB definition, DIBELS benchmark assessments at the middle and end of the year are considered to be progress monitoring assessments. However, the DIBELS researchers understood that two "progress monitoring" assessments a year are not enough to monitor struggling readers progress. They refer to the middle- and end-of-year assessments as benchmark assessments and consider them to be prudent screening for all children. DIBELS does not consider the second and third benchmark assessments to serve the purpose of effective progress monitoring, whereas other screening instruments may label the middle- and end-of-year assessments as progress monitoring.

DIBELS progress monitoring assessments are designed to be given only to children who are at risk of not meeting important early reading outcomes. Most often, these are the students who receive intervention instruction. Progress monitoring assessments are generally given every one to four weeks, with the specific intervals determined by administrators at the school, district, or state level. The more frequently progress monitoring measures are administered, the sooner any lack of progress can be identified so a change in intervention can be made. For that reason, the children with the most risk should receive the most frequent progress monitoring assessments.

An example of progress monitoring might involve a first grade student at the middle of the year who scores at or above the benchmark score in PSF but below the benchmark score in NWF. This student would be placed in an intervention group with instruction focused on early phonics skills. Every one to four weeks, every student in the intervention group would be given an NWF assessment using DIBELS progress monitoring materials. Each student's scores would be charted to determine whether that student is making enough progress to meet the end-of-year benchmark score within a specified time period (usually four to eight months, depending on the time of year intervention begins).

EXAMPLE OF DIBELS PROGRESS MONITORING FOR A STUDENT

Let's assume that Billy is a first grader with the following DIBELS scores on his middle-of-year (January) benchmark assessment:

PSF—49 (Established)

NWF—25 (Deficit)

ORF—10 (Some Risk).

Based on his scores, Billy would be placed in an intervention group with an instructional focus on early phonics, including reading connected text. There is apparently no need for phonemic awareness instruction because Billy's PSF score indicates his phonemic awareness skills are Established. Billy's Some Risk ORF score helps us determine that it is Billy's poor grasp of phonics, as demonstrated by his NWF score, that is hindering his reading abilities, not his phonological awareness skills.

When DIBELS progress monitoring assessments are administered, ample improvement in Billy's NWF score would demonstrate that the intervention instruction is working. In addition to monitoring Billy's phonics skills with NWF, some districts and schools also progress monitor his ORF skills because Billy also needs to meet the ORF benchmark score of 40 by the end of the year. By progress monitoring ORF in addition to NWF, teachers learn whether the intervention instruction focusing on phonics has generalized to his overall reading development so that he can achieve the benchmark score of 40 by the end of the year.

Billy's NWF progress monitoring chart as he begins his intervention for NWF would look like *Chart 4–1*. Notice that the progress monitoring chart is one used from the Appendix. It is slightly revised from the chart in the NWF progress monitoring Scoring Booklet. The two modifications are that the months have been written in by hand and the target icon is moved to March, rather than the end of the six-month period. (See Chapter 13 for more information about modifying progress monitoring charts for NWF.)

The line on the progress monitoring chart between Billy's benchmark assessment score and the target score, which is marked with a target icon, is called the *aimline*. The aimline shows the progress Billy must make in order to meet his intervention goal. Because Billy was supposed to meet the NWF benchmark of 50 by the middle of first grade, he is already behind in that measure. Billy's target is set to achieve a NWF score of 55 (5 more than the benchmark of 50) in March, after almost three months of intervention. By demonstrating mastery of early phonics skills before the end of the year, Billy can begin working on more advanced reading skills, including accuracy and fluency with connected text, so he can achieve the ORF benchmark of 40 by the end of the first grade.

Billy's Progress Monitoring Chart for NWF at the Beginning of Intervention Instruction   **Chart 4-1**

Name: _____*Billy*_____   Teacher: _____*Ms. Sample*_____

Nonsense Word Fluency - Progress Monitoring Chart

Month	*Jan*	*Feb*	*Mar*		
	Scores	Scores	Scores	Scores	Scores
Week 1	_____	_____	_____	_____	_____
Week 2	_____	_____	_____	_____	_____
Week 3	_____	_____	_____	_____	_____
Week 4	_____	_____	_____	_____	_____

Chart 4–2 and Chart 4–3 illustrate that Billy was given NWF progress monitoring assessments every two weeks. The charts show his scores under two scenarios. In Chart 4–2, Billy makes enough progress in his NWF progress monitoring scores to stay at or above the aimline. This means both that his intervention instruction for NWF is working and that he is on target to meet the benchmark score for NWF by March.

Chart 4-2	Billy's Progress Monitoring Chart for NWF After Six Weeks of Intervention Instruction: Instruction Is Effective

Name: _____Billy_____   Teacher: _____Ms. Sample_____

Nonsense Word Fluency - Progress Monitoring Chart

Month	Jan		Feb		Mar					
	Scores		Scores		Scores		Scores		Scores	
Week 1	25		40							
Week 2										
Week 3	32		42							
Week 4										

In *Chart 4–3*, Billy's scores were below the aimline for the first three progress monitoring assessments. This means that his intervention instruction is not effective enough. Given the level of improvement shown, he will not meet the benchmark score by March. Because Billy is not making enough progress to meet the March goal for NWF, his intervention would need to be changed so that it is more effective.

Billy's Progress Monitoring Chart for NWF After Six Weeks of Intervention Instruction: Instruction Is *Not* Effective Enough and Needs Modification   **Chart 4-3**

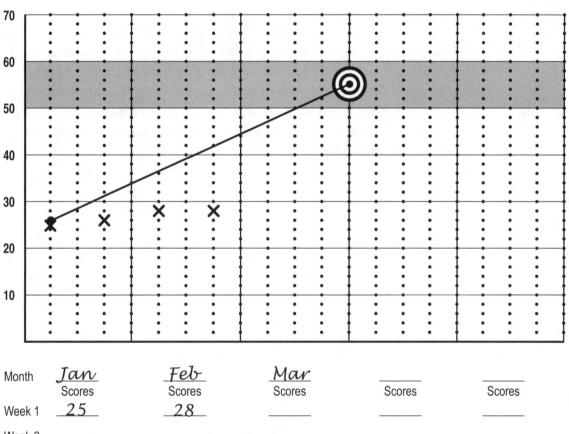

Name: _____ *Billy* _____   Teacher: _____ *Ms. Sample* _____

Nonsense Word Fluency - Progress Monitoring Chart

Month	*Jan*	*Feb*	*Mar*		
	Scores	Scores	Scores	Scores	Scores
Week 1	25	28			
Week 2					
Week 3	26	28			
Week 4					

Several options exist for changing intervention to make it more effective. Some of the changes are as follows:

(1) change the instructional materials

(2) move the student to a different group

(3) add more time to intervention instruction

(4) lower the student group size.

The first two choices offer the student more focus on his instructional needs. The second choice might also be used if the group dynamics were impeding learning. The last two choices increase the intensity of intervention, offer the student more opportunities to respond, or both. Other options might include adding instructional scaffolds, providing more explicit instruction, and giving more opportunities for practice.

Chart 4–4 shows the results of changing Billy's instruction after three progress monitoring scores were below the aimline. It shows that Billy made enough progress after his instruction was intensified to meet the NWF fluency benchmark by March.

It should be noted that the charts and the story about Billy are simply to illustrate the process involved in progress monitoring. Simply meeting the NWF benchmark score by March would not put Billy at the target level. The goal is for Billy to achieve an ORF score at or above the benchmark score of 40 by the end of first grade, and Billy would need to stay in intervention until his ORF progress monitoring scores were on or above the aimline for several consecutive progress monitoring assessments.

Billy's Progress Monitoring Chart for NWF After Three Months of Intervention Instruction   **Chart 4-4**

Name: _____*Billy*_____   Teacher: _____*Ms. Sample*_____

Nonsense Word Fluency - Progress Monitoring Chart

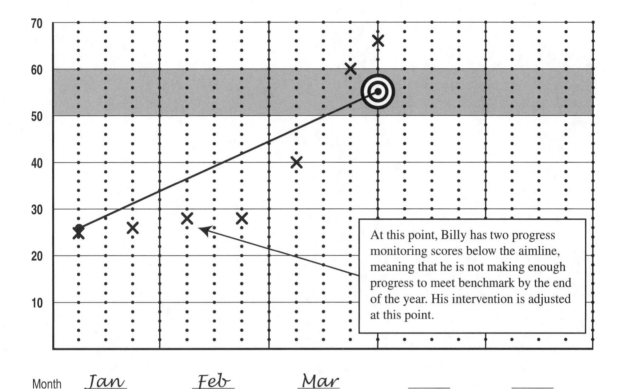

At this point, Billy has two progress monitoring scores below the aimline, meaning that he is not making enough progress to meet benchmark by the end of the year. His intervention is adjusted at this point.

Month	Jan Scores	Feb Scores	Mar Scores	Scores	Scores
Week 1	25	28	40		
Week 2					
Week 3	26	28	60		
Week 4			66		

Interpreting DIBELS Scores

5

DIBELS benchmark administration scores are designed to give two pieces of information:

1. whether a student is at risk for reading difficulties

2. the level of the student's risk.

For students who are in kindergarten and first grade, at some point DIBELS scores measure each of the five essential components of reading instruction.[1] Therefore, the general area of weakness is likely to be identified by DIBELS benchmark assessment for those students who need intervention. Because students in second and third grades take only ORF and RTF, further assessment may be needed to identify the underlying skill weakness that is causing reading difficulty. (Second graders also take NWF at the beginning of the year. WUF is an optional measure that can be administered to second and third graders.) The purpose of this chapter is to fully explain the purpose of DIBELS scores and to explain the levels of risk indicated by DIBELS scores.

MAJOR MILEPOSTS IN DIBELS

The major mileposts in DIBELS are shown in *Figure 5–1* (next page), which is the same as *Figure 1–2* in Chapter 1.

In general, intervention efforts need to focus on students achieving the major mileposts by the time indicated. Achieving the benchmark score for each measure at each benchmark assessment period will help students stay on track to achieve the major mileposts. Students who do not achieve one or more major mileposts by the time indicated will need to work toward reaching more than one major milepost during intervention. An example is Billy in Chapter 4, who did not reach the NWF milepost of 50 by the middle of first grade. Intervention efforts needed to focus on teaching him *beginning phonics skills and reading accurately and fluently in connected text*, helping him reach both the NWF milepost of 50 by March and the end-of-first-grade ORF milepost of 40 by year-end.

---

[1] The National Reading Panel concluded that the essential and most effective components of reading instruction are phonemic awareness, phonics, fluency, vocabulary, and comprehension (National Institute of Child Health and Human Development, 2000).

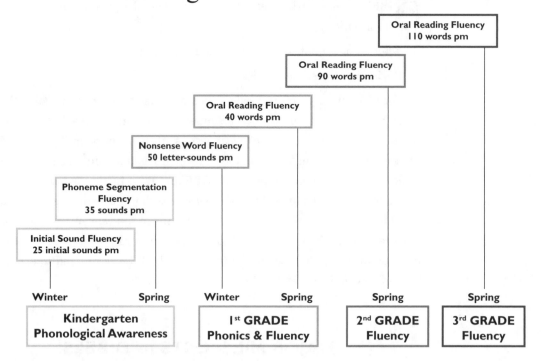

Figure 5-1   **Major Mileposts in DIBELS**

DIBELS Measures:
Learning-to-Read Continuum

ISF, PSF, and NWF scores are benchmark scores. All ORF scores are target scores.

Used with permission from Susan L. Hall. From *I've DIBEL'd, Now What?: Designing Interventions With DIBELS Data* (2006).

Benchmark Scores Table

The DIBELS Benchmark Scores Table in the Appendix shows the scores that determine a student's level of proficiency (risk level) in each foundational reading skill measured by DIBELS at each benchmark administration period. These scores were taken from the DIBELS Web site in January 2004. DIBELS users are encouraged to check the DIBELS Web site periodically for updates to the scores shown in the Appendix because scores determining risk levels may change from time to time.

Typically, schools choose to screen all children three times per year with DIBELS, and these are called benchmark assessment periods. Because many schools operate on year-round schedules, the headings "beginning," "middle," and "end" are used to define each of the benchmark assessment periods on the Benchmark Scores Table. (The DIBELS Web site lists benchmark scores and risk levels for schools that give DIBELS benchmark assessments four times a year, but we have not included those in this manual because the vast majority of schools elect to administer benchmark assessments three times a year.)

Depending on the time of year (beginning, middle, or end), a unique set of DIBELS measures is administered at each grade level. The DIBELS Benchmark Scores Table in the Appendix shows specifically which measures are administered at each benchmark assessment period by listing scores only for the measures given. *Table 5–1* is an excerpt from the Appendix and shows that ISF, LNF, and WUF (optional) are administered at the beginning of kindergarten. It also shows that ISF, LNF, PSF, NWF, and WUF (optional) are administered at the middle of kindergarten, with ISF dropped at the end of the year.

Kindergarten Benchmark and Target Scores   **Table 5-I**

	Beginning of Year		Middle of Year		End of Year	
	Score	Status	Score	Status	Score	Status
Initial Sound Fluency	0–3	At Risk	0–9	Deficit		
	4–7	Some Risk	10–24	Emerging		
	8+	Low Risk	25+	Established		
Letter Naming Fluency	0–1	At Risk	0–14	At Risk	0–28	At Risk
	2–7	Some Risk	15–26	Some Risk	29–39	Some Risk
	8+	Low Risk	27+	Low Risk	40+	Low Risk
Phoneme Segmentation Fluency			0–6	At Risk	0–9	Deficit
			7–17	Some Risk	10–34	Emerging
			18+	Low Risk	35+	Established
Nonsense Word Fluency			0–4	At Risk	0–14	At Risk
			5–12	Some Risk	15–24	Some Risk
			13+	Low Risk	25+	Low Risk
Word Use Fluency (optional)	No benchmark goals are established. The informal goal is for students in the lowest 20th percentile of a district to be considered At Risk; those between the 20th and the 40th percentile, Some Risk; and those above the 40th percentile, Low Risk.					

DESCRIPTION OF DIBELS RISK CATEGORIES

Examination of *Table 5–1* reveals that sometimes the DIBELS risk categories[2, 3] are labeled Low Risk, Some Risk, and At Risk. At other times, the risk categories are labeled Established, Emerging, and Deficit. These changes in labels for risk categories are explained fully in the next section.

For each measure administered during a benchmark assessment period, the DIBELS Benchmark Scores Table shows a range of scores for each risk level. The risk levels fall into one of three status categories: (1) Deficit or At Risk; (2) Emerging or Some Risk; and (3) Established or Low Risk.

---

[2] The exact percentages described in this paragraph for each risk category; for ISF, LNF, PSF, NWF, and ORF; and for each grade level are presented in the instructional recommendations section of the *DIBELS Administration and Scoring Guide*.

[3] The DIBELS risk categories have been shown in studies to be highly correlated to high-stakes tests in other states. See the DIBELS Web site for more information about these correlations (Good et al., 2002).

According to the instructional recommendations section in the *DIBELS Administration and Scoring Guide,* scores in the Established and Low Risk categories indicate that the student has an approximately 80% or better chance of achieving subsequent benchmark scores with appropriate core reading instruction. Scores in the Emerging and Some Risk categories indicate that the student has between approximately 20% and approximately 80% chance of achieving subsequent benchmark scores (or about 50–50 as a group). Scores in the Deficit or At Risk categories indicate that students have less than an approximately 20% chance of achieving the subsequent benchmark scores. (The exact percentages for individual DIBELS measures are discussed in the instructional recommendations section of the *DIBELS Administration and Scoring Guide.*) The different status levels for risk categories in the Benchmark Scores Table are described in detail below.

Established, Emerging, and Deficit Status Levels

One set of risk categories for DIBELS scores includes the labels Established, Emerging, and Deficit. These risk labels are used to indicate that mastery of the skill measured is or was expected by a certain time. (For example, in *Table 5–1* [previous page], these categories first appear for Phoneme Segmentation Fluency at the end of kindergarten, when the benchmark score is 35.) Once benchmark scores are labeled Established, Emerging, and Deficit for any measure, the scores in each risk category for that measure never change. Notice that in the DIBELS Benchmark Scores Table in the Appendix, the benchmark scores of 50 for NWF and 35 for PSF do not change after the risk levels are initially labeled as Established, Emerging, and Deficit. This is true of all scores once they are labeled Established, Emerging, and Deficit.

DIBELS scores with the category labels Deficit, Emerging, and Established indicate whether the student is on track to meet the benchmark score in the next different measure expected for benchmark. For example, a student who achieves an ISF score at the Established level in the middle of kindergarten is on track to achieve an Established score in PSF at the end of kindergarten with appropriate core reading instruction. A student who scores in the Emerging level for ISF at the middle of kindergarten may need intervention, in addition to appropriate core reading instruction, in order to achieve an Established score in PSF by the end of kindergarten. A student with a score in the Deficit level has a very low chance of achieving the end-of-year PSF benchmark without significant intervention.

ISF, PSF, and NWF. ISF, PSF, and NWF are the only three measures that have Established, Emerging, and Deficit risk categories. ISF, PSF, and NWF measure phonemic awareness and beginning phonics, the only foundational early reading skills that DIBELS researchers expect to fully mature by the end of third grade. LNF does not have these risk category labels because DIBELS researchers do not consider letter naming to be a foundational reading skill, as explained in Chapter 10. ORF does not have these risk category labels because students are expected to continue improving their fluency rates beyond sixth grade, the last year for which

DIBELS ORF benchmark scores are provided. WUF does not have any Established benchmark scores because this measure is still being studied.

Initial Sound Fluency Benchmark Scores. ISF is one of the three measures that have an Established benchmark score. Children who have mastered the skill of identifying initial phonemes by the middle of kindergarten are on track for meeting the PSF benchmark score by the end of kindergarten, given appropriate reading instruction. The DIBELS Benchmark Scores Table in the Appendix shows that the benchmark score for ISF is 25. Therefore, students who achieve the ISF benchmark score of 25 by the middle of kindergarten have an approximately 80% or better chance of achieving the PSF benchmark score of 35 by the end of kindergarten, when they have appropriate reading instruction.

Phoneme Segmentation Fluency Benchmark Scores. *Table 5–1* shows that students are expected to have mastered phoneme segmentation skills by the end of kindergarten, indicated by the PSF risk categories Established, Emerging, and Deficit. *Table 5–1* shows that the PSF benchmark score is 35 at the end of kindergarten.

The PSF benchmark score of 35 is labeled as Established because research has shown that if students can segment phonemes accurately and fluently by the end of kindergarten, they have a firm understanding of phonological awareness and have mastered the lowest level of the five essential reading components (National Institute of Child Health and Human Development, 2000). Those students who have achieved the benchmark score for PSF have an approximately 80% chance of meeting the next benchmark score, which is for Nonsense Word Fluency, in the middle of first grade. Achieving the PSF benchmark score by the end of kindergarten is also a strong indicator for achieving the ORF benchmark at the end of first grade.

Table 5–1 shows that, at the end of kindergarten, students who produce between 10 and 34 correct phonemes per minute have Emerging skills and students who produce fewer than 10 correct phonemes per minute have Deficit skills. If students at the end of kindergarten or thereafter earn a score in the Emerging or Deficit range, it is likely that additional instructional support is needed. Suggested levels of instructional help are discussed later in this chapter.

Nonsense Word Fluency Benchmark Scores. *Table 5–1* and *Table 5–2* show the benchmark scores given for NWF at the middle and end of kindergarten and at the beginning of first grade, respectively. The benchmark score of 50 as Established at the middle of first grade is valid only when the student reads the words and

> The benchmark score of 50 as established at the middle of first grade is valid only when the student reads the words and does not read sound by sound.

First Grade Benchmark and Target Scores for Nonsense Word Fluency						**Table 5-2**
	Beginning of Year		**Middle of Year**		**End of Year**	
	Score	Status	Score	Status	Score	Status
Nonsense Word Fluency	0–12	At Risk	0–29	Deficit	0–29	Deficit
	13–23	Some Risk	30–49	Emerging	30–49	Emerging
	24+	Low Risk	50+	Established	50+	Established

does not read sound by sound. DIBELS research shows that a score of 50, when the student reads words and not letter sounds, on NWF generally demonstrates competency in early phonics knowledge. When this competency is developed by the middle of first grade, students are on track to meet the ORF benchmark score for the end of first grade if they have appropriate reading instruction.

Retell Fluency Has Only Two Risk Categories

The RTF benchmark score is 25%. It is calculated by dividing the middle (median) RTF score by the middle (median) ORF score. (These scores may be from different passages.) As a general rule, the RTF percentage is considered reliable only if the student achieves a score of 40 or higher on ORF.[4] Students who score 40 or higher on ORF and have an RTF percentage score below 25% are considered to be at risk in the area of reading comprehension.

Low Risk, Some Risk, and At Risk Status Levels

Risk labels for the other type of status category are At Risk, Some Risk, and Low Risk. These labels are used if the skills measured are generally still in development at the time of the benchmark assessment, meaning complete mastery of the skill being measured is not yet expected. For example, *Table 5–1* (page 45) shows that the benchmark score for PSF at the middle of kindergarten is 18 and the risk levels are At Risk, Some Risk, and Low Risk. *Table 5–1* (previous page) also shows that the benchmark scores for NWF are 13 at the middle of kindergarten and 25 at the end of kindergarten, with the risk levels labeled At Risk, Some Risk, and Low Risk. *Table 5–2* shows the benchmark score for NWF at the beginning of first grade is 24, with the same risk levels. Beginning in the middle of first grade, NWF has a benchmark score of 50, and the risk levels change to Established, Emerging, and Deficit.

DIBELS scores with the category labels At Risk, Some Risk, and Low Risk indicate whether or not the student is on track to meet the next benchmark score in the same measure. Although the term "low risk" is used until a skill is expected to be mastered, the achievement of a score in the Low Risk category is meant to indicate that students are on track in the skill measured for reading success. Some educators interpret Low Risk to mean that the child has risk that should be addressed because the category is not labeled No Risk. This is not the case. Students who score in the Low Risk category are making progress as expected, and no intervention instruction is recommended. For example, *Table 5–1* shows that students are not expected to have mastered phoneme segmentation skills by the middle of kindergarten, indicated by the categories Low Risk, Some Risk, and At Risk, although they need a score of 18 or higher in order to be on track to master the skill by the end of kindergarten.

Students who have a PSF score of 18 (the benchmark score) or higher at the middle of kindergarten are identified as having Low Risk, meaning they have an

---

Benchmark scores are the minimum acceptable scores, not the goal.

---

[4] If a student scores lower than 40 on ORF, he or she may not have read accurately or fluently enough to accurately predict comprehension.

80% or better chance of achieving the benchmark score for PSF by the end of kindergarten. No intervention is recommended for these students with scores in the Low Risk range (although appropriate classroom instruction in phonemic awareness is generally necessary for the child to achieve the benchmark score by the end of the year).

Students with PSF scores of 7–17 by the middle of kindergarten are in the Some Risk range, meaning they are in the group with an approximately 50-50 chance of achieving the benchmark score for PSF by the end of kindergarten. Additional instructional support beyond that received in regular classroom reading instruction may be recommended for these students, although the recommended support is not as intense as for students in the At Risk range.

Students with PSF scores of 6 or lower by the middle of kindergarten are in the At Risk range and have only an approximately 20% chance of achieving a benchmark score for PSF by the end of kindergarten, meaning they are not likely to achieve the benchmark score (Established range) for that measure when expected without intensive intervention. With appropriate intensive intervention, the vast majority of these students can reach the benchmark score by the end of kindergarten.

Benchmark Scores Versus Classroom Instructional Goals

In this manual we are very careful to use the term "benchmark score" rather than "goal" when referring to the minimum score that is acceptable for any DIBELS measure. We use the term benchmark score instead of goal for a very specific reason. Benchmark scores are the minimum acceptable scores that predict reading success for a child; instructional goals should be significantly higher than minimum acceptable scores.

Development of DIBELS Risk Categories

DIBELS risk categories were developed by looking at the data (scores) gathered from children in the reference group. DIBELS researchers categorized the scores in the DIBELS Benchmark Scores Table so that children who are in the Established or Low Risk category have an approximately 80% chance of reaching the next benchmark score. Those in the Emerging or Some Risk category are in the group with an approximately 50-50 chance of success in meeting the next benchmark scores. Children scoring in the Deficit or At Risk category have a 20% or lower chance of meeting the next benchmark score (Good & Kaminski, 2003).

INTERVENTION RECOMMENDATIONS FOR STUDENTS WITH SCORES BELOW BENCHMARK SCORES

Specific policies for intervention recommendations for students who score below benchmark scores on DIBELS benchmark assessments are made on a local, district, or statewide basis. Some schools, districts, and states use the 3-Tier Model from the University of Texas (University of Texas Center for Reading and Language Arts, 2003) as the basis for developing intervention instruction. Some schools base instructional time on the recommendation given on the Class List Report from the DIBELS Data System. (See Chapter 9 for a description of the Class List Report.) Other schools develop their intervention policies based on the number of students who need intervention and the available resources, the most important resource being qualified instructors who have time to provide intervention.

DIBELS Instructional Recommendations

The DIBELS Class List Report provides instructional recommendations for each student. The *DIBELS Administration and Scoring Guide* explains the three categories of instructional recommendations:

- Benchmark—the student needs no intervention (appropriate classroom reading instruction should be sufficient).
- Strategic—the student needs additional intervention.
- Intensive—the student needs substantial intervention.

Each category of instructional recommendations is based on the overall performance of the student, including all measures administered, except RTF and WUF. The instructional recommendations are designed so that the odds in favor of achieving subsequent major mileposts without intervention are at least 80% for students with a benchmark recommendation and at most 20% for students with an intensive recommendation. The group of students with a Strategic recommendation has an approximately 50-50 chance of achieving the next major milepost, with the range of chances of achieving the next major milepost for these students being approximately 20%–80% (Good & Kaminski, 2003).

DIBELS researchers conducted longitudinal studies to develop overall predictive information for all combinations of DIBELS benchmark scores. The *DIBELS Administration and Scoring Guide*'s instructional recommendations section describes the profiles of instructional recommendations for each grade. The description shows that even though some students have an At Risk or Deficit risk level or a Some Risk or Emerging risk level on a measure, they will receive a Benchmark instructional recommendation, meaning no intervention is recommended. This happens because the overall profile of the student, when all measures administered (except WUF and RTF) are considered, indicates that the At Risk or Deficit score will improve because of the strength of other scores. For example, a student with either of the following risk profiles in the middle of kindergarten would receive a Benchmark instructional recommendation from DIBELS, even though the PSF score is in the Some Risk or Low Risk range:

- ISF = Established; LNF = Low Risk; PSF = Some Risk
- ISF = Established; LNF = Some Risk; PSF = Low Risk.

Intervention Instruction Guidelines

Ideal guidelines for intervention have not been defined precisely but can be loosely defined as:

- Providing students who have an Intensive instructional recommendation with 45–60 minutes of intervention instruction daily.
- Providing students who have a Strategic instructional recommendation with 20–40 minutes of intervention instruction daily.
- Maintaining core instruction for students who have a Benchmark recommendation. (These students do not require intervention, but an appropriate core reading program is recommended.)

In all cases, intervention instruction is to be provided in addition to the core language arts instruction. Students stay in intervention instruction until they achieve benchmark scores on all measures appropriate for their grade level and benchmark administration period. In some schools, intervention instruction works in conjunction with special education reading instruction for students who have been identified as having learning disabilities (University of Texas Center for Reading and Language Arts, 2003).

Intervention groups of three to five students are recommended for those with Strategic instructional recommendations. Groups of three or fewer are recommended for students with Intensive instructional recommendations. However, these recommendations are not always practical, and some schools make the decision to have larger groups, sometimes with as many as eight students in a group. The most important factors in structuring groups is that all students in a group have the same instructional need and that explicit, systematic instruction focuses on the skills that need improving.

> In all cases, intervention instruction is in addition to the core reading instruction. Intervention instruction does not replace any part of the core instruction.

Additional Information on Intervention Instruction

Not every school can provide the "ideal" intervention described above. Schools with limited resources have to make decisions about which students receive intervention and for how long, based on the available instructors and other resources. These schools proceed with the intention and expectation that the students who initially receive intervention instruction will achieve benchmark scores in a reasonable amount of time, making room for other students to be placed in and benefit from intervention instruction. For more information on interpreting DIBELS scores, grouping students, and designing intervention instruction, see *I've DIBEL'd, Now What?* by Susan Hall (2006).

Administering DIBELS Benchmark Assessments

DIBELS benchmark assessments are given three times a year[1] to screen *all* students in kindergarten–Grade 3. Increasingly, schools are also using DIBELS benchmark assessments to screen students in Grades 4–6. All DIBELS assessments are administered to children individually. The purpose of DIBELS benchmark assessments is to screen all children to determine if they are developing the necessary skills that will lead to at or above grade-level reading by the end of third grade, as measured by comprehension scores on standardized tests. Children who do not achieve benchmark scores are considered for additional instructional support to improve their skills and prevent future reading failure.[2] (The decision to provide intervention will be based on DIBELS scores and validated by comparing DIBELS results with knowledge about the student and other assessment information that may be available. In some cases in which DIBELS results are questioned, a DIBELS reassessment or additional assessments may be necessary to make the decision to provide intervention.)

SCHEDULE FOR ADMINISTERING BENCHMARK ASSESSMENTS

DIBELS benchmark assessments are given three times a year, as shown in *Table 6–1* (next page), which also shows specific measures given at each benchmark assessment period. The measures given at each benchmark assessment period vary from grade to grade, and they vary within every grade except third grade, which has the same measures for all three benchmark assessments.

Retell Fluency and Word Use Fluency are considered optional measures, as explained in Chapter 1. Because the National Reading First Assessment Committee[3] (NRFAC) has deemed RTF and WUF acceptable measures for comprehension and vocabulary, respectively, many schools include these two measures when administering benchmark assessments.

---

[1] Some states have elected to give DIBELS benchmark assessments four times a year. For these states, benchmarks for quarterly assessment are available on the DIBELS Web site.

[2] Not all schools have the resources available to provide intervention to all students who score below benchmark. In those cases, the schools give intervention to as many students as they can. They also may choose to progress monitor the rest of the students who do not meet the benchmark score in order to track their progress.

[3] Reading First schools must follow the recommendations of the NRFAC. Although other schools do not have to follow the NRFAC recommendations, many schools consider them when making decisions about assessments.

Table 6-1   Schedule of Individual Measures Administered at Each Benchmark Assessment Period

DIBELS Measure	Kindergarten B	M	E	First Grade B	M	E	Second Grade B	M	E	Third through Sixth Grade B	M	E
Initial Sound Fluency	x	x										
Letter Naming Fluency	x	x	x	x								
Phoneme Segmentation Fluency		x	x	x	x	x						
Nonsense Word Fluency		x	x	x	x	x	x					
Oral Reading Fluency					x	x	x	x	x	x	x	x

Optional Measures

	Kindergarten B	M	E	First Grade B	M	E	Second Grade B	M	E	Third through Sixth Grade B	M	E
Retell Fluency					x	x	x	x	x	x	x	x
Word Use Fluency	x	x	x	x	x	x	x	x	x	x	x	x

TIME TO ADMINISTER EACH MEASURE

Table 6–2 shows the approximate total time needed to administer DIBELS benchmark assessments to classrooms with 15, 20, and 25 students at each benchmark assessment period. The times are shown under two scenarios: (1) *Table 6–2*, Part A, shows times for schools that elect to administer all seven measures; and (2) *Table 6–2*, Part B, shows times for schools that elect not to administer RTF and WUF, the two optional measures.

Table 6-2   Approximate Time for One Examiner to Administer and Score Benchmark Assessments for Classrooms With 15, 20, and 25 Students

DIBELS Measure / Classroom Size	Part A — Schools That Give All Seven Measures (in hours) Kindergarten B	M	E	First Grade B	M	E	Second Grade B	M	E	Third Grade B	M	E
15 students	2¼	3¼	2½	2½	4	4	3½	2¾	2¾	2¾	2¾	2¾
20 students	3	4½	3½	3½	5	5	4½	3½	3½	3½	3½	3½
25 students	3½	5½	4¼	4¼	6½	6½	5½	4½	4½	4½	4½	4½

DIBELS Measure / Classroom Size	Part B — Schools That Give Five Measures, Opting Not to Administer Retell Fluency and Word Use Fluency (in hours) Kindergarten B	M	E	First Grade B	M	E	Second Grade B	M	E	Third Grade B	M	E
15 students	1¾	3	2¼	2¼	3	3	2½	2	2	2	2	2
20 students	2½	4	3	3	4	4	3¼	2½	2½	2½	2½	2½
25 students	3	4¾	3½	3½	5	5	4	3	3	3	3	3

Note: The letters **B**, **M**, and **E** stand for beginning, middle, and end of the school year.

Table 6–3 and *Table 6–4* show the detail supporting the times shown in *Table 6–2*, Parts A and B. The time it takes to complete each DIBELS measure varies, depending on the time needed to give standard directions and score the measure. Another variable is the time it takes to obtain the student responses:

- Four of the seven measures—LNF, PSF, NWF, and WUF—always take one minute for student responses, unless the discontinue rule is invoked.
- ORF takes three minutes for student responses because the student reads three passages for one minute each, unless the score on the first passage is lower than 10.
- Although RTF theoretically could take one minute, it is rare for a student to use the entire minute to retell the passage.
- The time to administer ISF includes several factors: (1) Student responses to ISF questions can vary from less than 16 seconds if the student responds instantly to 80 seconds if the maximum of 5 seconds per question is taken. (2) Naming the pictures and asking students questions associated with the pictures take time. (3) Turning the four pages of pictures also takes time. The approximate time it takes to give directions, mark student responses, and calculate the score for each measure is shown in *Table 6–3*.

Components for Timing Each DIBELS Measure for Benchmark Assessments   **Table 6-3**

DIBELS Measure	Total Minutes	Element of Administration (in Seconds)		
		Directions	Student Response	Scoring
LNF	1½	20	60	10
ISF	2½–3½	35–55	80–140	30
PSF	1½–2	20–35	60	20
NWF	2½	50–70	60	30
ORF*	4¾	45	180	60
RTF*	2	30	90**	5
WUF	1½	20–25	60	5

* Time is for three passages.

** Theoretically, RTF can be a one-minute measure. However, most children do not use the entire minute to retell what they have read and stop at no more than 40 seconds of retelling.

Table 6–4 shows the approximate time per student to administer DIBELS at each benchmark assessment period. Total times are shown: (1) if the school gives all seven measures; and (2) if the school elects not to give the two optional measures (WUF and RTF). Total times are a sum of the average time it takes to give each measure for the assessment period (based on *Table 6–2*), 30 seconds to greet the student and conclude the assessment, and 15 or 30 seconds to record the scores on the Summary of Scores page.

| Table 6-4 | | Approximate Time to Administer and Score Benchmark Assessments for One Student | | | | | | | | | | |

	Total Time											
	Kindergarten			First Grade			Second Grade			Third Grade		
	B	M	E	B	M	E	B	M	E	B	M	E
All seven assessments administered	6.75	11.25	8.25	8.25	12.5	12.5	10.25	7.75	7.75	7.75	7.75	7.75
Five assessments administered; WUF and RTF omitted	5.25	9.75	6.75	6.75	9.5	9.5	7.25	4.75	4.75	4.75	4.75	4.75

	Components of Total Time											
	Kindergarten			First Grade			Second Grade			Third Grade		
	B	M	E	B	M	E	B	M	E	B	M	E
Time to greet student and conclude assessment	0.5	0.5	0.5	0.5	0.5	0.5	0.5	0.5	0.5	0.5	0.5	0.5
Time to record scores on Summary of Scores page	0.25	0.25	0.25	0.25	0.5	0.5	0.25	0.25	0.25	0.25	0.25	0.25
Initial Sound Fluency	3.0	3.0										
Letter Naming Fluency	1.5	1.5	1.5	1.5								
Phoneme Segmentation Fluency		2.0	2.0	2.0	2.0	2.0						
Nonsense Word Fluency		2.5	2.5	2.5	2.5	2.5	2.5					
Oral Reading Fluency					4.0	4.0	4.0	4.0	4.0	4.0	4.0	4.0
Retell Fluency					1.5	1.5	1.5	1.5	1.5	1.5	1.5	1.5
Word Use Fluency	1.5	1.5	1.5	1.5	1.5	1.5	1.5	1.5	1.5	1.5	1.5	1.5

Note: The letters **B**, **M**, and **E** stand for beginning, middle, and end of the school year.

BENCHMARK MATERIALS

Examiners need to have certain materials in order to administer and score DIBELS benchmark assessments. *Table 6–5* is a checklist that an examiner can use to organize his or her benchmark assessment materials.

| Table 6-5 | Examiner's Checklist for Organizing Benchmark Materials |

❏ One Benchmark Assessment Scoring Booklet, at grade level, for every student being assessed.

❏ One set of Student Materials at each grade level being administered (for each examiner).

❏ Colored pen or pencil (any color that is not black and is easily seen against the white paper).

❏ Stopwatch

❏ Clipboard

❏ Calculator (necessary for ISF; may be helpful for totaling PSF, NWF, ORF, and WUF scores)

❏ Administration Rules table (Appendix)—optional

❏ Directions for all seven measures (Appendix)—optional because directions are also included in the scoring booklets

❏ Scoring and Marking Summary (Appendix)—optional; is for three passages

Description of Print Materials Used for Benchmark Assessment

When giving benchmark assessments, examiners will need to be prepared with appropriate print materials.

Scoring Booklet. Each grade level has a unique Benchmark Assessment Scoring Booklet that examiners use to *record* student responses and scores for each measure. Every student needs his or her own Scoring Booklet. The Scoring Booklet includes all DIBELS measures for all three benchmark assessments during the school year, as well as directions for each measure administered. Each Scoring Booklet contains scoring pages for the specific assessments given during each benchmark assessment period.

Summary of Scores Pages, Kindergarten–Grade 3　　　　　**Figure 6-1**

Kindergarten

Name: _____　　Teacher: _____

School: _____　　District: _____

	Benchmark 1 Beginning/Fall	Benchmark 2 Middle/Winter	Benchmark 3 End/Spring
Date			
Initial Sound Fluency			
Letter Naming Fluency			
Phoneme Segmentation Fluency			
Nonsense Word Fluency			
Word Use Fluency (Optional)	(Optional)	(Optional)	(Optional)

First Grade

Name: _____　　Teacher: _____

School: _____　　District: _____

	Benchmark 1 Beginning/Fall	Benchmark 2 Middle/Winter	Benchmark 3 End/Spring
Date			
Letter Naming Fluency			
Phoneme Segmentation Fluency			
Nonsense Word Fluency			
DIBELS Oral Reading Fluency		(Middle score)	(Middle score)
Retell Fluency (Optional)		(Middle score)	(Middle score)
Word Use Fluency (Optional)	(Optional)	(Optional)	(Optional)

Second Grade

Name: _____　　Teacher: _____

School: _____　　District: _____

	Benchmark 1 Beginning/Fall	Benchmark 2 Middle/Winter	Benchmark 3 End/Spring
Date			
Nonsense Word Fluency			
DIBELS Oral Reading Fluency	(Middle score)	(Middle score)	(Middle score)
Retell Fluency (Optional)	(Middle score)	(Middle score)	(Middle score)
Word Use Fluency (Optional)	(Optional)	(Optional)	(Optional)

Third Grade

Name: _____　　Teacher: _____

School: _____　　District: _____

	Benchmark 1 Beginning/Fall	Benchmark 2 Middle/Winter	Benchmark 3 End/Spring
Date			
DIBELS Oral Reading Fluency	(Middle score)	(Middle score)	(Middle score)
Retell Fluency (Optional)	(Middle score)	(Middle score)	(Middle score)
Word Use Fluency (Optional)	(Optional)	(Optional)	(Optional)

Examiners mark and record the student scores for each measure in the Scoring Booklets. The first page of the Scoring Booklet is referred to in this manual as the Summary of Scores Page. Figure 6–1 shows the Summary of Scores Page for each grade K–3. The examiner records all of a student's scores for each benchmark assessment on the Summary of Scores Page. The examiner can also use the Summary of Scores Page as a guide to which assessments are given at the beginning, middle, and end of the year by looking at open and shaded boxes for the assessment period in question. Open boxes indicate the measure is to be given during that benchmark assessment period, whereas shaded boxes indicate the measure is not to be given.

The numbers at the top of scoring pages are to help examiners quickly know whether they are using the measure for the correct time of year. For example, the scoring pages shown in *Figure 6–2* are for Nonsense Word Fluency. The benchmark number at the top of the page indicates whether the measure is for the beginning, middle, or end of the year. Benchmark 1 is used at the beginning of the year; Benchmark 2, in the middle of the year; and Benchmark 3, at the end of the year. Examiners who check the top of the scoring page before beginning the benchmark assessment will ensure that they are giving the correct assessment. (It is a common mistake for beginning examiners who do not understand the coding at the top of the page to give the midyear assessment at the beginning of the year or vice versa.)

Three passages are administered for ORF, and the median (middle) score is recorded as the DIBELS score for that benchmark period. For this reason, ORF

> The numbers at the top of Scoring Booklet pages and at the top or bottom of Student Materials pages show the benchmark assessment period for which the page is to be used.

Figure 6-2   **Benchmark Assessment Scoring Booklet Page, Nonsense Word Fluency—First Grade**

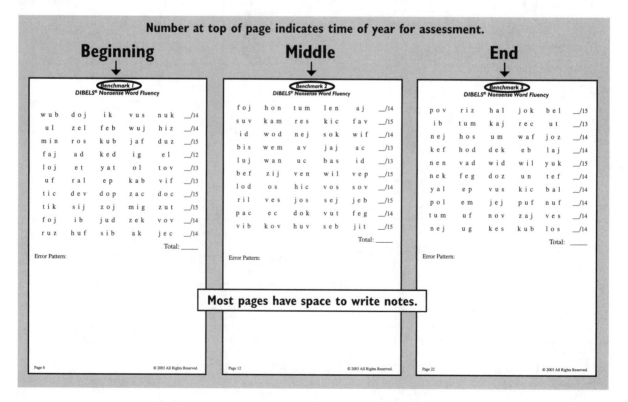

passages have a slightly different coding at the top of the scoring pages, as shown in *Figure 6–3*. The period in the number after the word *Benchmark* looks like a decimal point, but it is not. Benchmark 2.1, Benchmark 2.2, and Benchmark 2.3 are the numbers shown at the top of the middle-of-year ORF passages. The number to the left of the dot indicates the time of year, and in *Figure 6–3* all the passages are middle of the year because the number to the left of the dot is 2. The number to the right of the dot indicates the passage number. In *Figure 6–3*, the first passage, labeled Benchmark 2.1, is the first passage to be read in the middle of the year; Benchmark 2.2 is the second passage; and Benchmark 2.3 is the third passage. The labels Benchmark 3.1, Benchmark 3.2, and Benchmark 3.3 identify the three end-of-year ORF passages.

Benchmark Assessment Scoring Booklet Page, Oral Reading Fluency—Middle of First Grade   Figure 6-3

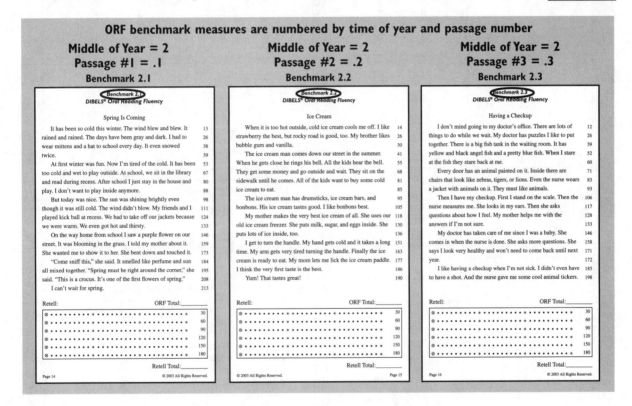

Student Materials Booklets. Student Materials booklets are grade specific and include all of the print materials students need to see during assessment. As with the Scoring Booklets, Student Materials booklets contain everything students need to see (including optional measures) for all three benchmark assessment periods. No pages are included in the Student Materials booklets for PSF, WUF, or RTF because these three measures do not require the student to look at anything in order to provide a response or answer. On Student Materials pages, the benchmark period is clearly marked at the top of the pages for LNF and NWF, as shown in *Figure 6–4* (next page).

The benchmark periods are indicated in a different place on the Student Materials pages for ISF and ORF. *Figure 6–5* (next page) shows that the benchmark periods are indicated at the lower corners of the pages.

Figure 6-4   **Student Materials Pages, LNF and NWF**

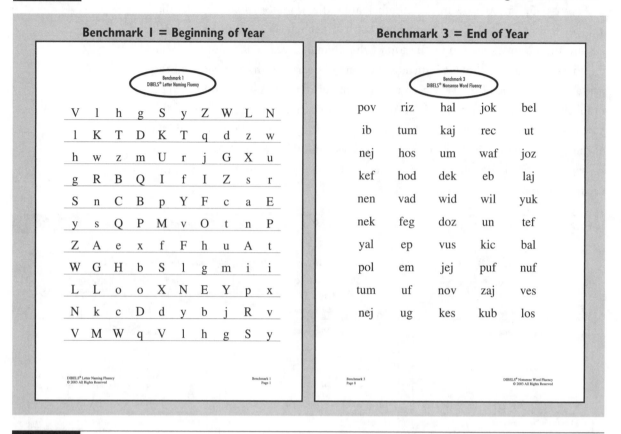

Benchmark 1 = Beginning of Year

Benchmark 1
DIBELS® Letter Naming Fluency

V	l	h	g	S	y	Z	W	L	N
l	K	T	D	K	T	q	d	z	w
h	w	z	m	U	r	j	G	X	u
g	R	B	Q	I	f	I	Z	s	r
S	n	C	B	p	Y	F	c	a	E
y	s	Q	P	M	v	O	t	n	P
Z	A	e	x	f	F	h	u	A	t
W	G	H	b	S	l	g	m	i	i
L	L	o	o	X	N	E	Y	p	x
N	k	c	D	d	y	b	j	R	v
V	M	W	q	V	l	h	g	S	y

Benchmark 1
Page 1

Benchmark 3 = End of Year

Benchmark 3
DIBELS® Nonsense Word Fluency

pov	riz	hal	jok	bel
ib	tum	kaj	rec	ut
nej	hos	um	waf	joz
kef	hod	dek	eb	laj
nen	vad	wid	wil	yuk
nek	feg	doz	un	tef
yal	ep	vus	kic	bal
pol	em	jej	puf	nuf
tum	uf	nov	zaj	ves
nej	ug	kes	kub	los

Benchmark 3
Page 8

Figure 6-5   **Student Materials Pages, ISF and ORF**

Benchmark K.2 = Middle of Year

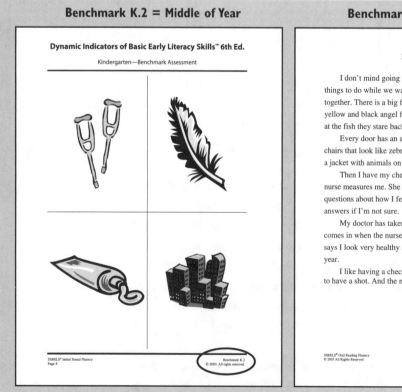

Dynamic Indicators of Basic Early Literacy Skills™ 6th Ed.

Kindergarten—Benchmark Assessment

Benchmark K.2
© 2003 All rights reserved.

Benchmark 2 = Middle of Year

Having a Checkup

I don't mind going to my doctor's office. There are lots of things to do while we wait. My doctor has puzzles I like to put together. There is a big fish tank in the waiting room. It has yellow and black angel fish and a pretty blue fish. When I stare at the fish they stare back at me.

Every door has an animal painted on it. Inside there are chairs that look like zebras, tigers, or lions. Even the nurse wears a jacket with animals on it. They must like animals.

Then I have my checkup. First I stand on the scale. Then the nurse measures me. She looks in my ears. Then she asks questions about how I feel. My mother helps me with the answers if I'm not sure.

My doctor has taken care of me since I was a baby. She comes in when the nurse is done. She asks more questions. She says I look very healthy and won't need to come back until next year.

I like having a checkup when I'm not sick. I didn't even have to have a shot. And the nurse gave me some cool animal stickers.

Benchmark 2
Page 7

Color Coding Downloaded Materials

For schools that download materials from the DIBELS Web site, it is extremely helpful to color code the cover page of the print materials by grade level. For example, both the kindergarten Scoring Booklets and Student Materials booklets would have the same color cover page, whereas the other grades each would have a different and individual color for cover pages. Color coding the cover pages makes it easy to select the appropriate print materials for each student. Color coding also minimizes both the time necessary to find materials and the errors made due to using incorrect materials. (Materials purchased from Sopris West are color coded by grade.)

Nonprint General Administration Materials

Certain items, in addition to print materials, are required to effectively administer all DIBELS measures. These materials, called general administration materials, consist of a clipboard, a stopwatch, and a colored pen or pencil. A calculator is also required for ISF and is suggested to help sum line-by-line scores for LNF, PSF, NWF, ORF, and WUF.

Clipboards. The clipboard provides a hard surface on which examiners can record student responses. Using a clipboard also allows the examiner to shield the Scoring Booklet from the student, which keeps the student from being distracted by the examiner's recording of his responses.

Stopwatches. Because each measure is timed, examiners need a stopwatch. Many examiners find it difficult at first to administer DIBELS while tracking time with a stopwatch. We are often asked if a digital kitchen timer can be used because it can be set for one minute and beeps when the minute is up. Kitchen timers are discouraged for two reasons: (1) Intermittent timing for ISF is virtually impossible with a kitchen timer. (2) Most kitchen timers have very loud ringers or beepers, which can be distracting to students and are disruptive when several examiners are working in close proximity to one another. With practice, virtually all examiners find using the stopwatch easy (even though they almost all find the stopwatch quite awkward when first learning to administer DIBELS). If you are new to DIBELS, please try using a stopwatch for at least 20 assessments (including at least five practice sessions) before you make the decision to give up and use a kitchen timer.

> Incorporating the use of stopwatches may be awkward for examiners at first, but they quickly adapt to using them.

Colored Pens or Pencils. Examiners need a colored pen or pencil as they score DIBELS measures because using it enables examiners to easily see their scoring marks. This reduces mistakes when counting the score for each measure. Using a colored pen or pencil also allows teachers to quickly identify student response patterns and errors when using the Scoring Booklets to plan for intervention instruction. Some schools elect to use a different colored pencil or pen for each benchmark assessment period, which makes scores easier to read and decipher on the Summary of Scores Page.

Calculators. Calculators are required to be able to quickly and accurately use the formula to calculate the ISF score. Calculators are useful for summing scores for LNF, PSF, NWF, and WUF. They are also useful for calculating ORF scores, especially when students skip lines or make a number of errors while reading the passage.

HELPFUL AIDS FOR SCORING AND ADMINISTERING DIBELS BENCHMARK MEASURES

Examiners need to have access to directions as well as administration and scoring rules when they give DIBELS benchmark measures. Many examiners find it helpful to reproduce and have immediate access to the following three handouts, available only in this manual (see the Appendix), while administering DIBELS benchmark assessments:

- Directions for each measure, with administration rules included
- Administration Rules table
- Summary of Scoring Rules for each measure.

Directions for Each Measure

DIBELS is a standardized test, and the directions for each measure *must be read exactly as written*. This ensures that all children receive the same opportunity to demonstrate their early literacy knowledge and that DIBELS scores provide a valid comparison among students. Although the directions for each measure are included in the more recent versions of the Scoring Booklets, many examiners find it cumbersome to use the directions in the Scoring Booklet. In addition, examiners expressed that they would like to have all the administration rules available on the same page as directions. For that reason, the Directions for Seven DIBELS Measures handout in the Appendix has both wording for directions and administration rules on the same page. Some examiners copy the directions in the Appendix, laminate the pages, and put them on a key ring to use when administering DIBELS measures. (Consider copying the scoring rules and the Benchmark Scores table from the Appendix for each measure on the back of the directions from the Appendix as a handy reference.)

Administration Rules

Administration rules consist of the following:

- *Stopwatch*—When to start the stopwatch
- *Timing*—Whether timing is continuous for one minute or intermittent (timing is intermittent only for ISF)
- *Discontinue*—When to stop the assessment before completing the entire measure because the student is obviously struggling with the concept being assessed

- *Wait Time*—How long to allow the child to hesitate before giving a prompt or moving to the next item so that the student will not use the entire time trying to figure out one answer or read one word
- *Prompt*—What to say, if anything, after the child hesitates for the required number of seconds
- *Additional information*—Any other information relevant to a measure.

Administration rules differ for each of the seven measures and can be difficult to remember. For that reason, administration rules are summarized in the Administration Rules table included in the Appendix. We recommend that examiners copy the Administration Rules table and review it prior to each benchmark assessment administration. Some examiners have told us that they keep it nearby for reference during assessments. (All the administration rules for each measure are also contained on the Directions for Seven DIBELS Measures handout in the Appendix, and some examiners prefer to use it to reference rules during benchmark administration.)

Scoring Rules

Consistency is important when marking student responses in Scoring Booklets. This is because DIBELS scoring is designed so that anyone who picks up a Scoring Booklet can recreate student responses as closely as possible. When scoring DIBELS measures, examiners must mark student errors according to DIBELS scoring rules.

Some examiners like to record the students' specific responses in addition to marking the responses according to DIBELS scoring rules. Recording specific errors can help guide instruction. However, scoring accurately is more important than recording the student's exact response. Therefore, only experienced examiners should consider recording the student's specific errors. In other words, examiners skilled at DIBELS scoring procedures should consider recording students' specific errors—especially for PSF, NWF, and ORF—only if they can do so without compromising the basic DIBELS scoring.

A way to note student errors that does not require recording specific errors as the student responds is to make a note on the scoring page after DIBELS has been administered about any consistent error patterns observed. Space is provided on scoring pages for examiner notations. Either the recording of specific errors or the notation of consistent error patterns observed can help guide instruction for the student.

Each DIBELS measure has its own set of scoring rules, which are detailed in the chapters about each measure (Chapters 10–16). However, among DIBELS measures, ORF and LNF are scored similarly, PSF and NWF are scored similarly, and WUF and RTF are scored similarly, whereas ISF is scored uniquely. Even those measures that are similarly scored have enough differences that it is not easy to remember the specifics of scoring each measure when an examiner gives benchmark assessments only three times a year. The Summary of Scoring and

Marking Rules in the Appendix has been included as a quick reference for examiners to use to answer questions about scoring. Examiners are encouraged not only to review these rules *prior* to benchmark assessment administration, but also to have a copy nearby *during* benchmark assessment administration.

MINIMIZING SCORING ERRORS

DIBELS scoring can be complex because each of the measures is scored differently. Therefore, scoring errors are likely to happen, especially when examiners are first giving DIBELS or when they have not given DIBELS for a while. The most effective way to minimize scoring errors is to make sure that all examiners have excellent training and that they practice before administering DIBELS. It also is effective to offer and require periodic ongoing training. (See Chapter 8 for a detailed explanation about selecting examiners and training opportunities.)

> The most effective way to minimize scoring errors is to make sure that all examiners have excellent training and that they practice before administering DIBELS.

Allowing examiners to shadow score is another way to help ensure that DIBELS scores are accurate. Shadow scoring occurs when two examiners score the same student. One examiner gives the directions to the student, but both examiners score the student's responses. The examiners then compare each other's scores. If both examiners are new, they can discuss any differences between their scores. If one examiner is new and the other experienced, the experienced examiner can check the new examiner's scoring. The Observer's Checklists in the Appendix give suggested tolerance ranges for differences in scoring.

> Shadow scoring occurs when two examiners score the same student and then compare each other's scores to ensure integrity of the data.

Besides offering DIBELS training and providing opportunities for shadow scoring, DIBELS coordinators can make certain that experienced examiners check all scores from first-time examiners and check at least a sample of Scoring Booklets from each examiner during all benchmark administrations. It is, of course, best to check all Scoring Booklets. However, this is often not practical. Checking a sample of Student Booklets from each examiner goes a long way toward ensuring that scoring is accurate. When errors are found, they can be corrected. It is not unusual for a sample check to find that specific examiners consistently mark the responses incorrectly or make computation errors. If this happens, it is easy to correct the inaccuracies and to educate the examiners about how to accurately compute scores or record answers. Three suggested methods for checking scores are:

- Divide each classroom's Scoring Booklets among two or three examiners and have each examiner recount the scoring for each measure and check to see that scores were accurately transferred to the Summary of Scores page.
- Conduct a random check of at least 20% of all Scoring Booklets for each examiner before data entry.
- Look at Class Reports (which list DIBELS scores for all students) with an eye toward scores that are suspicious. (For example, if a class is reported as having ISF scores of 60 for almost all students, that might indicate that a new examiner does not understand the formula used to calculate the ISF score.)

APPROVED ACCOMMODATIONS

When some children are assessed with DIBELS, they may need extra help in order to effectively demonstrate their abilities. The *DIBELS Administration and Scoring Guide* lists the entire set of Approved Accommodations. When these Approved Accommodations are used and student scores are submitted to the DIBELS Data System, the "Tested with DIBELS Approved Accommodations" box should be checked in the student demographics section.[4]

It is important for examiners to understand that DIBELS Approved Accommodations are to be used judiciously. Approved Accommodations are meant to be used selectively, usually after the examiner has attempted assessment without the accommodation; discussed the use of an Approved Accommodation for a particular student with the DIBELS team, which makes a collective decision about whether or not to use the Approved Accommodation. Some schools appoint one person, such as the reading coach, to make the decision about whether Approved Accommodations will be permitted for individual students.

> It is important for examiners to understand that DIBELS Approved Accommodations are to be used judiciously.

If an Approved Accommodation is used with a student, the scores generally can still be interpreted using the DIBELS Benchmark Scores Table found in the Appendix. If an examiner administers any DIBELS assessment and *uses any accommodation other than a DIBELS Approved Accommodation*, the resulting scores *cannot* be interpreted using this table. In addition, these scores should not be submitted to the DIBELS Data System or used when a school compiles its own data. An example of an *unapproved* accommodation would be giving a student extended time to complete a measure. *Under DIBELS procedures, in no case is an extended period of time or extra time ever given to a student.* Scores for a student who was given extra time or any other unapproved accommodation would not be comparable with students' scores who did complete the measures using standard DIBELS administration procedures or any DIBELS Approved Accommodation. DIBELS Approved Accommodations are summarized in the following sections.

> Under DIBELS procedures, in no case is extended or extra time ever given to a student for any measure.

Retesting. Any DIBELS measure can be repeated for any reason. When a retest for any measure is recommended, the examiner should write "retest" on the Summary of Scores Page for the measure that is to be retested and include the reason that retesting is recommended. The retest can then be scheduled for the follow-up testing day. The following apply for all DIBELS measures:

- Retest only the measure that is in question. There is no need to re-administer the entire set of measures given for the benchmark assessment.
- The same benchmark form cannot be used again for the retest. A different form must be used when the test is given again (use progress monitoring materials).

---

[4] At the time this manual was written, there was not a specific place in the Scoring Booklet to indicate that an Approved Accommodation was used. Most examiners write this information on the Summary of Scores Page so that the person entering data can see that an Approved Accommodation was used and, therefore, knows to check the "Tested with DIBELS Approved Accommodations" box when entering the data.

- Any conditions that adversely affect the student's performance during the first assessment should be changed before retesting. For example, if a noisy room caused the student to perform poorly, the retest should be given in a quiet room.
- The retest should be given no later than one week after the original test was given.
- The retest should be given the next day or even later. (Most schools and districts schedule a retest day or days at the same time they schedule DIBELS benchmark assessment days.)
- When the retest is given, the examiner must read the standard directions again, even though progress monitoring materials are used and the student may have very recently heard the standard directions.
- If only one retest is given, the student has two scores: the benchmark score and the retest score. The examiner should record the score he or she feels is most reflective of the student's skills. If two retests are given, the median (middle) score of the three assessments for that measure should be recorded as the student's score. (It is rare that two retests are given, resulting in three scores.)

Changing Testing Conditions. Sometimes a change in testing conditions will enable a student to better demonstrate his or her skills when taking a DIBELS measure. The change in conditions can be made during the normal benchmark assessment period if the teacher or examiner recognizes the need before the benchmark assessments are given. Or the change can be made for a retest if the need for a different condition is noticed during the benchmark assessment. The following Approved Accommodations can be used for all measures.

- Use an alternate setting, which might be a quiet room, a room with minimal visual distractions, or a room with special lighting.
- Have a different examiner than the one used for other children administer the assessments. A different examiner might be more familiar to the child, causing the child less anxiety. A speech–language pathologist or person who speaks an English Language Learner's native language might be helpful in interpreting a student's responses for more accurate scoring.
- A person who is familiar with the student and his or her relevant communicative strategies might be used to support the examiner. This person could help the examiner accurately interpret the student's responses.

Minor Alterations to Directions. The practice part of the directions in ISF, PSF, NWF, and WUF can be repeated, or one additional example may be provided. Additionally, the directions can be given in a manner more understandable to the student.

- ISF, PSF, NWF, and WUF—The child can be provided with an opportunity to repeat the examiner's example before being asked to respond to the next example. For example, for PSF, the examiner could say, "The sounds in 'sam' are /s/ /a/ /m/. *Do it with me, /s/ /a/ /m/.*" (Italicized words are the part of the directions that are an Approved Accommodation.)

- All measures—The child can be asked to repeat or summarize the directions if the examiner thinks the student's score will be negatively affected without doing so.

- All measures—Directions can be provided in sign language.

- All measures—For a child with limited English proficiency, the directions can be given in the primary language. However, the stimulus items in the directions to which the child responds should be presented in English.

  - For ISF, all pictures would be named in English. Directions and questions would be presented in the student's primary language, with the exception of the names of pictures.

  - For PSF directions, the examiner would ask the student to segment the sounds in the word *mop*, not its equivalent in the student's primary language.

  - Because stimulus items in NWF directions are not real words, there are no translation issues.

  - ORF and RTF directions would be given in the student's first language, but the student would need to read the story in English and retell the passage in English.

  - In WUF, the directions would be presented in the student's primary language, although the student would be asked to use a sentence in English using the word *rabbit*, named in English. The examiner would give all words in the WUF list in English, and the student's responses would need to be in English.

Changing Stimulus Materials. The Student Materials can be changed in various ways to accommodate a student's needs.

- ISF, NWF, ORF, and LNF—Large-print or enlarged editions of printed materials and pictures may be used. Large-print materials are available on the DIBELS Web site.

- ISF, NWF, ORF, and LNF—Closed-circuit TV can be used to enlarge print materials and pictures for students with impaired vision.

- ISF, NWF, ORF, and LNF—Colored overlays, filters, or lighting can be used if these accommodations improve vision or performance.

- NWF, ORF, and LNF—Braille materials may be created and used, although scores using braille materials may not be directly comparable. (DIBELS braille materials were in development at the time this manual was written.)

- NWF, ORF, and LNF—An alternate typeface for materials can be used, as long as it is one that would be used on reading materials used in first grade. (This generally means that the lowercase letters *a*, *g*, and *q* are presented in primer form instead of typeset form.) This is an accommodation that some kindergarten teachers tend to overuse. The benchmark score for LNF at the beginning of kindergarten is 8, which is low enough that the typeset forms of the letters *a*, *g*, and *q* should not affect whether or not the student needs intervention instruction for letter names. If the student does not meet the benchmark score of 27 at the middle of the year or 40 at the end of the year because of confusion with the typeset letter *a*, *g*, or *q*, intervention instruction should include teaching the student the difference between the typeset and the primer versions of these letters because most print materials use the typeset versions of these letters.

- ISF—The examiner can use alternate pictures to represent the target words if the examiner thinks using different pictures will help the child remember the names of the pictures. *In no case should the target words be changed*, which means the alternate pictures need to represent the same words.

- ISF—The examiner can ask the child to repeat unfamiliar vocabulary words that are names of pictures. For example, the examiner can say and ask, "This is 'cub.' *What is this?* This is 'skate.' *What is this?* This is 'refrigerator.' *What is this?* This is 'bump.' *What is this?*" (Words in italics are the Approved Accommodation.)

- ISF—Words in ISF that might not be part of a child's vocabulary can be taught prior to administration of DIBELS. For example, the teacher might explain in a lesson the week before DIBELS is administered that a cub is a "baby bear." *In no case should the teacher use the ISF picture names to practice identifying initial sounds.*

- All measures—An amplifier can be used to help students with hearing difficulties to hear directions, test questions, and stimulus words.

Using Markers or Rulers to Help the Student Track Letters or Words

One DIBELS Approved Accommodation is to provide a student with a marker or ruler to help the student keep his or her place while reading letters in LNF, words in NWF, and connected text in ORF. We find that some teachers, especially kindergarten teachers, overuse this accommodation. Students who cannot read without a marker may be showing signs of needing extra help with tracking. Only the students who have been tested at least once without using a marker or ruler to aid tracking and have scored below the benchmark should be allowed to use this accommodation.

- LNF, NWF, and ORF—The examiner can provide the student with a marker or ruler to put under the line of letters or words in the Student Materials. *Examiners should use this accommodation only for students who have great need for it.* If students who do not use a marker or ruler under each line skip a row, the skipped row does not penalize the student in terms of his or her score, and valuable information is gathered about the student's tracking skills. For that reason, examiners are warned to use this accommodation sparingly and only for children who would score significantly higher with an aid for tracking than without one.

Using Sign Language or a Computer for Communication

It is acceptable for examiners and students to use an alternate method of communication in ORF and WUF if oral language does not allow students to demonstrate the full extent of their early literacy skills when taking DIBELS measures.

- ORF and WUF—A student may use a mode of communication other than oral language to respond, if that mode is a stronger means of communication. For example, the student may sign to respond for ORF or WUF, or the student might use a computer to respond for WUF. The examiner will need to make a professional judgment regarding the fluency of the student's response. If the student's fluency is affected by the alternate form of communication, standard risk categories shown on the DIBELS Benchmark Scores Table will not apply, and caution should be used when interpreting these results.

FREQUENTLY ASKED QUESTIONS ABOUT BENCHMARK ASSESSMENT

Benchmark Assessment Procedures

1. During benchmark screening, do I have to give all the assessments at once?

The only time it is recommended not to give all assessments in one sitting is when the student's attention wanders so much that a true picture of the student's skills cannot be obtained unless assessments are given in "smaller doses."

2. Can we set up DIBELS administration so that teachers specialize in administering one part of the assessment? For example, one teacher would administer only LNF, and another, only PSF.

This is not an effective way to administer DIBELS. Schools that have tried this found it impractical for each examiner to administer only one measure because each measure takes such a short time (one to three minutes). Having students move from examiner to examiner or having an examiner move from student to student takes significantly more time than having one examiner administer all measures. One reason is that each measure takes a different amount of time to administer, and bottlenecking results when one examiner has a line of students while another examiner sits with no students. Furthermore, examiners do not get the "full flavor" of the student's skills under this arrangement, and important information about the child may be missed. Another reason not to use this arrangement is that young children are sometimes shy and do not perform optimally when they have a different examiner for each measure.

DIBELS General Scoring Questions

Questions about scoring a specific measure are included at the end of the chapters on each measure. The following questions are more general in nature than those answered at the ends of Chapters 10–16.

3. Can I write comments while I am scoring?

Every scoring page has room for comments. When administering DIBELS, it is most important to administer and score the assessment correctly. Therefore, comments may be written if you are able to make notations while administering the assessment without detracting from your scoring responsibilities. However, it may be helpful to simply mark an error and write notes after the assessment has stopped.

4. What do I do if the student starts asking me questions when I am giving the directions?

Most examiners find that if they continue reading the directions, the student will stop questioning when he or she understands the directions. Therefore, the best advice is to ignore the student and continue reading the directions. If you must answer a question, do so with as few words as possible.

5. What do I do if the student appears not to understand the directions?

If a student's questions or actions lead you to believe he or she does not understand the directions, several DIBELS Approved Accommodations are allowed (see the "Approved Accommodations" section in this chapter). You can check the student's understanding of the directions by asking him or her to repeat or summarize the directions. You can also repeat the practice item or give one additional example for ISF, PSF, and NWF. Either of these would be DIBELS Approved Accommodations, in which case the "Tested with DIBELS Approved Accommodations" box should be checked when entering scoring data into the DIBELS Data System.

6. Why can't we use timers that count down?

The Initial Sound Fluency measurement is almost impossible to score with a kitchen timer or other countdown timer. Therefore, it is easier for most examiners to use the same stopwatch for all measures. (Most teachers find the initial awkwardness with the stopwatch no longer exists after they finish 5 or 10 assessments.) In addition, most countdown timers have relatively loud ringers or beeping sounds that are distracting and anxiety provoking to many students. The beeps also can be distracting to students and examiners if several examiners are in the same room. Although some examiners insist on using countdown timers, we discourage their use. Virtually all examiners find that after they practice giving 5 to 10 DIBELS assessments the stopwatch is quite easy to use.

7. Why aren't extra words and sounds counted as errors?

Because these are fluency measures, the penalty for adding extra words in ORF and extra sounds in PSF and NWF is that extra time is used.

8. **What if children say the correct answer and then change it to an incorrect answer?**

Once a child says a correct answer, it is marked as correct. If the child changes the answer to an incorrect answer, it is counted as an added sound or word and ignored when scoring. However, because DIBELS measures fluency, as well as accuracy, the extra sound or word will use time and affect the student's score in that way.

9. **Can I make notes about the student's answers when they are incorrect or when an extra sound or word is inserted?**

Yes. Many examiners do this and use the information gathered to plan intervention instruction. However, examiners should make notes only if doing so does not affect their ability to administer and score DIBELS accurately. For example, in PSF, the examiner should not take notes if his or her ability to immediately give the next word is slowed.

10. **Why do the directions for LNF and NWF say "Put your finger *on* the word" instead of "*under* the word"? Students who take the directions literally won't be able to see the word.**

DIBELS is in the process of changing the directions to use the word *under* instead of *on*. If you want to substitute the word under for on, you may do so. This change does not affect the validity of DIBELS scores and does not have to be reported as a DIBELS Approved Accommodation.

DIBELS and ELL

11. **How do I use DIBELS with ELL students when their academic studies are in their native tongue?**

If the student's native language is Spanish and he or she is learning to read with Spanish language reading materials as the primary source, DIBELS offers a Spanish language version that can be used. The Spanish language version of DIBELS is available for benchmark assessments currently from the DIBELS Web site and beginning in fall 2005 from Sopris West. At this time, DIBELS does not offer assessments in any languages other than English and Spanish.

12. **How do I use DIBELS with ELL students when their academic studies are in mainstream English speaking classes?**

Students who are learning to read in English should take the English version of DIBELS, even if English is not their native language. Some students may benefit from having the directions given to them in their native language, which is a DIBELS Approved Accommodation (see the "Approved Accommodations" section in this chapter). Students who do not have strong English language vocabularies can be asked to repeat the word associated with each picture in ISF, or the vocabulary words for ISF can be taught prior to administration of ISF. (In no case should words from WUF or subjects for ORF passages be pretaught.) If any accommodation is used, the "Tested with DIBELS Approved

Accommodations" box should be checked in the student demographics section when entering scoring data into the DIBELS Data System.

DIBELS and Students With Speech Impairments

13. Does DIBELS allow any special accommodations for children who stutter or otherwise have impediments that slow their ability to respond quickly?

No, because the only reasonable accommodation would be to modify the time, which is not an Approved Accommodation under any condition. You can still give DIBELS to students who have speech or other difficulties that slow oral responses because some information about the student's skills might be obtained even though their scores will not be comparable to those in the risk categories shown in the DIBELS Benchmark Scores Table. (These scores should not be entered into the DIBELS data management system, nor should they be included when a district calculates its own norms.)

DIBELS Approved Accommodations

14. Does DIBELS offer large-print versions?

Yes, DIBELS does have large-print versions, which are available from the DIBELS Web site. Examiners also can create their own large-print versions of Student Materials. Another alternative is to use closed-circuit television to enlarge print and pictures in the Student Materials.

15. How is DIBELS used with students who read and comprehend well but who have neurological difficulties that slow speech and thus can't express their comprehension due to their expressive language difficulties?

The use of DIBELS for children with special needs varies from case to case. A DIBELS Approved Accommodation that may work in this case is to allow the student to respond using his or her strongest mode of communication. For example, the student may sign, use a word board, or use a computer for responses to WUF or for RTF. If any Approved Accommodation is used, the "Tested with DIBELS Approved Accommodations" box should be checked in the student demographics section when entering scoring data into the DIBELS Data System. If accommodations not approved by DIBELS are used, the scores should not be entered into the DIBELS Data System, and the risk categories shown in the DIBELS Benchmark Scores Table will not be valid.

16. There is no place on the Scoring Booklet for the examiner to indicate a DIBELS Approved Accommodation was used. If a DIBELS Approved Accommodation is used, how does the person entering data know to check the box marked "Tested with DIBELS Approved Accommodations"?

At the time this manual was written, there was no specific place in the Scoring Booklets to indicate that an approved accommodation was used. Most examiners write this information on the Summary of Scores Page, which is used for data input, so that the person entering data can see that an Approved Accommodation was used and can, therefore, check the "Tested with DIBELS Approved Accommodations" box when entering the data.

17. Do I have to indicate that an Approved Accommodation was used if my school does not submit scores to the University of Oregon database?

This is a decision that will be made by the school or district that collects the data from DIBELS benchmark assessments. Many districts and schools elect to exclude scores obtained with Approved Accommodations from their databases and to keep those scores separate. Other districts and schools include scores with Approved Accommodations in their databases. In no case should any school or district include any DIBELS scores that are obtained with accommodations that are not approved by DIBELS.

Reassessment

18. Under what conditions can I reassess a student?

A student can be assessed again for any reason. This includes reassessment because the examiner or someone else thinks the score is not reflective of the student's abilities. Other reasons for reassessing include an examiner who thinks the score may be incorrect because he/she forgot to start the stopwatch, couldn't hear, etc.

19. Do I have to reassess all measures?

No. Only the measure that is in question needs to be reassessed.

20. If I recommend reassessment because I couldn't hear the child's answers, how do I avoid the same thing happening during the reassessment?

The examiner can work with the student to help him or her talk in a louder voice before re-administering the assessment.

21. Can I give a reassessment on the same day that the original assessment was given?

In general, retests should be given no sooner than the next day but no later than the following week, if possible. (However, in some cases where there is an interruption, such as the child sneezing or the intercom interrupting an assessment, an immediate retest can be given.) Most schools and districts schedule a retest day at the same time they create the schedule for benchmark assessments. In all cases, use progress monitoring materials for the reassessment and give the standard directions. Never use the same benchmark materials for a reassessment.

7

Organizing DIBELS Benchmark Assessments

Administering DIBELS benchmark assessments takes considerable planning at the district, school, and classroom levels.[1] The planning begins months in advance of actually giving the benchmark assessments. Early in the planning process, decisions must be made about *who* will be doing the testing, *where* the testing will take place, and *when* the testing will be conducted.

SCHEDULING BENCHMARK ASSESSMENTS

Benchmark Assessments Three Times a Year

Most schools administer DIBELS benchmark assessments three times a year.[2] The beginning-of-year assessment generally is conducted in August, September, or October; the middle-of-year assessment in December, January, or February; and the end-of-year assessment April, May, or June. As a general rule, these assessments are most often given in September, January, and May, although schools that begin school unusually early or unusually late may give the assessments in different months.

Reserve Dates Well in Advance

The district needs to reserve the range of dates for DIBELS benchmark assessments well in advance. Doing so will enable schools to prevent scheduling conflicts and allow time to plan effective and well-implemented data collection. Start and end dates for benchmark assessments should be no longer than three weeks apart, including time for data input and reassessments. Whenever possible, assessments should occur on consecutive days. Also, schools and districts should avoid scheduling benchmark assessments just before or after a major school holiday because of the excessive absences that may be expected to occur.

---

[1] Responsibilities at the district, school, and classroom level may vary among states, districts, and schools. This chapter is meant as a guide to provide ideas for administering DIBELS on a widespread basis.

[2] Some states or districts, notably in Florida, elect to give DIBELS four times a year.

Avoid scheduling benchmark assessments just before or after a school holiday.

Schedule Benchmark Assessments Within a Defined Window

Schools or districts administering DIBELS decide on a window of administration for benchmark assessments. In order for scores across a district to be comparable, it is helpful for benchmark assessments to be administered within a defined time frame, which may be one day or several weeks. We recommend a period of not longer than three weeks so that children who are assessed later do not have more than three weeks of additional instruction compared with students assessed earlier. Small schools or small districts may schedule all benchmark assessments on the same one or two days, with retests scheduled within one week. When medium to large districts use one of the team approaches described in Chapter 8, they often use the entire three weeks for benchmark testing. The first two weeks are used for the schoolwide benchmark assessments, and the last week is used to conduct necessary retesting and to give benchmark assessments to students who were absent. Scores are entered throughout the three-week period or after all assessments are completed, depending on whether data input is centralized or conducted by a person who is part of the examining team. As previously mentioned, it is important to build time into the schedule for makeup assessments for those children who were absent and those children who need retesting on one or more measures.

Keep Teachers Informed

When using assessment teams, assessment coordinators need to develop a detailed schedule for the benchmark assessment window that informs teachers when an assessment team will be arriving so students will be available. (Alternatively, if teachers are the examiners, the schedule lets teachers know when they are expected to give the benchmark assessments.) Part of the purpose of a schedule is to navigate around special instruction such as art, music, and physical education and around times for lunch, recess, and library visits. Many assessment coordinators draft a preliminary schedule and solicit feedback from teachers about potential conflicts before finalizing the schedule.

The assessment coordinator also is responsible for posting reminders over e-mail, near the teachers' mailboxes, and in the teachers' lounge as the assessment window approaches. Even with early scheduling and these reminders, coordinators would be wise to expect some teachers to forget the benchmark assessment date. Often these teachers can be identified in advance, and making reminder calls both on the preceding day and 10 minutes before assessments begin to those teachers' classrooms can help keep DIBELS benchmark assessments on schedule.

Reschedule When Running Late

Occasionally, the team gets behind schedule when giving the assessments, often due to fire drills or other unexpected interruptions. If this happens and the team does not finish testing students on time, the team should leave that classroom in order to stay on schedule and plan to return to complete the unfinished assessments later. The teacher needs to be consulted when determining the time to reschedule assessments.

SELECTING LOCATIONS WITHIN SCHOOLS FOR ADMINISTERING DIBELS

DIBELS is given individually, and it requires both the student's and the examiner's full attention. Therefore, the space selected for benchmark assessments should have minimal distractions. When benchmark assessments are administered in a central location, examining stations should be far enough apart that students do not hear one another while being assessed. (A general rule is to try to have at least six feet between assessment stations.)

When a team approach is used for benchmark administration, there are several options for locations. The school library, gym, or cafeteria can be excellent spaces. Some schools give the assessments in the hallway, being careful to avoid active areas. Another option is to clear a classroom or two for the assessment period. Generally, the resource room, the music room, or other similar spaces make excellent benchmark administration locations.

If teachers give the assessments in their classrooms, they need to establish an examining station that is off limits to other children and that does not have distractions for the student being assessed. The teacher also needs to plan quiet activities for the rest of the class if benchmark assessments are given while the teacher is also responsible for classroom management.

> The school library, gym, and cafeteria are good locations for administering benchmark assessments when other activities in those locations have been rescheduled.

DATA MANAGEMENT

Most schools and districts want to be able to use the data (student scores) collected through benchmark assessments for purposes beyond just looking at a classroom in order to determine intervention groups and to plan for intervention instruction. A data management system is necessary in order to produce reports from aggregate data that can be used to compare DIBELS scores across the district and over time.

Selecting a Data Management System

Two basic options exist for managing DIBELS data (student scores). The first option is using the University of Oregon's DIBELS Data System. The second is developing an internal data management system on a school, district, or state level. (A few schools that use DIBELS by their own choice, not as part of a district or state program, use the Benchmark Scores Table in the Appendix to develop classroom reports because they use DIBELS scores only to identify and group children who are at risk for reading failure. They do not use the scores for any other purpose.)

University of Oregon DIBELS Data System. The University of Oregon DIBELS Web site (http://dibels.uoregon.edu) provides the DIBELS Data System, which is available for a minimal annual cost to schools ($1 per student as of 2004).[3] Schools enter students' scores into the database over the Web and can immediately request and receive reports incorporating the scores. (See Chapter 9 for a summary of some of the reports available from the Web site.)

Internal Data Management Systems. Some schools and districts elect to build their own data management systems. This can be done in a Microsoft® Excel spreadsheet or using other software.

Overall Supervision of Data Entry and Management

No matter which method is used for management of DIBELS data, one person needs to be responsible for data at the district level and one person needs to be responsible for data at the school level.

District-Level Responsibilities. The district-level DIBELS coordinator generally has data management as one of several responsibilities. One of the responsibilities is assigning user profiles and levels of authority for data access by school coordinators. This person rarely enters data but is responsible for coordinating data entry among the schools and downloading students demographic information into the system.

School-Level Responsibilities. The person responsible at the school level is often a reading coach or principal and is primarily responsible for setting up user profiles and levels of authority for data access by school staff. This person may also input the data or directly supervise the person who performs the actual data input.

Data Entry

Selecting Data Entry Personnel. Whether a district or school uses the University of Oregon's database or has its own system for gathering and presenting DIBELS scores, the scores need to be entered into a database. Responsibility for entering the students' scores varies depending on whether state-, district-, or school-level administrators are involved in oversight and management of DIBELS data. For Reading First schools, data entry responsibilities will be determined at the state level, and state-level administrators will designate the persons responsible for entering the DIBELS data (the reading coach, specially trained clerical staff, etc.). Some districts use DIBELS without state involvement or supervision, in which case administrators at the district level will appoint those responsible for data entry. Sometimes a school independently decides to use DIBELS, in which case the principal or another school administrator would determine whose responsibility it is to enter the data.

---

[3] Once a school district decides to implement DIBELS and use the DIBELS data management system, a district representative must log on to the DIBELS home page, complete and submit contact and billing information fields, and complete and fax the billing agreement form. Step-by-step directions are available in the Data System Manual, which is downloadable from the DIBELS Web site: http://dibels.uoregon.edu.

Methods for Data Entry. Most schools assign data entry responsibility to one or two people, sometimes a secretary or clerical employee, sometimes the reading coach or other support staff, and sometimes a volunteer who has been trained in DIBELS data entry. Some schools have teachers enter their own data, which is an approach that can result in less reliability. When teachers enter scores for only 20–30 students each benchmark assessment period, they may never enter enough data to become proficient at it. When a large- or small-team approach to benchmark assessment is used, any or all of the team members can be assigned the task of data entry if there is no other person assigned to enter data.

It is very efficient to have two people enter the data, one who reads the scores and one who enters the data. In addition, data entry errors are minimized when two people are involved in the process, especially if one person reads the scores and the other enters the data or if the two data entry persons spot-check one another's work. (Using the two-person method, data entry for a school with 500 students can be expected to take about 1.5 hours.)

MATERIALS MANAGEMENT

Obtaining Materials

Obtaining, distributing, collecting, and storing DIBELS materials is a huge task, even on the school level. If DIBELS is administered on the district level, the task can become gargantuan. Acquiring DIBELS materials can occur in two ways:

1. Purchasing all necessary materials from Sopris West (http://www.sopriswest.com)

2. Downloading master copies of all necessary materials from the DIBELS Web site and copying them locally.

Purchasing Materials From Sopris West. Sopris West offers DIBELS materials at very reasonable prices. Most schools purchase classroom kits and supplement their materials needs by purchasing additional materials individually or in small packages. Classroom kits are grade-level specific and contain:

- Twenty-five Benchmark Assessment Scoring Booklets
- Six grade-appropriate Progress Monitoring Scoring Booklets:
  - Kindergarten—ISF, PSF, and WUF
  - Grade 1—NWF, WUF, and ORF
  - Grades 2 and 3—ORF and WUF
- Two Benchmark Assessment Student Materials booklets
- One Progress Monitoring Student Materials booklet
- One *DIBELS Administration and Scoring Guide.*

It is a good idea to order materials four to six weeks in advance to ensure receiving materials in time for benchmark assessments.

Downloading DIBELS Materials From the DIBELS Web site. Districts that elect to download DIBELS benchmark materials from the DIBELS Web site need to consider two issues related to copying.

1. Although it is not mandatory to print ISF pictures in color, kindergarten children seem to like the color pictures better, and teachers report that they get better responses from some children with color pictures. Therefore, the school might consider the cost of having color copies made for ISF materials when weighing whether to download or purchase ISF materials.

2. DIBELS booklets look very much alike, and color coding cover pages for all booklets by grade makes the materials easier to identify. Schools that download materials quickly discover that materials are much easier to manage when the cover pages of all materials (Scoring Booklets and Student Materials) are color coded by grade. For example, the kindergarten booklets could be blue, the first grade booklets could be green, etc. It is not necessary to print all of the pages on colored paper, just the first page.

Some examiners laminate and bind the Student Materials booklets used by the examiner. Other examiners use the simpler procedure of inserting the Student Materials pages in plastic protective covers and placing them in three-ring binders. Both methods keep the Student Materials from becoming frayed and minimize necessary replacement of Student Materials as they deteriorate from extensive use.

ORGANIZING THE MATERIALS

Generally, the test coordinator, reading coach, or designated DIBELS coordinator at the school organizes all testing materials needed at the school site. Materials will need to be organized for each examiner and for each classroom.

Print materials[4] needed for each examiner include:

- One copy of the Student Materials booklet for each grade being assessed
- One student Scoring Booklet for each student, organized by classroom.

Equipment needed for each examiner includes:

- Stopwatch
- Colored scoring pen
- Clipboard
- Calculator.

---

[4] DIBELS materials are changed from time to time. The changes are often reflected first on the materials available to be downloaded from the DIBELS Web site. Because Sopris West materials are printed in advance, changes are not reflected until a new printing of the materials occurs, and printings are often months apart. Some schools have found that when they download student booklets from the DIBELS Web site, the student booklets do not match the Student Materials they have purchased from Sopris West or downloaded from the DIBELS Web site at an earlier date. Unfortunately, often these schools discover the mismatch only when examiners begin giving the benchmark assessments. To avoid this problem, we recommend that schools either: (1) download Student Materials and Scoring Booklets at the same time; or (2) check to make sure that student booklets downloaded from the DIBELS Web site match the scoring materials in hand.

Preparing and Distributing Scoring Booklets Before Benchmark Assessments

The DIBELS coordinator at the school site is responsible for ensuring that Scoring Booklets are properly labeled and that classroom teachers or examiners get one Scoring Booklet for each student in each class. Scoring Booklets generally are labeled with the child's name, classroom teacher, and other pertinent information, such as a student ID number. Almost all schools use computer-generated labels for this purpose. A clerical person, the DIBELS coordinator, or the teacher can place the labels on each Scoring Booklet. For general organization, it is helpful to group the student booklets by grade level and bundle them by teacher.

DIBELS coordinators who store the Benchmark Assessment Scoring Booklets in a central location distribute the Scoring Booklets to classroom teachers two or three days in advance of the benchmark assessment window. If classroom teachers store their own Scoring Booklets, the coordinator needs to distribute the Scoring Booklets at the beginning of the year and then check to make sure teachers have their Scoring Booklets during the other two assessment periods.

Storing Materials After Benchmark Assessments

Two options exist for storing benchmark assessment materials:

1. The DIBELS coordinator is responsible for storing all benchmark assessment materials for all students at the school. Storage is generally in a central location with only the DIBELS coordinator and the school administrator having access to the booklets.

2. The classroom teacher keeps the materials for each of his or her students.

Booklets are less likely to be lost or damaged when they are housed in a central location with one person responsible for storage. Also, when all DIBELS materials are stored centrally, teachers do not have access to DIBELS materials, and they are not tempted to use DIBELS materials for classroom activities. However, central storage can make teachers' access to the Scoring Booklets difficult, precluding them from using information in the Scoring Booklets for instructional planning.

ORGANIZATION CHECKLIST

Figure 7–1 is an organizational checklist for DIBELS Benchmark Administration that districts and schools may want to modify to meet their own needs.

Figure 7-1		Organization Checklist for Benchmark Administration	
Task	**Completion Date**	**Person Responsible**	**√**
Staff Preparation			
1. Present introduction			
2. Send background reading materials			
Parent Preparation			
1. Send introductory letter or article			
2. Present open house			
Scheduling Benchmark Assessment Dates			
1. Send preliminary schedule to teachers			
2. Create and post assessment and reassessment schedule			
3. Distribute final schedule			
Identifying and Training Examiners			
1. Identify and contact examiners			
2. Plan training sessions			
3. Train examiners			
4. Prepare training materials			
Finding Locations			
1. Arrange locations for assessments			
Assessment Materials			
1. Order or copy print materials for students and examiners			
2. Order administrative equipment for examiners			
At Least One Week Before Beginning Assessment Date			
1. Gather examiners' materials and equipment (stopwatches, clipboards, pencils, etc.)			
2. Send and post reminder notice about data collection			
3. Label student booklets			
4. Finalize last-minute training or review			
5. Obtain class lists to make sure all students have booklets			
6. Identify data entry person			

Organization Checklist for Benchmark Administration (continued)			Figure 7-1

Task	Completion Date	Person Responsible	√
Day of Assessment			
1. Meet with team prior to assessment to review measures and process			
2. Remind examiners to "score as they go"			
3. Have extra materials available			
4. Collect student booklets			
5. Identify students who need to be retested and the measure that needs to be retested			
6. List students who were absent and need to be assessed at a later date (checking student booklets against rosters is one way to do this)			
Retesting and Makeup Assessments			
1. Schedule retests and makeup assessments			
2. Circulate schedule for retesting and makeup assessment to appropriate schools and classrooms			
3. Give retests and makeup assessments			
4. Submit student booklets for data entry			
Data Entry			
1. Organize student booklets in alphabetical order by classroom			
2. Enter data into computer			
Filing DIBELS Materials			
1. File student booklets in predetermined storage location			
2. Store unused assessment materials for future use			
Using Data (Scores) From DIBELS Assessment			
1. Obtain classroom reports and distribute to teachers			
2. Set up meeting (e.g., grade level, cross-grade, reading team) to discuss results and plan intervention			

Note: Based on the data collection checklist from "Approaches and Considerations of Collecting Schoolwide Early Literacy and Reading Performance Data," by B. Harn (2000), available from the DIBELS Web site.

PARENT NOTIFICATION

Some schools and districts send a letter to parents stating when DIBELS benchmark assessments will be given and explaining the reasons for giving DIBELS. Other schools consider DIBELS a part of routine instructional activity and include discussions of DIBELS purposes and scores along with other topics at parent–teacher conferences.

Some schools decide to send a letter to parents partly to encourage them to make sure that their students attend school for DIBELS assessment, as well as to inform the parents about the purpose for and importance of DIBELS. *Figure 7–2* is a sample letter that schools may modify and use to notify parents.

| **Figure 7-2** | **Sample Letter to Parents** |

Dear Parent(s):

On DATE or RANGE OF DATES, we will be giving a very important assessment called DIBELS (Dynamic Indicators of Early Literacy Skills) to your child to determine how well his or her reading skills are progressing. This assessment is so important that we are requesting you to make a special effort to ensure that your child is at school for it. (For those children who cannot be present, a makeup assessment will be given during the week of DATE.)

The importance of the DIBELS assessment can be compared to that of the checkups given by doctors to our children. During the checkups, doctors use height and weight, among other markers, to check for growth and development. We all know how important it is for our children to "grow" in reading as well, because knowing how to read well is one of the most important factors in a child's learning, both inside and outside of school.

We know that early literacy, reading, and reading growth are very important. Therefore, our school is going to collect checkup information on a regular basis to let us and you know how well your child is reading. We do this by administering DIBELS three times a year.

DIBELS measures are simple and accurate. We will have each student participate in several short-duration literacy activities designed to allow the students to "show us what he or she knows." DIBELS takes approximately 5–10 minutes per student, depending on the student's grade level.

Teachers will use DIBELS scores to help plan reading instruction. This information will also help individualize instruction for those students who need help with their reading skills.

We are excited about our ability to know where all of our students are on their path to being successful readers and learners. We hope that you are excited as well.

We want you to know that there is nothing you need to do to prepare your child for the DIBELS assessment other than ensuring your child gets a good night of sleep and a good breakfast.

We look forward to talking with you regarding your child's progress. If you have any questions about DIBELS or your child's progress in reading, please feel free to contact me.

Sincerely,

NAME OF PERSON

TIME TO ADMINISTER DIBELS BENCHMARK ASSESSMENTS

The following tables provide a basis for determining the time that needs to be allotted for administering benchmark assessments. Both tables show the number of students that can be assessed in one hour by 1 to 10 examiners. *Table 7–1* assumes that all measures are being administered, including the optional measures RTF and WUF. *Table 7–2* assumes that the optional measures are not being administered.

Students Assessed in Approximately One Hour, Based on the Number of Examiners, *Including* Optional RTF and WUF   **Table 7-1**

Grade and Measures (Time per Student)	Number of Examiners	Number of Students Assessed in 60 Minutes		
		Beginning of Year	Middle of Year	End of Year
Kindergarten	1	7	5	6
Beginning	2	14	9	12
ISF and LNF	3	21	14	18
(8.5 minutes per student)	4	28	18	24
Middle	5	35	23	30
ISF, LNF, PSF, and NWF	6	42	28	36
(13 minutes per student)	7	49	32	42
End	8	56	37	48
LNF, PSF, and NWF	9	64	42	54
(10 minutes per student)	10	71	46	60
First Grade	1	6	4	4
Beginning	2	12	8	8
LNF, PSF, and NWF	3	18	12	12
(10 minutes per student)	4	24	16	16
Middle	5	30	20	20
PSF, NWF, and ORF	6	36	24	24
(15.25 minutes per student)	7	42	28	28
End	8	48	31	31
PSF, NWF, and ORF	9	54	35	35
(15.25 minutes per student)	10	60	39	39

Table 7-1   Students Assessed in Approximately One Hour, Based on the Number of Examiners, *Including* Optional RTF and WUF (continued)

Grade and Measures (Time per Student)	Number of Examiners	Number of Students Assessed in 60 Minutes		
		Beginning of Year	Middle of Year	End of Year
Second Grade	1	5	6	6
Beginning NWF and ORF (13.25 minutes per student)	2	9	11	11
	3	14	17	17
	4	18	22	22
Middle ORF (10.75 minutes per student)	5	23	28	28
	6	27	33	33
	7	32	39	39
End ORF (10.75 minutes per student)	8	36	45	45
	9	41	50	50
	10	45	56	56
Third Grade	1	6	6	6
Beginning ORF (10.75 minutes per student)	2	11	11	11
	3	17	17	17
	4	22	22	22
Middle ORF (10.75 minutes per student)	5	28	28	28
	6	33	33	33
	7	39	39	39
End ORF (10.75 minutes per student)	8	45	45	45
	9	50	50	50
	10	56	56	56

Table 7-2   Students Assessed in Approximately One Hour, Based on the Number of Examiners, *Excluding* Optional RTF and WUF

Grade and Measures (Time per Student)	Number of Examiners	Number of Students Assessed in 60 Minutes for a Benchmark Assessment Period		
		Beginning of Year	Middle of Year	End of Year
Kindergarten	1	9	5	7
Beginning ISF and LNF (7 minutes per student)	2	17	10	14
	3	26	16	21
	4	34	21	28
Middle ISF, LNF, PSF, and NWF (11.5 minutes per student)	5	43	26	35
	6	51	31	42
	7	60	37	49
End LNF, PSF, and NWF (8.5 minutes per student)	8	69	42	56
	9	77	47	64
	10	86	52	71

Students Assessed in Approximately One Hour, Based on the Number of Examiners, **Table 7-2**
Excluding **Optional RTF and WUF (continued)**

Grade and Measures (Time per Student)	Number of Examiners	Number of Students Assessed in 60 Minutes for a Benchmark Assessment Period		
		Beginning of Year	Middle of Year	End of Year
First Grade	1	7	5	5
Beginning	2	14	10	10
LNF, PSF, and NWF	3	21	15	15
(8.5 minutes per student)	4	28	20	20
Middle	5	35	26	26
PSF, NWF, and ORF	6	42	31	31
(11.75 minutes per student)	7	49	36	36
End	8	56	41	41
PSF, NWF, and ORF	9	64	46	46
(11.75 minutes per student)	10	71	51	51
Second Grade	1	6	8	8
Beginning	2	12	17	17
NWF and ORF	3	18	25	25
(9.75 minutes per student)	4	25	33	33
Middle	5	31	41	41
ORF	6	37	50	50
(7.25 minutes per student)	7	43	58	58
End	8	49	66	66
ORF	9	55	74	74
(7.25 minutes per student)	10	62	83	83
Third Grade	1	8	8	8
Beginning	2	17	17	17
ORF	3	25	25	25
(7.25 minutes per student)	4	33	33	33
Middle	5	41	41	41
ORF	6	50	50	50
(7.25 minutes per student)	7	58	58	58
End	8	66	66	66
ORF	9	74	74	74
(7.25 minutes per student)	10	83	83	83

8

Selecting, Training, and Organizing Examiners

Selecting examiners and then training and organizing them to administer benchmark assessments are perhaps the most important components of ensuring that DIBELS scores provide the best possible information to inform instruction. The ideas contained in this chapter are not exhaustive. They are meant to help schools and districts obtain the best examiners possible. This is so DIBELS scores will truly reflect students' abilities, and those students who need intervention instruction will get it.

EXAMINER QUALIFICATIONS

Many schools use classroom teachers as DIBELS examiners. Reading coaches and school psychologists are also common choices for examiners. Others who serve as DIBELS examiners are school personnel who do not have direct daily classroom responsibility. By including principals, assistant principals, special education teachers, librarians, school psychologists, speech and language pathologists, reading coaches, English as a second language instructors, Title I assistants, and classroom aides on the assessment team, a broader sense of ownership for improving reading performance on an individual and schoolwide basis is achieved.

DIBELS examiners must have a number of qualifications, including:

- Thorough training in how to administer and score DIBELS
- Practice before actually giving DIBELS to students for whom scores will count
- Knowledge and experience working in the areas of early literacy (phonemic awareness, phonics, fluency, vocabulary, and comprehension)
- Well-developed phonemic awareness, with the ability to hear and discriminate the phonemes in the English language.

The last qualification listed, well-developed phonemic awareness, is one of the most important. The examiner must be able to hear, discriminate, and process the sounds in words in order to accurately score ISF and PSF. The examiner who is not facile with phonemes will not be able to determine quickly whether the student's response to PSF is accurate.

To score NWF accurately, the examiners need to have a thorough understanding of the most common letter–sound correspondences. All vowels in DIBELS NWF words are scored correctly only if they are pronounced with their short vowel sounds. For that reason, it is especially important for NWF that examiners know and can discriminate the short vowel sounds.

Some people selected to be DIBELS examiners may have poor phonemic awareness. If an examiner admits to poor phonemic awareness or if it is otherwise determined that the examiner does not discriminate sounds well, do not punish that person. Rather, encourage these examiners to work with other examiners and teachers to develop their phonemic awareness, because research informs us that phonemic awareness can be taught (Gillon, 2004). (Indeed, this knowledge is driving much of our early literacy instruction.) By improving their phonemic awareness skills, these educators will not only be better DIBELS examiners, they will be better reading instructors. Also, it should be kept in mind that these examiners may be qualified to administer second and third grade benchmark assessments, which do not include ISF, PSF, or NWF and do not require the ability to quickly identify whether a student articulated the correct phoneme.

In addition to phonemic awareness skills and excellent training, examiners must have time to commit to administering DIBELS. After the scores are obtained, examiners may be involved in checking Scoring Booklets for accuracy as well. Further, it is important for examiners to be available for additional professional development training, which may involve learning to interpret DIBELS data and use it to plan intervention instruction.

DIBELS TRAINING AND WORKSHOPS

Administration and Scoring Workshops

Examiners need to attend a DIBELS scoring and administration workshop to learn the intricacies of scoring each DIBELS measure. Reading this manual will help examiners understand the assessment and will introduce the examiners to DIBELS and each of the seven measures. However, this manual is intended as a resource for those administering and scoring DIBELS when they have questions. It is not intended to take the place of a scoring and administration workshop for any DIBELS examiner.

Workshops for administering and scoring DIBELS are generally one or two days long and most effectively given to no more than 50 participants. The workshops vary in format depending on the trainer, audience, and time frame. One-day workshops generally cover the scoring and administration rules and include some interactive practice for most or all measures. Two-day workshops often allow time to practice all seven measures, sometimes offering hands-on practice with children. Two-day workshops also may go more in depth for additional information about DIBELS.

Sopris West offers DIBELS scoring and administration workshops. To learn about Sopris West workshops, go to http://www.dibelsassessment.com/training. htm. The DIBELS Web site also provides a list of individuals who offer DIBELS scoring workshops. The authors of this book are available to give DIBELS scoring and administration workshops and can be contacted at their e-mail addresses: Linda Farrell, lindadibels@earthlink.net; Carrie Hancock, drcarriehancock@cox. net; and Susan Smartt, susandibels@comcast.net.

PRACTICING DIBELS

After examiners attend a workshop to learn to score and administer DIBELS and before they actually administer any official benchmark assessments, they should practice giving any DIBELS measures they will be administering at the benchmark assessment. This practice helps the examiner learn to juggle the materials, operate the stopwatch, read the directions, and score accurately. At first, administering DIBELS benchmark assessments can be daunting because there is so much to do and there are so many intricacies for scoring each measure (much like learning to drive a car!). However, most DIBELS examiners are completely comfortable with the assessment after giving 5 to 10 complete DIBELS benchmark assessments. That is why we recommend that new examiners give *at least* 5 practice assessments for each measure.

Examiners need to be careful not to use materials that the practice students might encounter in benchmark assessment. There are three ways to avoid this happening:

1. Use the materials in the Appendix for practice assessments. These materials are appropriate for students ages six and older who are at least beginning readers and can comfortably read some connected text. By using these materials, examiners ensure that students will not inadvertently be shown DIBELS assessments that they may encounter while taking a benchmark assessment.

2. Use DIBELS benchmark assessment materials only if it is a certainty that the students with whom they practice will not have DIBELS benchmark or progress monitoring assessments with the same materials. The best way to do this is to select children older than those in the grade for the benchmark materials used for practice. For example, use a student who is older than kindergarten age to practice LNF, ISF, PSF, NWF, and WUF, and use the kindergarten benchmark materials for those assessments. Work with a student who is beyond first grade to practice ORF and RTF and use the first grade benchmark materials for that practice session.

3. Use DIBELS progress monitoring materials for practicing. This is the last alternative presented because practicing with progress monitoring materials does not give the examiner experience using the benchmark Scoring Booklet and Student Materials.

Selecting Practice "Students"

Although it is ideal to practice with students, this may not be practical given the busy workdays that many examiners have. If they cannot find students, it is sufficient for examiners to practice scoring DIBELS by giving it to spouses, friends, other teachers, or anyone else. The purpose of the practice is twofold: (1) for the examiner to learn to handle all the materials while scoring and timing; and (2) for the examiner to make initial mistakes with someone whose score will not be recorded. By giving at least five practice assessments for each measure, even to older students or adults, new examiners will be prepared to administer DIBELS to students and obtain valid scores.

We cannot stress enough how important it is for new examiners to practice giving measures before giving assessments "for real." Students selected for practice should be able to read because nonreaders do not allow for enough practice with the measures. Other teachers make excellent practice subjects because they can easily emulate the behaviors of students.

Shadow Scoring

Another recommended strategy to use when practicing DIBELS or when first administering assessments for real is to participate in shadow scoring. Shadow scoring involves two examiners scoring the assessment for one student. One examiner gives directions, but both examiners time the assessment and score the student's answers. When both examiners are new, they compare scores and discuss any differences. When one examiner is experienced, the new examiner can learn by comparing scores with those of the experienced examiner.

Mentoring

Some schools and districts offer an extra training step for examiners. They have all the new examiners administer their first "official" benchmark assessments under the supervision of a more experienced examiner or a DIBELS trainer. The experienced examiner or trainer is available on site to answer the new examiners' questions and to check their Scoring Booklets for accuracy.

Another way to provide mentoring is to have an experienced examiner watch a novice examiner and use the Observer's Checklist, found in the Appendix, to provide feedback about the areas in which the new examiner shows competence and the areas in which there is room for improvement. Some schools or districts decide to use this technique occasionally even with experienced examiners so that scoring integrity is assured.

ORGANIZING EXAMINERS TO ADMINISTER DIBELS

A decision about the approach to administering DIBELS benchmark assessments is usually made at the district level. Many choices exist for organizing examiners to administer DIBELS benchmark assessments in the schools. The suggestions in this chapter are not exhaustive but are meant to give ideas that schools and districts can use when developing their own DIBELS assessment procedures. Often, a combination of the discussed approaches is selected.

When determining which approach to DIBELS benchmark assessment to take, many factors must be considered. Regardless of choice, there are strengths and limitations that must be considered with regard to each district's or school's available resources. The goal is for DIBELS scores to be accurate, useful, and reflective of a student's individual and collective instructional needs for reading.

Choices are School-Based or District-Based

The choices for organizing examiners fall into two categories: school-based and district-based. School-based DIBELS assessment teams use personnel from the school as examiners. Members of a school-based team give assessments to all students at their own school. District-based teams travel from school to school, and their members are district-level or district-hired personnel.

Our recommendation is for schools and districts to use the team approach for benchmark assessments. The team approach generally gives more accurate scoring because team members consistently administer and score DIBELS and, therefore, are always developing their scoring skills.

A question that is often discussed is whether classroom teachers should assess their own students. There are both advantages and disadvantages. The advantages center on the teacher being able to observe the students' performance, including observing error patterns made by struggling students. The disadvantages are based on the perception that teachers may want to coach or otherwise help their students because they want them to get higher scores. Many schools do not have teachers assess their own students so that there is no such perception. Some schools have the teacher work as part of an assessment team and assess some, but not all, of his or her own students.

Three Basic Choices for Organizing Benchmark Assessments

The three basic choices for organizing both school-based and district-based teams are described below. We have seen many variations on the three basic choices. We describe these three approaches in order to provide ideas for schools and districts to begin thinking about how best to organize DIBELS benchmark assessments.

For purposes of this discussion, the three basic choices for organizing school-based DIBELS assessment teams are as follows:

1. Small team

2. Large team

3. Classroom teacher.

Each of the three approaches to administering DIBELS is discussed below.

Small Team

General Description. This approach requires one small team of examiners who administer DIBELS benchmark assessments in a school over multiple days. The exact number of team members and the time devoted to administering each benchmark assessment to an entire school will vary based on the size of the school. In general, the assessment team typically has four to seven people who administer DIBELS all day each day over a two- to four-day period in one school.

School-Based or District-Based? The small-team approach can be implemented on a school-by-school or districtwide basis. If the approach is *school-based*, the assessment team will be formed from personnel based at the school or district personnel directly affiliated with the school. A *district-based* approach might have several small teams that serve the entire district, depending on the number of schools to be assessed. Another alternative is to combine district and school personnel. Whether the small teams are school-based, district-based, or a combination of the two, each member of the team will need to be thoroughly trained in DIBELS scoring and administration techniques.

Team Members. Examiners on a school-based team may or may not be classroom teachers, depending on whether funds are available to hire substitutes for the classroom teachers on the examining team. The school-based team may include a combination of the following:

- Classroom teachers (for whom substitutes have been hired)
- Building staff (principals, assistant principals, etc.)
- Substitutes specially trained to give DIBELS
- Classroom aides
- Specially trained volunteers
- Reading coaches
- Support instructors such as special education or resource instructors; speech pathologists; and music, art, or physical education teachers who do not have regular classroom responsibilities
- District personnel with responsibility for the school (area reading coaches, area language arts directors, school psychologists, social workers, etc.).

District-based examiners on small teams may be district staff or may be hired specifically to give DIBELS benchmark assessments. Some districts appoint a team of school psychologists, speech therapists, and other support personnel to be part of small teams that devote one or two weeks to giving benchmark assessments throughout the district. Examiners hired specifically to give DIBELS benchmark assessments may be retired teachers, substitute teachers, and university students.

Facility Considerations. If a small, multiple-day team approach is selected, adequate space must be available in the schools to allow the team to administer assessments over several days. The design of a school building may dictate where the assessments occur. Working in hallways is an option if disruptions can be minimized. Using hallways makes it easy for examiners to move desks, chairs, and materials to locations near the classrooms they are assessing. Other options include using the library, an empty classroom, a multipurpose room, or a gymnasium. When the assessments are given in these locations, scheduled activities will need to be moved or postponed. It is also important to consider transition time from the classroom to one of these larger rooms. If it takes several minutes to walk from the classrooms to the larger room, this may not be an efficient choice. It is possible to administer benchmark assessments in the classroom, but it is not always advisable because of the noise level, student distractions, and limited space.

Scheduling Time. Teams schedule a block of time, depending on team size and classroom size, to administer benchmark assessments in each classroom. (See *Table 7–1* and *Table 7-2* in Chapter 7 to estimate the amount of time it will take to assess each class.) The size of the examining team needs to be set so that the examiners spend from two to four days in the school to complete benchmark assessments for all the classes. Additionally, one or more team members will need to schedule time to administer retests and to assess students who were absent during benchmark screening.

Advantages and Disadvantages. The advantages and disadvantages of the small-team approach are:

Small-Team Approach

ADVANTAGES	DISADVANTAGES
Fewer people require training than if every classroom teacher gives assessments. Therefore, multiple schools or districts can combine resources to pay for examiners to be trained.	Teachers are less involved in data collection. While this may be an advantage in increasing efficiency, it is also a disadvantage as teachers may not accept ownership of the DIBELS data or be invested in the "data driven instruction" viewpoint.
Scores from a small team of examiners can be more reliable because these examiners quickly become experts in how to score accurately. Also, when examiners have questions, it is easy for them to meet to discuss their administration and scoring issues.	
With fewer examiners, not as many stopwatches, clipboards, calculators, colored pens or pencils, and Student Materials booklets need to be purchased.	This approach increases responsibilities surrounding materials management. Instead of managing materials for a single classroom, the team is responsible for the entire school's DIBELS materials.
This approach allows for minimal disruption to instructional activities. Children are pulled from each class in a short period of time, and teachers do not have to disrupt their classroom routines to administer DIBELS to their classes. As a result, teachers can concentrate on teaching rather than administering benchmark assessments.	While classroom disruption is minimized, it still occurs. Teachers must plan activities conducive to DIBELS assessments collection as students constantly leave and reenter the classroom during the assigned time block for DIBELS administration.
Using a small team makes finding a location for administering DIBELS less problematic because having a smaller team means needing less space than using a large team over a shorter period of time.	Scheduling time for each classroom may be difficult because special-area activities (P.E., music, and art), lunch, release time, recess, and sometimes special education classes limit the amount of available blocks of time.
Teachers are not assessing their own students, minimizing the perception that teachers might coach their own students or otherwise affect their scores.	Teacher involvement in administering DIBELS to their own students is minimal or nonexistent, so teachers do not benefit from observing their students taking the assessments. Even if they are part of the assessment team, teachers are likely to have the opportunity to assess only a few of their own students.

Large Team

General Description. This approach requires assembling one large team of examiners; the team administers DIBELS benchmark assessments to all the schools in a district. Teams spend no more than one day in any school, which is the purpose of having a large team. The exact number of team members varies based on the number of schools and students in the district. A large assessment team typically has 12–20 people. A very large district will need several large examination teams, whereas a small district may need only one examination team.

School-Based or District-Based? The large team approach can be implemented on a school-by-school basis or on a district basis. If the approach is *school-based*, the assessment team will be formed from personnel based at the school or from district personnel directly affiliated with the school. Some schools pair up and have one large team that administers one day to one of the schools and another day to the other school. A *district-based* approach might have several large teams that travel from school to school, depending on the number of schools to be assessed. Whether the large teams are school-based or district-based, each member of the team will need to be thoroughly trained in DIBELS scoring and administration techniques.

Team Members. A large school-based team can be organized to administer DIBELS to one school in one day. Depending on the size of the school, this generally requires approximately 12–20 examiners. Because team members need to be out of the classroom for only one day, it is feasible to have a few classroom teachers on the school-based assessment team because substitutes would need to be hired for only one day. Because of the size of the team, it is more likely that district-level personnel will be part of the team even if it is school-based. This team may include a combination of the following:

- Classroom teachers (for whom substitutes have been hired)
- Building staff (principals, vice principals, etc.)
- Substitutes
- Classroom aides
- Retired teachers
- Specially trained volunteers
- Reading coaches
- Support instructors such as special education or resource instructors, librarians, speech pathologists, and music, art, or physical education teachers who do not have regular classroom responsibilities
- District personnel with responsibility for the school (area reading coaches, area language arts directors, school psychologists, social workers, etc.)
- Other district personnel (curriculum specialists, program specialists, etc.).

District-based examiners on large teams may be district staff or may be hired specifically to give DIBELS benchmark assessments. Some districts appoint a team of school psychologists, speech therapists, and other support personnel to be part of large teams giving benchmark assessments throughout the district. Examiners hired specifically to give DIBELS benchmark assessments may be retired teachers, substitute teachers, and university students. Whatever the composition of the large team, all members will need to be thoroughly trained in DIBELS scoring and administration techniques.

Scheduling Time. Teams schedule a block of time for each classroom, depending on classroom size, to administer benchmark assessments. (See *Table 7-1* and *Table 7-2* in Chapter 7 to determine the time required for each classroom.) The team needs to be large enough to be able to give benchmark assessments to all students in a school in one day. Additionally, some team members will need to schedule time to administer retests and to assess students who were absent during benchmark assessment.

Facility Considerations. When choosing the large-team approach, it is necessary to have access to a sizeable room and waiting area. Efficiency may be increased if this space is centrally located in, for example, a library, a multipurpose room, a gymnasium, or adjoining empty classrooms. As an example of this efficiency, while one group of students is participating in assessment, another group is outside the library reading quietly. When applying the large-team approach, it is helpful to

97

have one or two people dedicated to transitioning students from the waiting area to the assessment space and from the assessment space back to their classroom.

Advantages and Disadvantages. The advantages and disadvantages of the large-team approach are:

Large-Team Approach

ADVANTAGES	DISADVANTAGES
An important and significant strength of using this approach is minimal class disruption. With a large number of examiners, a teacher can have all of his or her students assessed in less than 20 minutes, and an entire school can be tackled in one day.	Scheduling may be difficult, especially with half-day kindergarten. Canceling special-area classes (art, music, and P.E.) for the day may be necessary. (However, this may provide an opportunity for these educators to be part of the assessment team.)
	Significant advance planning is required, and rescheduling due to last-minute changes or unforeseen circumstances is more difficult.
	Finding a central location spacious enough to accommodate a large assessment team may be challenging.
	DIBELS assessment coordinators must schedule time to collect data on those students who were absent or need to be retested.
The speed of this approach allows reports to be generated in a timely manner. Many schools structure this approach so that one person is continually entering data as students are being assessed.	
Because many people from the school are involved with DIBELS, enthusiasm is generated toward the commitment to reading achievement and improving DIBELS scores.	Teacher involvement in administering DIBELS to their own students is minimal or nonexistent, so teachers do not benefit from observing their students taking the assessments. Even if they are part of the assessment team, teachers are likely to have the opportunity to assess only a few of their own students.
Teachers are not assessing their own students, minimizing opportunities for the perception that the teacher coached students or otherwise affected their scores.	

Classroom Teachers Assessing Their Own Students

Using teams as described previously is our recommended approach for administering DIBELS benchmark assessments. However, having classroom teachers assess their own students may be the only available option for administering DIBELS benchmark assessments. If this is the case, we suggest that schools and districts move toward a team approach to benchmark assessments as soon as is practicable.

General Description. With this approach, classroom teachers administer DIBELS benchmark assessments to their own students. This can be done in several ways, two of which are described below:

1. A substitute teacher is hired, and the classroom teacher administers DIBELS until all students have been assessed. This generally takes one to two days, depending on the size of the class.

2. The classroom teacher administers benchmark assessments during regular classroom time.

School-Based or District-Based? This is a school-based approach.

Team Members. There is no official team when all the teachers give benchmark assessments to their own classrooms. In essence, the teachers are the assessment team, each responsible for assessing his or her own students.

Scheduling Time. Teachers need to schedule their classroom activities so that benchmark assessments are all given in the specified time frame. This can involve hiring substitutes or otherwise giving the teachers enough time to administer all the benchmark assessments.

Facility Considerations. If a substitute is hired while the teacher gives the assessments, the teacher will need a space outside the classroom to administer the assessments. (Giving assessments in the classroom is too distracting for both the teacher and the students.) If the teacher is required to give the assessments in the classroom without a substitute or other help (this is not recommended), distractions to the teacher, as well as to the students, need to be minimized while assessment occurs.

Advantages and Disadvantages. The advantages and disadvantages of the classroom teacher approach are as follows:

Classroom Teachers Assess Their Own Students

ADVANTAGES	DISADVANTAGES
Teachers have ownership of DIBELS data, and the children's progress may be stronger because the teacher is involved.	When teachers administer benchmark assessments only to their own students, there are more chances for inaccurate administration and scoring practices because the assessments are so seldom given.
	The amount of responsibility placed on teachers in addition to their instructional responsibilities may be overwhelming and place a negative light on DIBELS and its purpose.
This approach avoids the common complaint from teachers that when someone else collects data on their students, the students don't know the examiner and therefore the students may not perform maximally.	
There is minimal schoolwide disruption of scheduled activities. Teachers collect their data in their own classrooms on their own time without disrupting other school activities.	It is much more difficult to supervise DIBELS benchmark administration when assessment is occurring in multiple settings at the same time.
	Assessment activities must occur over several days, which may reduce the efficiency and timeliness of data entry.
	The teacher's instructional time is interrupted in order for the teacher to administer DIBELS.

9

DIBELS Web-Based Reports

The Web-based DIBELS Data System offers numerous reports that are easily accessed immediately after scores are entered into it. Various DIBELS reports show benchmark assessment scores for any period (beginning, middle, or end of the school year) or for any series of periods in various formats. The reports show scores for individual students, for individual classrooms, by grade level, by individual school or for a cluster of schools, by district or for a cluster of districts, and by state or in comparisons between states. Reports are also available for progress monitoring scores. DIBELS reports present data in various formats so that educators can engage in professional dialogue with objective information and make effective decisions for a student's reading instruction.

This chapter highlights only several of the many reports available from the DIBELS Data System. The reports explained in this chapter are those most often used by teachers, reading coaches, and administrators. This chapter focuses only on understanding information contained in reports for benchmark assessments. It does not include a detailed discussion about advanced use or data analysis, nor do we discuss reports specifically for progress monitoring.

Table 9–1 (next page) shows reports described in this chapter and the levels at which they can be viewed. A description of each level follows.

Table 9-1		Reports Discussed in This Chapter and Most Common Levels for Viewing			
		Most Common Level for Viewing			
Figure #	**Report and Description**	District/ Project	School/ Grade	Classroom	Student
9-1	**Histogram** — bar chart showing the distribution of scores on a single test	X	X		
9-2	**Box Plot** — "box and whiskers" graph showing percentiles over time	X	X		
9-3	**Class List Report** — list of individual student scores and instructional recommendations			X	
9-4 and 9-5	**Scatter Plot** — "dots" in four quadrants show relationship of students' performance on one DIBELS measure against performance on another measure at a later time.	X	X		
9-6	**Summary Report** — shows means, standard deviations, and number and percent of students by risk level for all measures given at one benchmark period	X	X		
9-7	**Summary of Effectiveness Report** — shows the effectiveness of instruction from one benchmark period to another, by instructional recommendation	X	X	X	
9-8	**Distribution Report** — disaggregated results by school, class, or demographics	X	X		
9-9	**Class Progress Graph** — graphs individual scores for each student in a class over an entire year			X	
9-10	**Individual Student Performance Profile** — one-page summary of a student's performance on all measures, also called Summary Report or Student Report				X

COMMON CHARACTERISTICS OF DIBELS REPORTS

DIBELS Web-based benchmark reports share several common characteristics:

- All benchmark reports must be viewed by grade level. Therefore, when viewing any report, users must first select a grade level.
- Benchmark reports are organized by time of year. Many reports show data for one benchmark period. Box Plots, Scatter Plots, and Summary of Effectiveness reports are viewed over two or three benchmark periods, always within the same year. The Individual Student Performance Profile covers kindergarten through third grade. When viewing reports, it is necessary to select a benchmark period (beginning, middle, or end of year).
- Benchmark reports display data based on scores, percentiles, status categories (Deficit/At Risk, Emerging/Some Risk, and Established/Low Risk), and instructional recommendations (Intensive, Strategic, and Benchmark). The report chosen dictates which specific categories are displayed.
- Most DIBELS benchmark reports can be viewed at multiple levels. The levels available include project, district, school (grade), classroom, and student.

- District-level reports include data for the district overall and for all schools subscribing to the DIBELS system within a district. Only district-level administrators can view these reports.

- Reports can also be generated for "projects," which might be defined to include several districts within a state or several schools within a district. All reports available on a district level are also available for projects.

- School- and grade-level reports show school progress in reading *by grade level*. The school-level reports also may include classroom-level data. They can be viewed only by district- and school-level administrators.

- Classroom-level reports include data for individual classrooms. Only district- and school-level administrators and the classroom teacher can view these reports. Another teacher in the school cannot view these reports.

- Student-level reports show data for an individual student and can be viewed only by the student's teacher and district- and school-level administrators. Student reports cannot be viewed by other teachers, students, or parents.

ACCESSING REPORTS

At the time of this manual's publication, approximately 20 different reports were available for downloading, printing, and viewing online. Any state, district, or school with a DIBELS Data System account (established by paying an annual fee of $1 per student) has access to DIBELS reports. Individuals authorized to use the DIBELS Data System can access various reports, depending on the level of access they have been granted. DIBELS Data System users need to click on the "View/ Create Reports" link to get into the reports homepage.

The reports are divided into two groups: those available in PDF format and those available in HTML format. The reports included on the PDF list are already formatted for downloading and printing. Those reports included under the heading "Web Reports for Viewing Online" (HTML) are formatted to fit the screen but may not print well.

DESCRIPTION OF REPORTS

Histogram

Histogram is a fancy word for bar graph. Each Histogram is specific to one DIBELS measure and includes all students in one grade level at a district or school at a particular time of year. Histograms may be viewed at the school, district, or project level. The Histogram is a compilation of data with neither student nor teacher names attached to the graph.

Most Frequent Use. Histograms are most often used by district and school administrators to see the distribution of scores across a grade level. A Histogram gives a general picture of the efficacy of instruction in a particular reading-related skill.

Interpreting the Report. Figure 9–1 shows a schoolwide Histogram for midyear NWF scores in kindergarten. Several important parts to this report are identified with a number on *Figure 9–1*. An explanation for each number follows.

Figure 9-1   **Histogram**

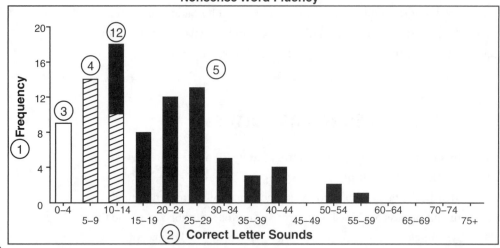

Dynamic Indicators of Basic Early Literacy Skills
Kindergarten School Report

District: Test District
School: Adams
Date: January 2001–2002

⑥ **Benchmark Goal:** The benchmark goal is for all children to have established alphabetic principle skills of 50 or more on Nonsense Word Fluency by the middle of first grade.

⑦ **January Status:** In the middle of kindergarten, students should be beginning to learn some letter–sound correspondences.

⑧ ▮ **63% (n=56) Low Risk**
Children scoring 13 or more letter sounds per minute are likely to achieve the benchmark goal if provided with effective alphabetic principle instruction. For these students, progress toward benchmark goals should be checked at the end of kindergarten to ensure adequate growth.

⑨ ▨ **27% (n=24) Some Risk**
Children scoring between 5 and 12 letter sounds per minute in the middle of kindergarten are at some risk for difficulty achieving the benchmark goal. Additional instructional support in alphabetic principle may be needed to achieve the middle-of-first grade benchmark goal. Progress toward benchmark goals should be monitored monthly.

⑩ ☐ **10% (n=9) At Risk**
Students scoring below 5 letter sounds per minute in the middle of kindergarten are at risk for difficulty achieving the alphabetic principle goal. For students in this range, intensive intervention in alphabetic principle may be needed to achieve the benchmark goal. Progress toward benchmark goals should be monitored at least every two weeks.

⑪ Note: Split bars where the bottom part indicates At Risk and the top part indicates Some Risk or where the bottom part indicates Some Risk and the top part indicates Low Risk are used when the cutoff scores for At Risk or Some Risk occur in the middle of a score range. The number of students is indicated by the size of the bar part.

---

① The number of students is shown on the vertical axis, or y axis, which is labeled "Frequency." Each bar represents the number of students who scored within a specific range on the measure.

② The ranges of scores are specified along the horizontal axis, or x axis, which is labeled "Correct Letter Sounds" on *Figure 9–1*.

③ ④ ⑤ The individual bars in the Histogram have different patterns to indicate whether the scores are Deficit/At Risk, Emerging/Some Risk, or Established/Low Risk. In this example, the white bar (③) shows scores in the At Risk range, bars with stripes (④) show scores in the Some Risk range, and black bars (⑤) show scores in the Low Risk range. In this school, 9 students scored in the At Risk range (represented by the white bar); 24 students scored in the Some Risk range: 14 with scores in the 5–9 range and 10 in the 10–14 range; and 56 students scored in the Low Risk range: 8 students in each of the 10–14 and 15–19 ranges, 12 in the 20–24 range, 13 in the 25–29 range, 5 in the 30–34 range, 3 in the 35–39 range, 4 in the 40–44 range, 2 in the 50–54 range, and 1 in the 55–59 range. (Exact numbers are determined by looking at the bars to estimate the number of students in each range and making the numbers add up to the total described in ⑧ ⑨ and ⑩ below.)

Below the graph portion of the Histogram report, an interpretation guide or key is displayed in text. Both important features of the key are numbered and explained in the following paragraphs.

⑥ The Benchmark Goal is the score children are expected to achieve to show mastery in a subject. ⑦ The Current Status is the score children are expected to achieve for the period of the Histogram. On this Histogram, the Benchmark Goal is 50, the NWF score that children are expected to achieve by the middle of first grade in order to demonstrate mastery of early phonics skills. The January Current Status goal is not defined on this report, but is stated as "students should be beginning to learn some letter–sound correspondences." The DIBELS Benchmark Scores Table in the Appendix shows that the benchmark score for the middle of the year in kindergarten is 13.

⑧ ⑨ ⑩ This part of the key shows the *percentage* of students scoring in each range, the *number* of students scoring in each range, an *explanation* of what skills typically look like in that range, a recommendation for instruction support, and a recommendation for progress monitoring intervals. For example, on this Histogram, the numbers next to the black square (⑧) show that 63%, or 56 students, scored in the Low Risk. The numbers next to the striped box (⑨) show that 27%, or 24 students, scored between 6 and 12 in the Some Risk range; additional instruction in the alphabetic principal may be needed, with monthly progress monitoring recommended. The white square (⑩) shows that 10%, or 9 students, scored in the At Risk range, and the recommendation is for these children to receive intensive instruction in the alphabetic principal, with progress monitoring every two weeks.

⑪ Occasionally, the graph part of a Histogram will show a bar that has two shades, such as the third bar from the left, labeled ⑫ on this Histogram. These are called split bars.

⑫ The bar for the score in the range of 10–14 is partly black and partly striped. The split bar shows that the cutoff score between Some Risk (striped portion of bar) and Low Risk (black portion of bar) is within the specified range shown along the "correct letter sounds" axis. The cut point on this bar is 12. (On this bar, the cut point means that a score of 12 is considered Some Risk and one of 13 is considered Low Risk for midyear in kindergarten, as shown on the Benchmark Scores Table in the Appendix.) The size and pattern scheme of the bar distinguish the number of students in each risk category. On this chart, 10 students are in the Some Risk range, scoring 10, 11, or 12. Eight students are in the Low Risk range, scoring 13 or 14.

Box Plot

Box plots are often referred to as "box and whisker graphs" because of their appearance. Box Plot Reports show the range of scores and the percentiles on one measure (NWF, PSF, etc.) at two or three benchmark assessment periods.

Most Frequent Use. Box Plots are most frequently used by school- and district-level administrators to see the impact of instruction over time for a specific grade level. Box Plots are also a quick way to see how different groups of students are progressing when charts for schools or classes are compared.

Interpreting the Report. Understanding the purpose and content of the Box Plot report is important for both administrators and teachers because the report shows the progress of students for one measure over time. The important parts of the Box Plot in *Figure 9–2* are explained in the following text.

Box Plot   Figure 9-2

Dynamic Indicators of Basic Early Literacy Skills
Kindergarten School Progress Report

District: Test District
School: Adams
Date: 2001–2002

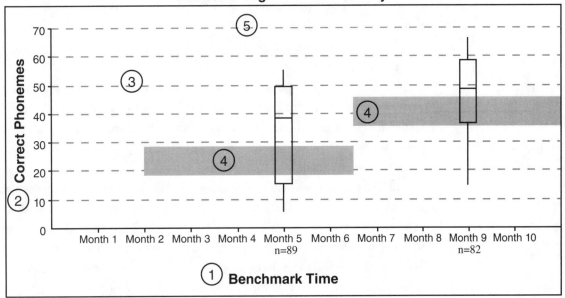

Phoneme Segmentation Fluency

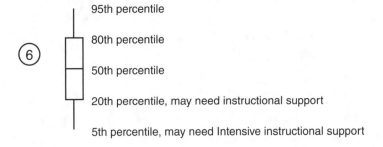

(5) Benchmark goal for all students:
35–45 correct sounds per minute at the end of kindergarten or beginning of first grade.

– Students scoring 18 or more in the middle of kindergarten are likely to achieve the benchmark
goal with effective instruction.

(6)
95th percentile

80th percentile

50th percentile

20th percentile, may need instructional support

5th percentile, may need Intensive instructional support

① The horizontal axis, or x axis (labeled "Benchmark Time" in *Figure 9–2*), identifies the times of year for which scores are being shown, which is midyear and year-end, or month 5 and month 9 on this report. Below the text identifying the time of year, the number of students included in the benchmark assessment is shown. For example, in this report, n = 89 for month 5 means 89 students were tested on PSF during the midyear benchmark.

② The vertical axis, or y axis (labeled "Correct Phonemes" in *Figure 9–2*), shows the unit of measurement and the number of correct responses for that measure.

③ The dotted lines within the body portion of the graph aid in approximating scores in each box.

④ The gray bars highlight the benchmark score for students at each benchmark assessment period. In this example for kindergarten PSF, at midyear students should be producing at least 18 correct phonemes per minute and by year-end they should be producing at least 35 correct phonemes per minute, which is the benchmark goal.

⑤ The benchmarks and the benchmark goal for each period on the Box Plot are stated in verbal form below the chart. On this report, the benchmark and the benchmark goal are the same at year-end, which is when children are expected to achieve a score of at least 35, indicating they have phonemic awareness. The benchmark for midyear is 18 or more, the score students need to achieve in order to be on the way to meeting the benchmark goal at the end of the year.

⑥ This graphical key helps interpret the boxes on the chart. This key shows the meaning of the lines and boxes on the chart. The top of the line represents the 95th percentile. The box itself represents scores in the average range (20th percentile to 80th percentile), with the top of the box showing the 80th percentile, the line in the middle of the box showing the 50th percentile, and the bottom of the box showing the 20th percentile. Finally, the bottom of the line below the box represents the 5th percentile. The exact scores that correspond to these percentiles are not available on this report. However, teachers and administrators can get this information using the Norms Report.

Class List

The Class List Report presents every score for each measure, except WUF and RTF, for all students in one class for one benchmark assessment period. Raw scores, percentile ranks, and status are shown for each measure given for each student. An instructional recommendation is also given for each student. (Technical explanations for the derivation of the instructional recommendations are included in the *DIBELS Administration and Scoring Guide* in the "Instructional Recommendations" section at the back of the guide.)

Most Frequent Use. The Class List Report is used by teachers to identify students At Risk and group them for intervention.

Class List Report

Figure 9-3

Dynamic Indicators of Basic Early Literacy Skills
Kindergarten Class List Report

District: Test District
School: Adams
Date: January 2001–2002
Class: Smith, A.

Note: Scores provide an indication of performance only. If there is any concern about the accuracy of scores for an individual student, performance should be verified by retesting to validate need for support.

① Student	② Initial Sound Fluency			③ Letter Naming Fluency			④ Phoneme Segmentation Fluency			⑤ Nonsense Word Fluency			⑥ Instructional Recommendations
	Score	Percentile	Status	Score	Percentile	Status	Score	Percentile	Status	Score	Percentile	Status	
B, JUDY	5	2	Deficit	6	10	At Risk	3	7	At Risk	6	16	Some Risk	Intensive - Needs Substantial Intervention
R, CHRISTIAN	9	6	Deficit	20	41	Some Risk	7	11	Some Risk	12	34	Some Risk	Strategic - Additional Intervention
Y, SAMANTHA	14	14	Emerging	7	12	At Risk	9	14	Some Risk	6	16	Some Risk	Intensive - Needs Substantial Intervention
W, KATHLEEN	15	17	Emerging	11	20	At Risk	10	15	Some Risk	5	14	Low Risk	Intensive - Needs Substantial Intervention
M, AUSTENE	17	22	Emerging	15	29	Some Risk	25	32	Low Risk	20	55	Low Risk	Strategic - Additional Intervention
H, ADRIAN	20	32	Emerging	64	98	Low Risk	41	61	Low Risk	44	95	Low Risk	Benchmark - At Grade Level
P, NYSHEL	23	41	Emerging	49	89	Low Risk	38	55	Low Risk	14	40	Low Risk	Benchmark - At Grade Level
R, MICHAEL	24	47	Emerging	19	39	Some Risk	22	30	Low Risk	0	3	At Risk	Strategic - Additional Intervention
B, CHELSEA	25	51	Established	29	60	Low Risk	29	38	Low Risk	21	58	Low Risk	Benchmark - At Grade Level
M, CLAY	27	57	Established	7	12	At Risk	27	35	Low Risk	10	28	Some Risk	Strategic - Additional Intervention
W, NICHOLAS	28	60	Established	11	20	At Risk	2	6	At Risk	11	31	Some Risk	Strategic - Additional Intervention
V, IRIS	30	66	Established	10	17	At Risk	29	38	Low Risk	9	25	Some Risk	Strategic - Additional Intervention
J, AUSTIN	31	69	Established	23	49	Some Risk	31	41	Low Risk	32	81	Low Risk	Benchmark - At Grade Level
B, KAYLEE	32	72	Established	41	80	Low Risk	40	59	Low Risk	9	25	Some Risk	Benchmark - At Grade Level
D, KAI	40	88	Established	21	43	Some Risk	39	57	Low Risk	4	11	At Risk	Benchmark - At Grade Level
G, WILLIAM	42	90	Established	19	39	Some Risk	48	74	Low Risk	24	64	Low Risk	Benchmark - At Grade Level
C, BRIANNA	43	91	Established	28	58	Low Risk	51	82	Low Risk	23	61	Low Risk	Benchmark - At Grade Level
M, JUSTIN	50	94	Established	41	80	Low Risk	46	71	Low Risk	37	88	Low Risk	Benchmark - At Grade Level
C, LEXINGTON	51	94	Established	61	96	Low Risk	43	65	Low Risk	18	50	Low Risk	Benchmark - At Grade Level
D, MARIAH	60	95	Established	14	27	At Risk	38	55	Low Risk	19	52	Low Risk	Strategic - Additional Intervention
B, EMERALD	70	98	Established	27	56	Low Risk	42	63	Low Risk	19	52	Low Risk	Benchmark - At Grade Level
E, CALEM	70>99		Established	47	87	Low Risk	55	90	Low Risk	25	66	Low Risk	Benchmark - At Grade Level
	32 Mean			25.9 Mean			30.7 Mean			16.1 Mean			

⑦ ⑧

Available from the DIBELS Web site, http://dibels.uoregon.edu. Used by permission of the Center on Teaching and Learning (CTL), Institute for the Development of Educational Achievement (IDEA), College of Education, University of Oregon.

Interpreting the Report. Figure 9–3 is a Class List Report for A. Smith's kindergarten class at the midyear benchmark assessment period. A detailed explanation of the Class List Report features follows.

① This column lists student names. The last name is listed first. (However, on this report the last name is represented only by an initial to maintain confidentiality.) The names are not in alphabetical order because the report is sorted by scores in one of the columns. A complete discussion of how the scores are sorted on this report is in the explanation for the Initial Sound Fluency column in ② below.

② ③ ④ Each of these sections has three columns that provide the same information, as described below:

First column: *Score* refers to the student's raw score, which is the number correct for that measure.

Second column: *Percentile* refers to the student's percentile rank based on all scores reported by a school or district. If a school is the only school in a district participating in DIBELS, the percentile rank will be based on students in the school. However, if multiple schools are using DIBELS in a district, the percentile rank will be based on all students participating in the district.

Third column: *Status* lists the risk category for a measure. When mastery of the skill being measured is expected, the status levels are as follows:
- Established—Students who have met the benchmark for that measure
- Emerging—Students who are making progress toward the benchmark but have not yet achieved it
- Deficit—Students who are significantly behind and are at risk for reading failure.

When mastery of the skill is not expected but students need to show progress toward mastery, the status levels are as follows:
- Low Risk—Students are making enough progress in this skill to be considered on track to master the skill
- Some Risk—Students are not making enough progress in this skill to ensure mastery and likely need additional instructional support in the skill being measured
- At Risk—Students are making so little progress with this skill that they are considered at risk for mastering the skill and are highly likely to need additional instructional support in the skill being measured.

② This section provides information on Initial Sound Fluency. The students' names on this report are sorted by their scores on this measure, with the student having the lowest score at the top and the student with the highest score at the bottom. ISF is used as the measure for sorting because students are expected to meet the ISF benchmark goal of 25 by midyear in kindergarten, the time of this report. Generally, Class List Reports are sorted by the measure that is expected to be mastered at the time of the report. For example, midyear first grade reports will be sorted by NWF, because the benchmark goal for that measure is expected to be met by that time.

③ This section provides information on Letter Naming Fluency. The information in each column is explained previously.

④ This section provides student information on Phoneme Segmentation Fluency. The information in each column is explained previously.

⑤ This section provides student information on Nonsense Word Fluency. The information in each column is explained previously.

⑥ The final column, *Instructional Recommendations*, communicates the intensity of instruction recommended for each student by the University of Oregon. The instructional recommendations offered by the University of Oregon are based on the scores in the student's profile, excluding WUF and RTF. Instructional recommendations rely on studies that show the overall level of risk for a particular combination of skills. For students identified as "Intensive," the research data show that, unless intensive instructional support is provided, these students have less than an approximately 20% chance of meeting later reading benchmarks. Students identified as "Strategic" have between an approximately 20% and 80% chance of meeting later reading benchmarks. (This Strategic group is the "iffy" group and will likely—but not necessarily—require additional instructional support in order to meet benchmark scores.) Finally, students identified as "Benchmark" have an approximately 80% or greater chance of meeting later reading outcomes. Essentially, for those at or above benchmark, the provided instruction is working and teachers should continue "doing what they're doing" with these students. Schools determine their own guidelines for providing instructional support. Some general guidelines that many schools use are that students with strategic recommendations receive between 20 and 30 minutes of extra instruction in groups of three to five, and students with intensive recommendations receive 45 minutes or more of additional instruction in groups of three or fewer. All intervention instruction should be targeted toward the skills for which DIBELS scores are below benchmark.

⑦ This student has an "Intensive" instructional recommendation. The combination of her scores indicated that she needs strategic intervention (at least 45 minutes daily) in early reading skills. She is At Risk for Letter Naming Fluency, and Emerging or Some Risk for all other measures, indicating that she needs intervention instruction in phonemic awareness, letter names, and letter sounds.

⑧ This student has a "Strategic" instructional recommendation, indicating the student may need some intervention. This student's scores show that he is Emerging in ISF and Some Risk in LNF, although he has Low Risk scores on PSF and NWF. Further investigation into this student's specific difficulties and whether they are with accuracy or fluency may provide clues about the level of intervention to give this student, if any.

Scatter Plot

Scatter Plots are used to show the connection between DIBELS scores at different times of the school year. Essentially, these reports are a visual representation of the link between early reading skills and later reading skills. For a more detailed description of Scatter Plot charts, see Good, Gruba, and Kaminski (2001). Scatter Plots are generated at the end of year if the "School, District, and Project PDF Reports" link is chosen. As with the previous reports, teachers can also choose to view some Scatter Plot Reports throughout the school year by selecting the Scatter Plot link under "Web Reports for Viewing Online."

Most Frequent Use. Teachers and administrators use Scatter Plots to determine how reliably one DIBELS score predicts another. For example, administrators may want to know how year-end PSF scores in kindergarten connect to ORF scores at the year-end in first grade. *Figure 9–4* is an example of a Scatter Plot Report for all first graders in a district showing the connection between year-end ORF and year-end PSF scores in kindergarten.

Figure 9-4   **Scatter Plot**

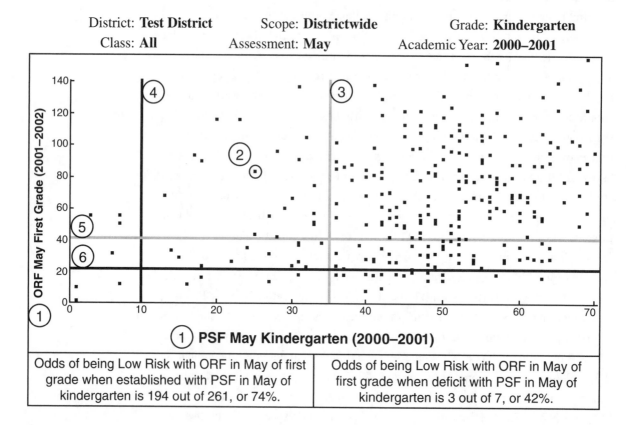

Dynamic Indicators of Basic Early Literacy Skills, University of Oregon
Scatter Plot

District: **Test District**   Scope: **Districtwide**   Grade: **Kindergarten**
Class: **All**   Assessment: **May**   Academic Year: **2000–2001**

Odds of being Low Risk with ORF in May of first grade when established with PSF in May of kindergarten is 194 out of 261, or 74%.	Odds of being Low Risk with ORF in May of first grade when deficit with PSF in May of kindergarten is 3 out of 7, or 42%.

Interpreting the Report. Initially, the Scatter Plot Report may seem overwhelming. Scatter plots, however, are worth understanding because they provide some critical information about the impact of early literacy instruction across time. The school level Scatter Plot Report contains both a graph and student list. For purposes of our discussion, we will focus on a district-level Scatter Plot. Within the Scatter Plot graph are several important component parts that are numbered and discussed here.

① The horizontal (x) and vertical (y) axes show the DIBELS measures and benchmark periods being compared. In *Figure 9–4*, kindergarten year-end PSF scores (horizontal axis) are being compared with first grade year-end ORF scores (vertical axis).

② Each dot represents a student. (Darker dots represent more than one student.) In order to have a dot on this graph, the student must have scores for both measures being compared. On this Scatter Plot, the dot that is circled near ② represents a student who scored 25 on the year-end PSF in kindergarten (the dot is above the midpoint between 20 and 30 on the horizontal axis representing PSF scores) and 80 on year-end ORF in first grade (the dot is to the right of the 80 on the vertical axis representing ORF scores).

③ This gray line shows the cut point between Established and Emerging scores for year-end PSF scores in kindergarten. In the Web reports version, this line is green. Notice that this line intersects the horizontal axis at 35, which is the benchmark score for PSF at the end of kindergarten. All dots to the right of this line represent scores at or above 35 on PSF at year-end in kindergarten. All dots to the left represent PSF scores below 35 at year-end in kindergarten.

④ This black line shows the cut point between Emerging and Deficit scores for year-end PSF in kindergarten. In the Web reports version, this line is red. The line intersects the x axis at 10, which is the cut point between Emerging and Deficit score for PSF at the end of kindergarten. All dots between this line and line ③ represent scores between 10 and 35 on PSF at year-end in kindergarten. All dots to the left of line ④ represent scores below 10 on PSF at year-end in kindergarten.

⑤ This gray line shows the cut point between Low Risk and Some Risk scores for first grade year-end ORF. In the Web reports version, this line is green. This line intersects the vertical axis at 40, which is the benchmark score for ORF at year-end in first grade. All dots *above* this line represent first grade year-end ORF scores above 40, and all dots *below* this line represent first grade year-end ORF scores below 40.

⑥ This black line shows the cut point between Some Risk and At Risk scores for first grade year-end ORF. In the Web reports version, this line is red. This line intersects the vertical axis at 20. All dots between the horizontal axis and this line represent ORF scores between 20 (Some Risk) and 40 (Low Risk) at year-end in first grade. All dots below this line represent ORF scores lower than 20 (At Risk).

In order to simplify interpretation of this graph, teachers may want to divide it into quadrants. *Figure 9–5* is an example of the Scatter Plot in *Figure 9–4* divided into quadrants.

Figure 9-5   **Scatter Plot With Quadrants Defined**

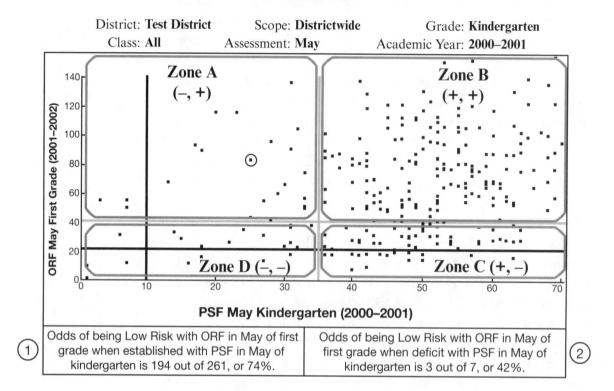

**Dynamic Indicators of Basic Early Literacy Skills, University of Oregon
Scatter Plot**

District: **Test District**   Scope: **Districtwide**   Grade: **Kindergarten**
Class: **All**   Assessment: **May**   Academic Year: **2000–2001**

| | Odds of being Low Risk with ORF in May of first grade when established with PSF in May of kindergarten is 194 out of 261, or 74%. | Odds of being Low Risk with ORF in May of first grade when deficit with PSF in May of kindergarten is 3 out of 7, or 42%. | |

Zone A shows students who met the ORF benchmark at year-end in first grade but did not meet the PSF benchmark at year-end in kindergarten. This profile is summarized with minus and plus symbols (–, +) to show that students were not on track at year-end in kindergarten for PSF, but were on-track by year-end in first grade for ORF.

Zone B shows students who met or exceeded the PSF benchmark at year-end in kindergarten *and* met or exceeded the ORF benchmark at year-end in first grade. This profile is summarized with plus symbols (+, +). This means that these students were on track at year-end in kindergarten for PSF *and* at year-end in first grade for ORF.

Zone C shows students who met the PSF benchmark at year-end in kindergarten but did *not* meet the ORF benchmark at year-end in first grade. This profile is summarized with plus and minus symbols (+, –), which means that students met year-end PSF benchmark in kindergarten (+) but did not meet the year-end ORF benchmark in first grade (–).

Zone D shows students who did not meet the PSF benchmark at year-end in kindergarten and did not meet the ORF benchmark in year-end in first grade. Minus symbols (–, –) show that students did not meet either benchmark.

Below the Scatter Plot are two boxes that summarize the likelihood that students at a particular school will meet the end-of-year ORF goal if they have or have not met the year-end PSF goal in kindergarten.

① This summary box shows the likelihood that students will meet the end-of-year ORF goal *if* they met the end of year K PSF goal. In this case, the likelihood is 74%. This percentage is based on the number of dots in Zone B compared with the total number of dots in Zones B and C combined. When considering actual students, this information also tells you that in this district, at year-end in kindergarten 261 students met the PSF goal. Of those students, 194 (74%) met the ORF year-end goal in first grade. (Counting the dots on this sample Scatter Plot will not yield these numbers because some darker dots represent more than 1 student.)

② This summary box shows the likelihood that students will meet the year-end ORF goal in first grade *if* they had a deficit PSF score at year-end in kindergarten. At this school, the likelihood is 42%. When considering actual students, 7 students did not meet the year-end PSF in kindergarten (dots to the left of the vertical black line in Zones A and D). Of these 7 students, only 3, or 42%, met the year-end ORF goal in first grade. (The 3 students are the dots to the left of the vertical black line in Zone A.)

When Scatter Plots are downloaded and printed as part of the year-end school and district PDF reports, they are accompanied by a list of students, their individual scores, and their status for the measures shown on the Scatter Plot. The school and/or class for each student is also listed.

Summary Report

The Summary Report (see *Figure 9–6*, next page) is the third link under "PDF Reports for Downloading and Printing." It is a one-page summary of all data collected during a school year, and it does *not* include a graph. These reports are downloaded by grade level and can be viewed at the school, district, and project level. Data within the Summary Report are organized by measure and time of year.

Most Frequent Use. Administrators at the school, district, and project level use Summary Reports most often to review data reflecting an entire grade level of scores.

Figure 9-6 **Summary Report**

Dynamic Indicators of Basic Early Literacy Skills
(1) First Grade Summary Report

District: Test District
School: Adams (1)
Date: 2001–2002

(3)

	September	January	May
LNF	Goal: 37 letter names		
Students tested	77		
Mean (SD)	37.2 (17.8)		
	49% Low Risk		
	25% Some Risk		
	26% At Risk		
PSF	Goal: 35 phonemes	Goal: 35 phonemes	Goal: 35 phonemes
Students tested	77	73	75
Mean (SD)	40.7 (18.1)	52.5 (16.4)	54.5 (13.3)
	73% Established	86% Established	91% Established
	18% Emerging	12% Emerging	9% Emerging
	9% Deficit	1% Deficit	
NWF	Goal: 24 letter sounds	Goal: 50 letter sounds	Goal: 50 letter sounds
Students tested	77	73	75
Mean (SD)	31.4 (25)	61.3 (33.4)	80.6 (34.3)
	60% Low Risk	62% Established	77% Established
	21% Some Risk	27% Emerging	23% Emerging
	19% At Risk	11% Deficit	
ORF		Goal: 20 words per minute	Goal: 40 words per minute (4)
Students tested		73	75 (5)
Mean (SD)		37.7 (35.9) (6)	62.4 (40)
		62% Low Risk	68% Low Risk
		29% Some Risk (7)	19% Some Risk
		10% At Risk	13% At Risk
RTF		Goal:	Goal:
Students tested		73	75
Mean (SD)		15.7 (11.8)	30.3 (15.7)
20th percentile		7	16
40th percentile		12 (8)	24
WUF	Goal:	Goal:	Goal:
Students tested	77	73	75
Mean (SD)	17.1 (8.4)	24.3 (10.2)	32.1 (16.0)
20th percentile	7	12	24
40th percentile	14	19 (9)	29

(2)

Interpreting the Report. The information contained in the Summary Report is easily interpreted. However, it is important to understand the layout of the report. Numbers ①–③ describe the structure of the report. Once the structure of the Summary Report is understood, it is possible to interpret the information, which is described in a uniform way. The goal, mean, standard deviation, skill status, and percentile are reported for each measure administered at each benchmark time. Explanations of figures provided in numbers ④ through ⑨ follow.

① Identifying information is provided at the top of the report. *Figure 9–6* is a First Grade Summary Report for Adams School in a Test District during the academic year 2000–2001.

② Each measure given during the assessment periods shown on the report is found on the far left of the page. In this case, the measures administered include LNF, PSF, NWF, ORF, RTF, and WUF. The information in this report is sorted by both DIBELS measure and time of year (shown in ③ below).

③ The benchmark time of year can be found across the top of the Summary Report. This report shows the months September, January, and May. Not all measures are administered during each benchmark period. For example, in this First Grade Summary Report, LNF is given at the beginning of the year, but not at midyear or year-end, as indicated by blank columns for LNF during those periods. Similarly, ORF is not given at the beginning of the year, but is administered at midyear and year-end.

④ Goal—Each measure has a benchmark (called *goal* on this report) that may change with the time of year. For example, the ORF benchmark for midyear is 20; it increased to 40 at year-end. (WUF and RTF do not have goals on Summary Reports.)

⑤ Students Tested—This is the total number of students tested on a measure at a particular benchmark time. For example, at the school for this report there were 77 students assessed on all measures in September, 73 in January, and 75 in September.

⑥ Mean (SD)—*Mean* is another word for average. The mean score is reported for each measure at each benchmark time and is unique to the school, district, or project examined. For example, the mean score for ORF at Adams School at midyear is 37.7. Next to the word *mean*, *SD* appears in parentheses. SD stands for *standard deviation* and is a unit of measurement used when the distribution of scores is normal. Teachers and administrators rarely use this figure when interpreting DIBELS because it is a measurement understood easily only by those with knowledge of statistical concepts. The standard deviation score for ORF at Adams School at midyear is 35.9.

⑦ Skill status is the final piece of data included in the Summary Report. Skill status provides the percentage of students scoring within a particular range. Skill status is shown for LNF, PSF, NWF, and ORF, but not for WUF or RTF. For ORF at the middle of the year, 62% of students had Low Risk scores, 29% had Some Risk scores, and 10% had At Risk scores.

⑧ RTF data do not include skill status information because an RTF score lower than 25% of ORF defines the At Risk category for that measure, and this information was not calculated by the DIBELS Data System at the time of publication. Information about RTF scores that define the 20th and 40th percentiles at the local level is provided for these measures. On this report, a score of 7 marked the 20th percentile and a score of 12 marked the 40th percentile for midyear RTF scores. The cut points for RTF are informational only (because an RTF score that is lower than 25% of the ORF score is At Risk, and DIBELS reports did not provide this calculation at the time of press).

⑨ WUF data do not include skill status information because formal WUF benchmarks have not yet been established. Information about scores that define the 20th and 40th percentiles at the local level is provided for WUF. As suggested by DIBELS, these cut points can be used as guides for determining the student's level of risk for reading difficulties in WUF. On this report, at midyear a WUF score of 12 was at the 20th percentile and a score of 19 was at the 40th percentile.

Summary of Effectiveness Report

The Summary of Effectiveness Report shows the impact of curriculum and instruction over time. Specifically, it shows the number and percentage of students who meet benchmark goals in each Instructional Recommendation category from one benchmark period to the next. These reports may be viewed at the classroom and school level.

Most Frequent Use. The Summary of Effectiveness Report is most frequently used by classroom teachers and building administrators to view the progress of their students from one benchmark period to the next.

Interpreting the Report. This report can be generated for a specific classroom or for an entire grade level. In order to interpret this report, it is important to read the small print. *Figure 9–7* is an example of a Summary of Effectiveness Report at Adams School for the beginning of year and midyear benchmark periods in A. Jones' kindergarten classroom for ISF.

Summary of Effectiveness Report

Figure 9-7

Dynamic Indicators of Basic Early Literacy Skills
Summary of Effectiveness of Core Program

District: Test District
School: Adams
Date: September 2001–2002
Class: A. Jones
Step: Beginning of kindergarten to middle of kindergarten ①

② Effectiveness of Core Curriculum

Students at Benchmark at Beginning of Year	⑥ Beginning ISF Score	⑦ Middle ISF Score	⑧ Check If Reached Middle ISF Benchmark of 25
B, EMERALD	25	60	√
B, KAYLEE	26	32	√
C, LEXINGTON	45	50	√
E, CALEM	21	70	√
G, WILLIAM	17	42	√
H, ADRIAN	18	20	
J, AUSTIN	20	31	√
M, JUSTIN	9	48	√

| School: | Adams | Count: | 7/8 |
| Class: | A. Jones | Percent: | 88% |

③ Effectiveness of Strategic Support Program

Students at Benchmark at Beginning of Year	⑥ Beginning ISF Score	⑦ Middle ISF Score	⑧ Check If Reached Middle ISF Benchmark of 25
B, CHELSEA	6	25	√
D, KAI	14	40	√
M, AUSTENE	23	7	
P, NYSHEL	11	23	
R, CHRISTIAN	4	9	
V, IRIS	23	30	√
W, KATHLEEN	8	15	
W, NICHOLAS	18	28	√
Y, SAMANTHA	10	14	

| School: | Adams | Count: | 4/9 |
| Class: | A. Jones | Percent: | 44% |

④ Effectiveness of Intensive Support Program

Students at Benchmark at Beginning of Year	⑥ Beginning ISF Score	⑦ Middle ISF Score	⑧ Check If Reached Middle ISF Benchmark of 25
B, JUDY	2	5	
D, MARIAH	5	51	√
R, MICHAEL	0	24	

| School: | Adams | Count: | 1/3 |
| Class: | A. Jones | Percent: | 33% |

⑨

Available from the DIBELS Web site, http://dibels.uoregon.edu. Used by permission of the Center on Teaching and Learning (CTL), Institute for the Development of Educational Achievement (IDEA), College of Education, University of Oregon.

① The Summary of Effectiveness Report for a classroom compares DIBELS scores at two different benchmark times. For example, this report is comparing ISF from the beginning of kindergarten to midyear.

② ③ ④ The report is divided into three sections: (②) effectiveness of core curriculum; (③) effectiveness of strategic support program; and (④) effectiveness of intensive support program. These categories correlate directly with the instructional recommendations from the Class List Report. Several pieces of information are included within each section relating to program effectiveness.

⑤ The first column under each category related to program effectiveness is a list of students in the classroom who scored at or above benchmark for the measure at the first time period on the report. For example, eight students listed in this column under ② "Effectiveness of Core Curriculum" earned a Benchmark instructional recommendation. Nine students listed in this column under ③ "Effectiveness of Strategic Support Program" were in the "Strategic" category for instructional recommendations. Three students listed in this column under ④ "Effectiveness of Intensive Support Program" were in the "Intensive" category for instructional recommendations. (Instructional recommendations for each student are shown on the Class List Report.)

⑥ ⑦ The next two columns in each category list each student's scores for one measure for the two time periods being compared. This report shows ISF scores for the beginning and middle of kindergarten benchmark periods. *(Only students who were tested during both benchmark periods are included in this report.)*

⑧ The final column shows a check mark if the student reached the benchmark score for the second period included on the report. On this report, the top of the column reads "Check If Reached Middle ISF Benchmark of 25." This column tells the teacher how effective instructional programs were by showing how many children in each instructional recommendation category met benchmark scores. From this report we know the following:

- Seven of 8 students in the core curriculum who met benchmark have check marks, meaning that, of the 8 students who had beginning-of-year ISF scores indicating they were on track to meet the midyear ISF benchmark score, only 1 did not meet the midyear benchmark score of 25.
- Of the 9 students who were recommended for strategic support after beginning-of-year benchmark testing, 4 met the midyear ISF benchmark score of 25 and 5 did not.
- Three students were recommended for intensive instruction after beginning-of-year benchmark testing, and only 1 of those students met the midyear ISF benchmark score of 25.

⑨ The final piece of information contained in this report is at the bottom of the page and is basically a summary of the data above. These cells describe the number and percentage of students who met the midyear ISF benchmark score in each category. For example, 7/8, or 88%, of students in the core curriculum met the midyear ISF goal; 4/9, or 44%, of students in the strategic support program met the midyear ISF goal; and 1/3, or 33%, of students in the intensive support program met the midyear ISF goal.

Distribution Report

The Distribution Report is viewed for a specific benchmark time (beginning, middle, or end) and presents a graphic and numerical summary of student scores and instructional recommendations for each DIBELS measure administered. The reports may be viewed at the classroom level, school level, district level, and project level. When schools enter demographic information (e.g., gender, ethnicity, English proficiency, and socioeconomic status) into the DIBELS Data System, this report will also disaggregate the graphic and numerical data by those demographics.

Most Frequent Use. The Distribution Report is most often used by administrators at the school, district, and project level because it gives a brief synopsis of student achievement by grade and by teacher.

Interpreting the Report. The data displayed on the Distribution Report include (1) the number and percentage of students scoring in each skill status category (Deficit, Emerging, and Established or At Risk, Some Risk, and Low Risk) for each DIBELS measure administered during one benchmark period; and (2) the total number and percentage of students in each instructional recommendation category (Benchmark, Strategic, and Intensive).

Figure 9–8 (next page) is an example of a district-level Distribution Report for kindergarten at midyear. Users can choose to obtain the DIBELS data broken down by specific categories. These choices include school, class, secondary class (used if a student has a different reading teacher), race/ethnicity, gender, free/reduced-cost lunch, special education, disability status/special education category/services provided, additional codes, and DIBELS Approved Accommodations. Regardless of choice, the data displayed will include the skill status category for each measure administered and instructional recommendation category.

① This part of the report identifies how the data are broken down. In the case of this midyear kindergarten report at the district level, the data are broken down by school.

② The total number of students tested is shown at the left of the report. Underneath this number, data are broken down by school and indicate how many students in each school were tested. In this example, 235 kindergarten students were tested in the Sample District. The numbers of students tested in each school were Adams, 89; Garfield, 77; and Jefferson, 69.

③ This row shows the data for the entire district by DIBELS measures administered. WUF and RTF will not be included on this report because benchmarks for these measures are not provided on DIBELS reports.

④ Data for each school's students are reported by DIBELS measure.

⑤ Number and percentage of students in each risk category is shown for each measure by school. For example, the total number of students at Garfield scoring in the Deficit category on ISF was 5, which translates into 6% of the kindergarten students in this school; 34 (44%) of Garfield kindergarten students scored in the

Distribution Report

Figure 9-8

Dynamic Indicators of Basic Early Literacy Skills
Kindergarten Distribution Summary

District: Sample District
School: All Schools
Date: January 2001–2002

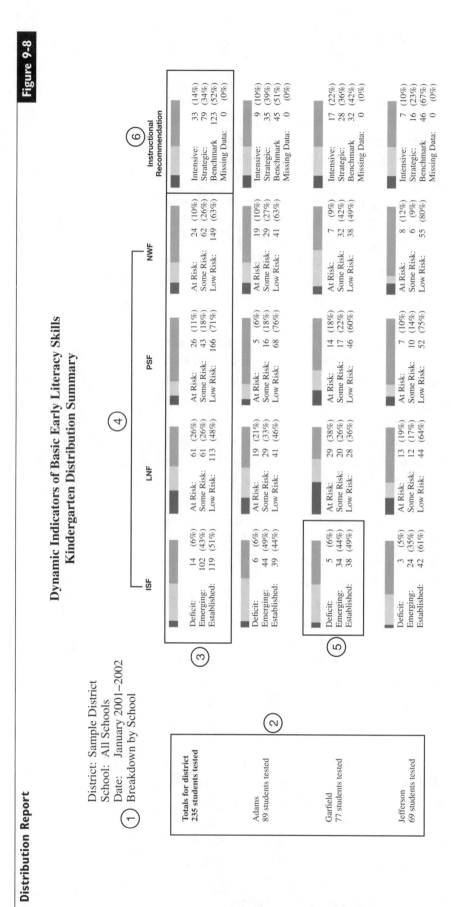

Note: "Missing Data" refers to students who have been tested on some measurements for the requested assessment period, but are missing some scores that are required to determine the Instructional Recommendation.

Available from the DIBELS Web site, http://dibels.uoregon.edu. Used by permission of the Center on Teaching and Learning (CTL), Institute for the Development of Educational Achievement (IDEA), College of Education, University of Oregon.

Emerging range on ISF; and 38 (49%) Garfield kindergarten students scored in the Established range on ISF.

⑥ On the far right of the report is a column entitled "Instructional Recommendation." The data in this column are derived from the Instructional Recommendation section of the Class List Report. The Distribution Report combines that information into a summary for the entire grade level at each school. On this report, Intensive instruction across the district in kindergarten was recommended for 33 students (14%), Strategic intervention was recommended for 79 students (34%), and Benchmark instruction (continued core instruction) was recommended for 123 students (52%).

Class Progress Graph

The Class Progress Graph (*Figure 9–9*) shows student progress across a school year by plotting beginning, middle, and end scores for one measure. Teachers may obtain one report for each measure assessed for children in their class.

Class Progress Graph—ORF   **Figure 9-9**

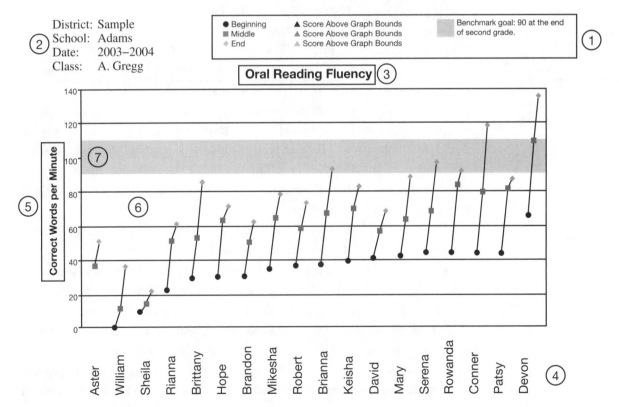

Kindergarten teachers may obtain Class Progress Graphs for ISF, PSF, and NWF. The Class Progress Graph for ISF will reflect only beginning and middle scores because it is administered only at these two benchmark times. In kindergarten, PSF and NWF Class Progress Graphs reflect only midyear and end-of-year benchmark scores because these measures are administered only during these two benchmark periods.

First grade teachers get Class Progress Graphs for PSF, NWF, and ORF. ORF is reflected only for middle-of-year and end-of-year scores because ORF is administered only at these times in first grade. Second grade teachers may obtain both NWF and ORF at the beginning of the year. After that, second and third grade teachers can access Class Progress Graphs for ORF only.

Class Progress Graphs are not produced for LNF because no benchmark score is available for that measure. (See Chapter 10 for an explanation of why LNF does not have a benchmark score.) This report is not produced for WUF and RTF because DIBELS reports do not have benchmarks for these measures.

Most Frequent Use. Teachers most often use Class Progress Graphs as a quick reference to students' scores at each benchmark. The graphic representation shows students' scores at each benchmark and the progress made between benchmark assessments.

Interpreting the Graph. Class Progress Graphs are produced by grade level for specific DIBELS measures: ISF, PSF, NWF, and ORF. *Figure 9–9* is an example of a Second Grade Class Progress Graph for ORF.

① A key is located at the top of the report. The key reveals that a circle (●) marks the beginning-of-year ORF score, a square (■) marks the middle-of-year ORF score, and a diamond (♦) marks the end-of-year ORF score. (On the graphs, circles are black, squares are red, and diamonds are blue.) If a black, red, or blue triangle appears on the graph, it means that the score for that student was so high that it was out of the bounds of the graph. On this report, the ORF score would have to be above 140, and no student scored that high. The final piece of information included in the key is the gray bar. This bar shows the benchmark score. In this case, the ORF benchmark score for year-end of second grade is 90 words read correctly in one minute (WRC).

② This shows the name of the classroom teacher for the students shown on the report, along with the district, school, and academic year.

③ The name of the measure graphed is shown at the top of each class progress report. This Class Progress Graph displays ORF scores for second grade students.

④ The horizontal axis, or x axis, shows the names of every student in the class. Students are listed from lowest to highest scores on the initial benchmark score shown on the graph. On this report, Aster is farthest left because she had no beginning-of-year ORF score; she has only middle and end scores (as displayed by ■ and ♦). She may have enrolled after the first assessment period and did not have a score. William had the lowest ORF score at the beginning of the year, and Devon had the highest.

⑤ The vertical axis, or y axis, defines the score for the measure. In this case, Correct Words per Minute are measured for ORF.

⑥ Lines connect each series of dots, squares, or diamonds. This is done to visually display growth from beginning to middle and from middle to end.

⑦ The gray bar shows the benchmark goal at the end of the periods measured. On this graph, the benchmark for the end of second grade is 90. The gray bar shows that only five students met or exceeded the 90-word goal. Those five students were Brianna, Serena, Rowanda, Conner, and Devon.

Individual Student Performance Profile
(also called Student Report)

The Individual Student Performance Profile (see *Figure 9–10*, next page) shows individual student progress for all DIBELS scores across kindergarten–Grade 3 for an individual student.

Most Frequent Use. Classroom teachers and reading coaches are the most common users for this report because it gives a snapshot of all the student's DIBELS scores over the entire time DIBELS has been given to the student. This report is available for benchmark assessments and for progress monitoring.

Interpreting the Report. This report is organized by measure, grade level, and time of year, and it can show both benchmark and progress monitoring data for individual students over time. LNF is not included on the report. (See Chapter 10 for a discussion of why LNF is not included.) *Figure 9–10* is an Individual Student Performance Profile for Timothy D, who is a third grade student at Adams School in Test District. Components of the profile are explained as follows:

① The legend at the top of the page provides a helpful guide to interpreting this report. As with other DIBELS reports, the gray bar represents the benchmark scores. Black dots and triangles represent benchmark assessment scores, and white dots and triangles represent progress monitoring scores. (Triangles represent high scores that are outside the bounds of the graph.)

② ③ ISF and PSF scores are shown under the category "Phonemic Awareness" because they measure a student's phonemic awareness.

② ISF scores are shown only for the beginning and middle of kindergarten because ISF is administered only during those benchmark assessment periods. This student scored near zero on ISF at the beginning of the year and around 11 at midyear. The dots are located below the gray box, showing that he did not meet benchmark at either assessment period.

③ PSF scores are shown for midyear in kindergarten through year-end in first grade because PSF is administered at those assessment periods. This student never scored at or above benchmark on PSF, although he was close in May at the end of first grade.

④ NWF measures the student's understanding of early phonics and the alphabetic principle (that letters represent sounds). NWF scores are shown for midyear in kindergarten through beginning-of-year in second grade because NWF is administered at those assessment periods. This student never scored at or above benchmark on NWF.

Figure 9-10   Individual Student Performance Profile (also called Summary Report or Student Report)

Name: D, TIMOTHY
ID: 02921
Class: Adams 3rd #1
Grade: Third
Year: 2001–2002
School: Adams
District: Test District

Dynamic Indicators of Basic Early Literacy Skills
Student Report

Legend
● Benchmark Assessment   ▲ Score Above Graph Bounds
▨ Target Goal   ○ Progress Monitoring Assessment   △ Score Above Graph Bounds

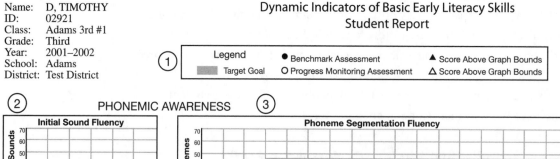

PHONEMIC AWARENESS

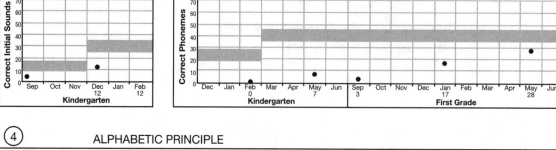

ALPHABETIC PRINCIPLE

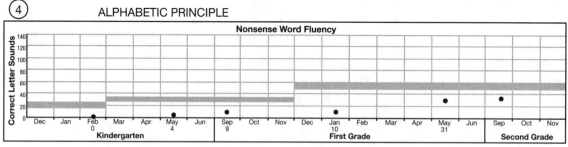

VOCABULARY

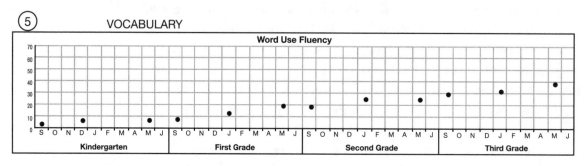

FLUENCY AND COMPREHENSION

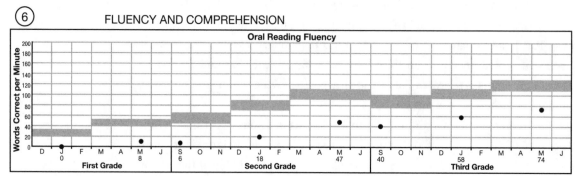

⑤ No gray boxes are shown for WUF because there is no established benchmark for the measure. This student shows steady improvement in WUF scores over the period from kindergarten through third grade.

⑥ The student's ORF score measures fluency and comprehension. The ORF score is shown, but the RTF score is not charted on this report. ORF scores are shown for midyear in first grade through year-end in second grade because ORF is administered at those assessment periods. This student did not meet benchmark at any time from the middle of first grade through the end of third grade.

10

Letter Naming Fluency (LNF)

LNF Student Materials Page and Student Booklet Page
Benchmark Assessment, Kindergarten, Middle of Year

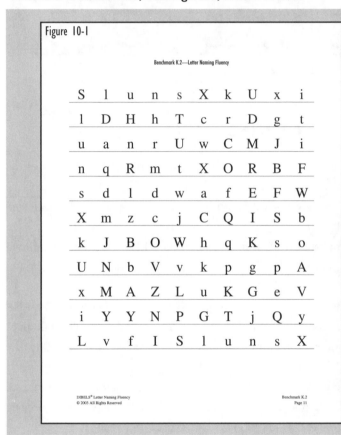

Figure 10-1

Benchmark K.2—Letter Naming Fluency

S	l	u	n	s	X	k	U	x	i
l	D	H	h	T	c	r	D	g	t
u	a	n	r	U	w	C	M	J	i
n	q	R	m	t	X	O	R	B	F
s	d	l	d	w	a	f	E	F	W
X	m	z	c	j	C	Q	I	S	b
k	J	B	O	W	h	q	K	s	o
U	N	b	V	v	k	p	g	p	A
x	M	A	Z	L	u	K	G	e	V
i	Y	Y	N	P	G	T	j	Q	y
L	v	f	I	S	l	u	n	s	X

DIBELS® Letter Naming Fluency
© 2003 All Rights Reserved

Benchmark K.2
Page 11

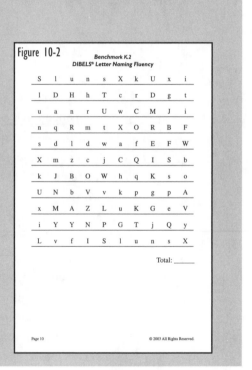

Figure 10-2

Benchmark K.2
DIBELS® Letter Naming Fluency

S	l	u	n	s	X	k	U	x	i
l	D	H	h	T	c	r	D	g	t
u	a	n	r	U	w	C	M	J	i
n	q	R	m	t	X	O	R	B	F
s	d	l	d	w	a	f	E	F	W
X	m	z	c	j	C	Q	I	S	b
k	J	B	O	W	h	q	K	s	o
U	N	b	V	v	k	p	g	p	A
x	M	A	Z	L	u	K	G	e	V
i	Y	Y	N	P	G	T	j	Q	y
L	v	f	I	S	l	u	n	s	X

Total: _____

Page 10

© 2003 All Rights Reserved.

BASIC INFORMATION

Purpose	Measures whether the student can name letters accurately and fluently.
Description	The student names randomly sorted uppercase and lowercase letters for one minute.
Relationship to NRP's five essential components	Recognizing letters so they can be matched with sounds is essential to understanding *phonics*.
Approximate time to administer per student	1.5 minutes

LNF BENCHMARK ASSESSMENT SCHEDULE AND RISK LEVELS

LNF is given as a benchmark assessment throughout kindergarten and at the beginning of first grade.

Table 10-1												LNF Benchmark Scores

Letter Naming Fluency	Kindergarten			First Grade			Second Grade			Third Grade		
	B	M	E	B	M	E	B	M	E	B	M	E
Low Risk	8+	27+	40+	37+								
Some Risk	2–7	15–26	29–39	25–36								
At Risk	0–1	0–14	0–28	0–24								

Note: The letters **B**, **M**, and **E** stand for beginning, middle, and end of the school year.

LNF DISCUSSION

LNF is unique in that it does not directly measure one of the five essential components of reading. DIBELS researchers included LNF scores in the benchmark assessments because LNF gives additional information that may not be indicated by other measures when determining a student's risk for reading difficulties in kindergarten and at the beginning of first grade. When LNF scores are combined with ISF scores, PSF scores, or both, the combination is a stronger predictor of reading success than when LNF is excluded.

DIBELS researchers do not provide progress monitoring materials for LNF because they do not consider letter naming to be an essential instructional target to enhance early literacy or reading outcomes. (See further discussion in the "Progress Monitoring" section of this chapter.)

The benchmark score for LNF decreases from 40 at the end of kindergarten to 37 at the beginning of first grade. This decrease may be attributable to summer lag, but the reason for the decrease is not known with certainty.

DIRECTIONS

The examiner will read these directions to the student:

LNF Directions   **Figure 10-3**

Here are some letters (point to the page with the letters). *Tell me the names of as many letters as you can. When I say, "Begin," start here* (point to first letter), *and go across the page* (underline the first row with your finger). *Point to each letter and tell me the name of that letter. If you come to a letter you don't know, I'll tell it to you. Put your finger on the first letter. Ready, begin.*

Start your stopwatch after you say "begin."

These directions are sometimes taken literally by kindergarteners, and they understand them to mean "read the first line and then stop." The kindergarteners will proudly read the first line and look up as if they have accomplished the task! All the examiner needs to do in this case is use the three-second hesitation prompt, which is to point to the first letter on the next line, give its name, point to the next letter, and ask, "What letter?"

Another incorrect response given by some children is to give the letter sound instead of the letter name. The examiner is allowed to say *one* time, "Remember to tell me the letter name, not the sound it makes." If the student continues to give letter sounds after receiving the prompt, the answers are to be scored incorrectly, even if they are the correct letter sound. In this case, the examiner should note in the Scoring Booklet that the student accurately named sounds instead of letters. Students who provide letter sounds may need to be retested if the teacher or examiner thinks the student knows letter names and the initial assessment may not be indicative of the student's knowledge.

LNF ADMINISTRATION RULES

Timing:	One minute continuous.
Stopwatch	Start the stopwatch immediately after saying "begin" at the end of the directions.
Hesitation time allotment	3 seconds.
Hesitation prompt	Provide the correct letter name, point to the next letter, and ask, "What letter?"
Discontinue rule	Stop administering the assessment if the student gets none of the 10 letters in the first line correct.
Additional prompt	When a student gives letter sounds instead of letter names, the examiner is allowed to say, one time only, "Remember to tell me the letter name, not the sound it makes."

SCORING

Marking Student Responses

- Correct answers—Do not mark.
- Incorrect answers—Mark with a slash (/) through the letter. Exceptions are:
  - If the child mistakes an uppercase *I* ("eye") for a lowercase *l* ("el") or vice versa, do not record the response as an error. These letters look very much alike, and we do not expect kindergarten or first grade students to be able to distinguish them.
  - The misreading of *b* for *d*, *p* for *q*, or *m* for *n* and similar reversals *are* counted as errors. The letters have obvious differences and are marked as incorrect if they are mistaken for one another.
- Omissions—Letters that the child skips or omits are counted as errors and marked with a slash (/) through the letter.
- Skipped lines—Draw a line through any line that is skipped and do not count these letters as correct.
- Self-corrections—If a student self-corrects an error within three seconds, write "sc" above the letter, and do not count it as an error.
- Final letter—Put a bracket ( ]) after the last letter the student names or attempts to name.

Figure 10–4 is an example of an LNF page that has been marked and scored for the midyear kindergarten benchmark assessment.

Figure 10-4   **LNF Scoring Booklet Page—Marked**

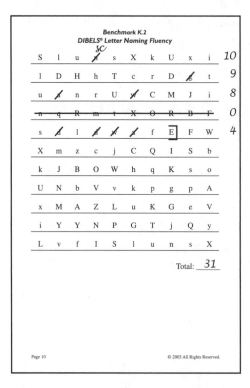

Counting Correct Answers

To get the LNF score, count the number of letters that the student names correctly. Counting is made easier because each line has 10 letters. The examiner can put the number of correct responses to the right of each line and sum the numbers to get the total scores. In *Figure 10–4*, the student named 10 letters correctly in the first line, named 9 letters correctly in the second line, named 8 letters correctly in the third line, skipped the fourth line (naming no letters correctly), and named 4 letters correctly in the fifth line. (In the first line, the student self-corrected 1 letter within three seconds and the response is counted as correct.) The sum of the numbers of letters named correctly is 31. This is the score that will be recorded on the Summary of Scores Page at the beginning of the Scoring Booklet.

PROGRESS MONITORING

The DIBELS researchers intentionally omitted progress monitoring materials for LNF. This decision was made to discourage teachers from focusing intervention instruction on letter naming at the expense of phonemic awareness and letter sound knowledge, which are two of the Big Ideas (foundational skills of early reading).

A number of studies have shown accurate letter naming by young children to be a strong predictor of early reading skills (Adams, 1990; Ehri & Sweet, 1991; Henry, 2003; Wolf, 1991; Wolf & Bowers, 1999). Another important aspect of LNF is measuring fluency during a serial naming exercise. The LNF is similar to a RAN, or rapid automatic naming task, which studies show to be a strong predictor of future reading abilities (Wolf, 2001). Teachers know that letter naming instruction is important for spelling, alphabetizing, and letter recognition, all important skills for success in school. For these reasons and others, the DIBELS researchers believe the teaching of letter names should be strategically integrated with teaching the Big Ideas, especially phonemic awareness and the alphabetic principle.

To improve letter naming skills, some teachers engage children in several short letter naming activities throughout the day rather than focusing intervention time on letter naming. Alternatively, some teachers strategically integrate letter naming instruction with phonemic awareness and alphabetic principle instruction during intervention lessons. These teachers prudently spend as few as 3 minutes and rarely more than 10 minutes on letter naming activities during intervention lessons with students who do not achieve benchmark scores on LNF.

If teachers decide to teach letter names to their students and want to monitor the progress on an informal basis, we suggest that teachers prepare lists of uppercase and lowercase letters to use for practice with and for timing their students. *In no case should any DIBELS benchmark assessment materials be used for practicing letter names or for monitoring progress in letter naming skills.* (As discussed many places in this manual, using any DIBELS benchmark materials for any purpose other than benchmark assessment is inappropriate. It is a misuse of assessment materials to use them for progress monitoring or to teach items directly. There are many other, better ways to teach the letters to children than using DIBELS materials.)

HELPING CHILDREN PREPARE FOR LNF DIRECTIONS

Sometimes kindergarten students, and even a few first graders, taking LNF do not know to read the letters from left to right and they do not know to continue to the next line. That some letters are listed more than once can be confusing to some children. Therefore, it may be helpful for kindergarten and first grade teachers to prepare their children for the LNF measure before the benchmark assessment, especially at the beginning of the year. By no means do we mean that teachers should "teach to the test" when we suggest that teachers "prepare their students for this assessment." Rather, we mean that teachers might consider helping their students, during regular reading instruction, to understand that, when letters are presented in rows, the letter names are to be read from left to right and the rows are read from top to bottom. Teachers can structure letter naming activities so that a letter shows up more than once in letter naming activities. When children are first learning their letter names, teachers can instruct students that it is helpful to point to each letter while students read the letter names. If letter names and letter sounds are being taught, it is important that the student's core instruction include explicit explanations, demonstrations, and practice in the differences between letter names and sounds.

INTERPRETATION OF LNF SCORES

LNF measures both accuracy and fluency when children name letters. A low score can mean that the student doesn't know the letter names (accuracy), that he or she is slow to remember and produce the letter names from memory (fluency), or a combination of poor accuracy and fluency. If a child has a score below benchmark, we can determine if the problem is accuracy or fluency only by looking at the student's Scoring Booklet. If the student made many mistakes when attempting to name letters, he or she has an accuracy problem and needs to learn to name the letters accurately before working on fluency. If the student accurately named all the letters attempted, he or she is likely to not have an accuracy difficulty and can begin working on fluency. (If a student did not name all the letters during LNF and did not meet benchmark, the teacher should check whether the student can accurately name all the letters.)

Children who are good readers recognize and process the letter patterns in words very quickly. They are able to generalize spelling patterns from one word to another. A child who is slow to learn letter names or slow to retrieve letter names from memory is exhibiting behaviors that indicate the child may have difficulty learning and using abstract symbols (letters) related to language.

Children who have difficulties with language-related symbols sometimes have difficulty recognizing or remembering common spelling patterns and generalizing them to other words. These children may also have difficulty remembering words that have uncommon spelling patterns (sight words). Children who are accurate in their letter naming but are very slow are indicating a slower processing of language symbols, or possibly language in general, which may affect their reading fluency when they learn to read.

By teaching children to name the letters accurately and rapidly when they are very young, we are helping them to solidify their knowledge of the symbols that will later be matched with sounds when they read words. We are also teaching them to process language-related symbols fluently. If a child is inaccurate or slow in naming a letter, it is an indicator that the child may be inaccurate or slow in matching a sound to a letter. By teaching children to name letters accurately and fluently, we are helping the child take the first steps toward accurate and fluent word recognition.[1]

MISTAKES MADE WHEN ADMINISTERING LNF

We find that teachers consistently score LNF accurately. The only observation we have is that some teachers put a check mark above or an underline below each letter the student names correctly instead of leaving these letters unmarked. In DIBELS, no mark is made for letters named correctly.

Deciding how to score skipped lines is confusing to some teachers. It will help if the teacher recognizes that in LNF we are not counting errors, but counting the number of letters named accurately. A student who skips a line did not read any letters correctly in the skipped line, and therefore no credit is given for those letters. The skipped letters are not "wrong"; they are simply not counted as correct answers.

FREQUENTLY ASKED QUESTIONS ABOUT LNF

1. Why aren't all the letters included on every LNF page?

In order to create a scientifically valid instrument, the letters for LNF were randomly generated. Randomly generated letters ensure that there is no specific pattern in any set of letters. As a screening instrument, DIBELS will provide information about whether or not the student can name letters accurately and fast enough to be considered "on target" for reading success. Teachers

---

[1] Eventually, children will learn to recognize chunks of letters with automaticity, which helps to make reading efficient and fluent.

will need to provide further assessment using all the letters to determine specifically which letters the child needs to learn.

2. What is the score if the student names the lowercase *l* or the uppercase *I* as the numeral *1*?

Naming lowercase *l* or uppercase *I* as the numeral *1* is scored as an error because *1* is a numeral, not a letter, and children need to know the difference between a letter and a number.

3. Why is it acceptable for children to misread lowercase *l* and uppercase *I*?

These letters look almost identical in certain typefaces, particularly Times New Roman, which is used in DIBELS materials for LNF and in many printed publications. Because LNF is given only in kindergarten and the beginning of first grade, we do not expect children to be able to easily differentiate these letters. Indeed, many adults confuse these letters in isolation because they look so much alike in the most commonly used typefaces in print.

4. Why does misreading *b* and *d*, *p* and *q*, or *m* and *n* count as an error when misreading lowercase *l* and uppercase *I* is not counted as an error?

The typeset letters lowercase *l* ("el") and uppercase *I* ("eye") are confusing even to some adults when they are seen in isolation. These letters are more easily discriminated, even by many good readers, when in the context of a word. Because only very young children are given LNF, we do not expect them to accurately discriminate between lowercase *l* and uppercase *I* out of context. It is true that young children often also confuse the letters *b* and *d*, *q* and *p*, and *m* and *n*. However, unlike *l* and *I*, these letters have obvious differences and are confused consistently only by children who may be displaying signs of difficulty with recognizing letters that are formed with similar shapes. This is a problem that needs to be recognized so that appropriate instruction can be designed to help students.

5. Why does the typeface used for LNF use the typeset *a*, *g*, and *q*, which can be confusing to kindergarten students, instead of using a primer alphabet?

The creators of DIBELS selected typefaces that students are likely to see in printed materials. It is true that many younger children do not recognize the typeset versions of the letters *a*, *g*, and *q*. Indeed, these letters may be confusing to many younger children. However, the benchmark score for the beginning of kindergarten is to name only eight letters accurately in one minute. The use of the typeset versions of the letters *a*, *g*, and *q* will not keep even children who are familiar with the names of only a few letters from meeting the benchmark score. Older children who remain confused by the typeset versions of the letters *a*, *g*, and *q* and who do not meet benchmark scores will need explicit instruction to learn to recognize and name these letters.

6. **I had a student who named the letters in lines one and two. He began naming letters in line three, then his eyes skipped back to line two again and he renamed some of the letters. Do we give credit only once for those letters that were read two times or do we credit them twice?**

Give credit for the letters that are reread only once. In this case, when the student skips up to a line previously read, point to the place where he or she should be and ask, "What letter?" If this doesn't work and the student's score is below benchmark, note the tracking problem in the Scoring Booklet.

7. **How do I score if the student names some lines of letters from right to left?**

This is a good opportunity for the examiner to point to where the student should be reading. This redirects the student's attention until he or she might begin reading from left to right and from top to bottom. However, if the student persists in reading from right to left, the student's score does not count. The student should be recommended for a retest, with an explanation that the student is reading letters from right to left. Before giving the retest, the teacher or examiner should review left-to-right reading of letters and the importance of pointing to the letters as they are named. If the problem persists after retesting and the student's score is below benchmark, the teacher should design instruction to teach the student left-to-right directionality.

8. **How do I score if the student points to letters in a seemingly random fashion but accurately names the letters to which he or she points?**

In our experience, this happens most often when a student is looking for letters that he or she knows (generally, the letters in his or her name). The best strategy is to put your finger where the student should be naming letters. However, if the student persists in naming letters in this fashion, the student's score does not count. The student should be recommended for a retest, because the student is reading letters in a random order or looking for letters that he or she knows. Before giving the retest, the teacher or examiner should review left-to-right reading of letters and the importance of pointing to the letters as they are named. Examiners may consider using a ruler or marker to track the lines for this student, if necessary. Using a marker such as a ruler or index card is an Approved Accommodation and should be so indicated when scores are entered into the DIBELS Web site.

9. **If a student names the uppercase letters "capital *a*," etc., and gets a score below benchmark, can I reassess the student because saying the word *capital* took extra time?**

Any time an examiner thinks that the student's score is not reflective of the student's ability, the assessment for that measure can be given again. In this case, before giving the retest, the examiner could instruct the student that he needs only to name the letter and not to say the word *capital*.

10. What materials do I use to retest Letter Naming Fluency given that there are no progress monitoring materials?

There are several choices for selecting materials for a DIBELS retest of LNF. The preferred option is to use the same LNF page used for the benchmark assessment but to start on the line after the student finished the original assessment. If there are not enough lines remaining, an alternative is to use an assessment from a previous benchmark period and start on the line after the student finished the original assessment. If a previous benchmark page is not available, use an LNF page from a future benchmark assessment. If you use a future assessment. There is no need to mark the lines already used because the length of time between benchmark assessments is enough so that there are no practice effects.

11. Can students use a ruler or other marker to track letters?

A marker such as a ruler or an index card can be used if it is *required* in order to get the most accurate measure of what the student knows. However, the use of a marker or ruler should be judicious and allowed only when absolutely necessary. We recommend using a marker or ruler only after a student has scored below benchmark without the use of an aid. Our goal is to find out how well the child is reading without aids, if at all possible. Using a marker such as a ruler or index card is an Approved Accommodation and it should be so indicated when scores are entered into the DIBELS Web site.

12. Is it ever appropriate to give LNF to students beyond the beginning of first grade?

It would be appropriate to give LNF to students of any age who achieve benchmark scores on PSF but fall below benchmark on NWF. This pattern indicates that the child cannot match letters and sounds well or that he or she is not fluent at letter naming. The issue in this case may be that the child does not recognize letters accurately enough or fast enough to read nonsense words accurately or quickly. For this student, we recommend using LNF to assess whether the student knows letter names and is quick to name them. A student of any age who cannot achieve the de facto benchmark score of 40 on LNF may need intervention to practice letter names. Another skill to check in this case is whether or not the student knows the sounds for each letter and can name the sounds with fluency.

13. Should I practice letter–sound relationships with my students even though they aren't measured on DIBELS benchmark assessments?

In DIBELS, NWF measures the student's knowledge of and fluency with letter–sound relationships. The teaching and practice of letter–sound relationships are a part of all SBRR (Scientifically Based Reading Research) programs.

11

Initial Sound Fluency (ISF)

ISF Student Materials Page and Scoring Booklet Page
Benchmark Assessment, Kindergarten, Beginning of Year

Figures 11-1 and 11-2

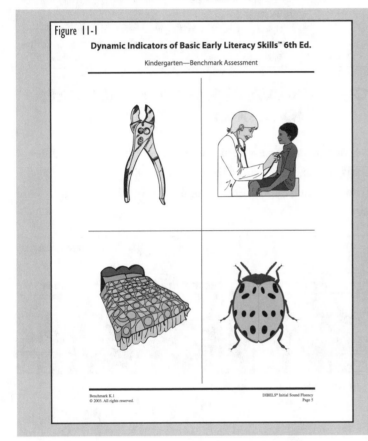

Figure 11-1

Dynamic Indicators of Basic Early Literacy Skills™ 6th Ed.

Kindergarten—Benchmark Assessment

Benchmark K.1
© 2003. All rights reserved.

DIBELS® Initial Sound Fluency
Page 5

Figure 11-2

Benchmark K.1
DIBELS® Initial Sound Fluency

This is **tomato, cub, plate, jail** (point to pictures).

1. Which picture begins with /j/?	0	1
2. Which picture begins with /t/?	0	1
3. Which picture begins with /k/?	0	1
4. What sound does "plate" begin with?	0	1

This is **bump, insect, refrigerator, skate** (point to pictures).

5. Which picture begins with /sk/?	0	1
6. Which picture begins with /r/?	0	1
7. Which picture begins with /b/?	0	1
8. What sound does "insect" begin with?	0	1

This is **rooster, mule, fly, soldier** (point to pictures).

9. Which picture begins with /r/?	0	1
10. Which picture begins with /fl/?	0	1
11. Which picture begins with /s/?	0	1
12. What sound does "mule" begin with?	0	1

This is **pliers, doctor, quilt, beetle** (point to pictures).

13. Which picture begins with /b/?	0	1
14. Which picture begins with /pl/?	0	1
15. Which picture begins with /d/?	0	1
16. What sound does "quilt" begin with?	0	1

Time:_____ Seconds   Total Correct:_____

$$\frac{60 \times Total\ Correct}{Seconds} = \text{_____} \text{ Correct initial sounds per minute}$$

Page 2   © 2003 All Rights Reserved.

BASIC INFORMATION

Purpose	To measure the student's ability to match and produce initial phonemes or blends.
Description	The student answers 16 questions, presented in sets of 4 questions. To answer the first 3 questions in each set, the student selects a picture or word that begins with a target sound. To answer the fourth question, the student produces the initial phoneme or blend for a given picture.
Relationship to the NRP's five essential components	Measures the student's earliest phonemic awareness skills, which are identification and production of initial phonemes and blends in words.
Approximate time to administer per student	3 minutes

Additional information	• All 16 questions are given to every student (unless the discontinue rule applies), regardless of the cumulative time it takes the student to answer the questions. There is a five-second limit on the time allowed to answer each question.
	• The student's answer is either correct or incorrect, with correct answers marked as "1" and incorrect answers marked as "0."
	• The timing for this measure is intermittent, meaning that the examiner starts the timer immediately after giving each question and stops the timer immediately after the student answers.
	• The examiner accumulates the time for answering all 16 questions on the stopwatch.
	• A formula is used to calculate the student's ISF score. The formula incorporates both the number of questions answered correctly and the cumulative time for all 16 questions.

ISF BENCHMARK ASSESSMENT SCHEDULE AND RISK LEVELS

ISF is given as a benchmark assessment at the beginning and middle of kindergarten. Students are expected to achieve a score of 25 or higher by the middle of kindergarten in order to be on track to meet the PSF benchmark score at the end of kindergarten.

Table 11-1   **ISF Benchmark Scores**

Initial Sound Fluency	Kindergarten			First Grade			Second Grade			Third Grade		
	B	M	E	B	M	E	B	M	E	B	M	E
Low Risk or Established	8+	25+										
Some Risk or Emerging	4–7	10–24										
At Risk or Deficit	0–3	0–9										

Note: The letters **B**, **M**, and **E** stand for beginning, middle, and end of the school year.

HISTORY OF INITIAL SOUND FLUENCY

Initial Sound Fluency was originally called "Onset Recognition Fluency" because it is designed to measure whether the student could recognize and produce the onset of a word. (Examples of onset are as follows: *sk* is the onset in *skate*, and *ate* is the rime; *shr* is the onset in *shrimp*, and *imp* is the rime; *t* is the onset in *tail*, and *ail* is the rime; the word *on* has no onset, and the entire word is a rime.) The name of this measure was changed because Initial Sound Fluency is a friendlier name for the measure. The onset (the part of the syllable before the vowel) is presented in ISF as the "first sound" in the word because developmentally it is easier for a child first learning phonemic awareness to hear the onset in a word than to isolate the individual phoneme. For most words in ISF, the onset is a single phoneme, but for a few words, the onset is a blend.

Some teachers question the use of blends in ISF questions because they teach individual phonemes in their core reading instruction, and they correctly do not teach blends as single unit sounds. Our observation is that some children take a bit longer to answer a question about which picture begins with an onset such as /sk/ when they have been learning about phonemes in their classroom lessons. For example, the correct answer to the question "Which picture begins with /sk/?" is *skate*. Children with solid beginning phonemic awareness skills generally can figure out the correct answer to this question, even though the student may have been taught (correctly so) that the first sound in skate is /s/.

ISF DISCUSSION

Children who reach the ISF benchmark score of 25 by the middle of kindergarten are on track to reach the PSF benchmark score of 35 by the end of kindergarten. The ISF benchmark score of 25 can be applied to students of any age who are developing the ability to identify and produce initial phonemes. Once a student of any age reaches the score of 25 on ISF, he or she is ready to begin learning to blend and segment all sounds in one-syllable words. (Segmenting sounds in two- to five-sound words is the skill assessed in PSF.)

DIRECTIONS

Directions, including example pictures, are the same for both ISF benchmark assessments. ISF directions have two parts, with each part preparing the student to respond to one of the two types of questions asked in ISF. The first part of the directions prepares the student to answer the first three questions in each set of four questions by demonstrating *identification* of a picture with given initial sounds. The second part of ISF directions prepares the student to answer the last question in each set of four questions by demonstrating *production* of the initial sound in a word.

When giving the student directions for ISF, the examiner selects one of two different scripts for responses to the student's answer, depending on whether the student responds correctly or incorrectly to the question in the directions.

First Part of ISF Directions Explained

The first part of the ISF directions is shown in *Figure 11–3* (next page). This part of the ISF directions prepares the student to select a picture or word that begins with the sounds /fl/. A correct answer occurs when the student points to the picture of flowers or says "flowers" or "flower."[1] If the student gives a correct answer, the examiner responds with the words in the box on the left ("Good. *Flowers* begins with the sounds /fl/.") and then moves to the second part of the directions.

---

[1] If the student points to the wrong picture and says a word that begins with /fl/, such as *fluffy* (while pointing to the pillow), this would be counted as a correct answer for ISF. However, the wording in the directions implies that, for the directions only, the examiner would respond to the student pointing to the pillow and saying "fluffy" as if it were an incorrect answer.

Figure 11-3   **ISF Directions—1st Part**

This is mouse, flowers, pillow, letters (point to each picture while saying its name). **Mouse** (point to mouse) **begins with the sound /m/. Listen, /m/, mouse. Which one begins with the sounds /fl/?**

CORRECT RESPONSE: Student points to flowers, you say	INCORRECT RESPONSE: If student gives any other response, you say
Good. Flowers begins with the sounds /fl/.	**Flowers** (point to flowers) **begins with the sounds /fl/. Listen, /fl/, flowers. Let's try it again. Which one begins with the sounds /fl/?**

An *incorrect answer* occurs when the student does one or more of the following:

1. Points to any picture other than flowers

2. Says the name of any other picture

3. Says a word or sound other than *flowers* or *flower*

4. Does not respond within 5 seconds.

If the student gives an incorrect answer, the examiner responds with the words in the box on the right ("*Flowers* (point to flowers) begins with the sounds /fl/. Listen, /fl/, *flowers*. Let's try it again. Which one begins with the sounds /fl/?") and then gives the student a second chance to respond. Whether the student's second response is correct, incorrect, or to say nothing, the examiner continues by moving to the second part of the directions.

Second Part of ISF Directions Explained

Figure 11–4 shows the second part of ISF directions. The second part of the directions prepares the student to articulate the first sound in a word. A correct answer occurs when the student says the sound /l/.[2] If the student gives a correct answer, the examiner responds with the words in the box on the left ("Good. *Letters* begins with the sound /l/.") and then says the following before asking the first question: "Here are some more pictures. Listen carefully to the words."

An *incorrect response* occurs when the student says any sound other than /l/ or says nothing. If the student gives an incorrect answer, the examiner responds with the words in the box on the right ("*Letters* (point to letters) begins with the sound /l/. Listen, /l/, *letters*. Let's try it again. What sound does *letters* (point to letters) begin with?" and then says the following before asking the first question: "Here are some more pictures. Listen carefully to the words." It is important that examiners understand the box on the right is to be read only *once*, even if the student answers incorrectly again.

---

[2] If the student gives a longer part of the first part of the word *letters*, such as /le/ or /let/, this would be counted as a correct answer when scoring ISF. However, the wording in the directions implies that, for the directions only, the examiner would respond to the student who gives either of these answers as if it were an incorrect response.

Pillow (point to pillow) ***begins with the sound /p/. Listen, /p/, pillow. What sound does letters*** (point to letters) ***begin with?***

CORRECT RESPONSE: Student says /l/, you say	INCORRECT RESPONSE: If student gives any other response, you say
Good. Letters begins with the sound /l/.	***Letters*** (point to letters) ***begins with the sound /l/. Listen, /l/, letters. Let's try it again. What sound does letters*** (point to letters) ***begin with?***

Here are some more pictures. Listen carefully to the words.

Script for ISF Directions

The examiner reads these directions to the student:

This is mouse, flowers, pillow, letters (point to each picture while saying its name). ***Mouse*** (point to mouse) ***begins with the sound /m/. Listen, /m/, mouse. Which one begins with the sounds /fl/?***

CORRECT RESPONSE: Student points to flowers, you say	INCORRECT RESPONSE: If student gives any other response, you say
Good. Flowers begins with the sounds /fl/.	***Flowers*** (point to flowers) ***begins with the sounds /fl/. Listen, /fl/, flowers. Let's try it again. Which one begins with the sounds /fl/?***

Pillow (point to pillow) ***begins with the sound /p/. Listen, /p/, pillow. What sound does letters*** (point to letters) ***begin with?***

CORRECT RESPONSE: Student says /l/, you say	INCORRECT RESPONSE: If student gives any other response, you say
Good. Letters begins with the sound /l/.	***Letters*** (point to letters) ***begins with the sound /l/. Listen, /l/, letters. Let's try it again. What sound does letters*** (point to letters) ***begin with?***

Here are some more pictures. Listen carefully to the words.

The examiner then names four sets of pictures and asks questions about each set of pictures, as scripted in the Scoring Booklet.

The examiner must read the description of the pictures exactly as written. For example, the directions might read, "This is sun, cup, banana, pie." The examiner should not change the script to read, "This is *a* sun, *a* cup, *a* banana, *and a* pie."

Naming Pictures and Asking Questions for ISF

Before each set of questions, the examiner points to four pictures and names them. The examiner must read the description of the pictures exactly as written in the Scoring Booklet. The script does not include articles before the names of the pictures, nor is there a conjunction between the names of the last two pictures. For example, the directions might read, "This is sun, cup, banana, pie." It is incorrect to change the script and read, "This is *a* sun, *a* cup, *a* banana, *and a* pie." Adding the articles may lead the children to think the name of the picture is *asun* or *andapie*, causing them difficulty when answering the questions.

Examiners must also be careful to name the sound (not the letter) in the ISF questions that ask what picture begins with a specific sound. Questions are phrased, "Which picture begins with /__ /?" When one letter or two letters are inside the two slashes, such as /p/ or /ch/, it means to name the sound, not the letter or letters.

ISF ADMINISTRATION RULES

Timing	The timing for this measure is intermittent, because the examiner starts the stopwatch after he or she finishes asking each question and stops the stopwatch after the student answers. In some cases, it can take less than a second for the student to answer a question. Because of the hesitation rule, the time for any single question will never be more than 5 seconds. This means that the maximum time for ISF would be 80 seconds (16 questions times 5 seconds). The minimum time could be less than 16 seconds if a student responds quickly to every question.
Stopwatch	Start the stopwatch after asking each question and stop it after the student answers. Do this 16 times, one time for each question.
Hesitation time allotment	5 seconds
Hesitation prompt	Ask the next question. (No prompt exists.)
Discontinue rule	Stop administering ISF if the student does not get any of the *first 5* answers correct. (If the student misses any other 5 answers in a row, ask the student all 16 questions.)
Additional prompt for incorrect answers	The following prompt may be given only once: "Remember to tell me a picture that begins with the sound (repeat stimulus sound)." Use this prompt the first time the student gives any incorrect answer only if he or she answered the questions in the directions accurately.[3]

OBTAINING AN ISF SCORE

ISF is the only DIBELS measurement that is not timed continuously for one minute and for which scores are calculated using a formula. For ISF, a formula is used to calculate the number of questions the student would have answered had

---

[3] The *DIBELS Administration and Scoring Guide* (Good & Kaminski, 2003) states that this prompt is allowed only if the student answered the examples correctly. The authors have found that, when examiners are giving many assessments continuously, they cannot easily remember which child answered the examples correctly and which child didn't without conscious attention to thinking back to the example. We, therefore, recommend that examiners who cannot easily attend to which children answered the examples correctly use this prompt once only for any child who might benefit from it.

he or she been able to continue answering questions for one minute continuously, without counting the time it takes to ask the questions.

The formula to calculate the student score is found at the bottom of the ISF scoring page, which can be seen in *Figure 11–6*. The formula incorporates both the cumulative time recorded and the total number of correct answers. To calculate the ISF score, the examiner first plugs in the number of correct answers for "total correct" into the formula. Next, the examiner plugs in the total cumulative time from the stopwatch, with hundredths of seconds rounded up or down to the nearest second. "Cumulative time" is the number of seconds it took the student to answer the 16 questions. The formula is as follows:

$$\frac{\textbf{60 x \textit{Total Correct}}}{\textbf{\textit{Seconds}}} = \underline{\hspace{2cm}} \text{ Correct Initial Sounds Per Minute}$$

In *Figure 11–6*, the total number of correct answers is 9 and the number of seconds is 33. When these numbers are plugged into the formula, the ISF score is 16 correct initial sounds per minute. (The actual answer is 16.36 seconds, but we round down because the decimal is lower than 0.5.)

ISF Scoring Booklet Page—Marked   **Figure 11-6**

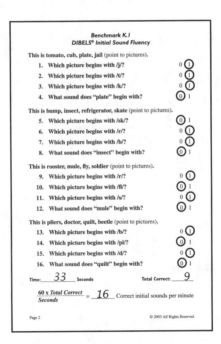

Recording Student Responses

The examiner asks all 16 ISF questions for every student (unless the discontinue rule applies). Every student has an opportunity to get 16 correct answers regardless of the time on the stopwatch. The student's answer to each question will be either correct or incorrect, and the examiner records whether the student's answer is correct or incorrect immediately after the student answers each question and the timer is stopped. Correct answers are marked by circling *"1"* and incorrect answers are marked by circling *"0."* In the set of four questions below, the first two answers were correct and the final two were incorrect.

Which picture begins with /t/?	0	①
Which picture begins with /j/?	0	①
Which picture begins with /m/?	⓪	1
What sound does quilt begin with?	⓪	1

The total number of correct answers is recorded at the bottom right side of the page, as shown on *Figure 11–6*. It is important for examiners to understand this number is not the student's score, but rather is plugged into the formula used to record the student's score, as explained below.

Accumulating and Recording Time

ISF is the only DIBELS measure not administered for one minute continuously. For ISF, the examiner uses a stopwatch to determine the cumulative time it takes the student to answer all 16 questions. To get the time for each question, the examiner starts the stopwatch immediately after asking each question and stops the stopwatch immediately after the student answers each question. This means that the examiner will start and stop the stopwatch 16 times while giving ISF. The examiner should not clear the stopwatch between questions because the time recorded is an accumulation of the total time the student takes to answer all 16 questions.

When the examiner finishes asking all 16 questions, the time on the stopwatch is rounded to the nearest second and recorded at the lower left side of the ISF scoring page, as shown on *Figure 11–6*. The cumulative time is plugged into the formula used to record the student's score, as explained in the preceding and following sections.

Calculating ISF Score

The ISF score is determined by using the formula below, which is found at the bottom of the ISF Scoring Page in the Student Booklet:

$$\frac{60 \times \textit{Total Correct}}{\textit{Seconds}} = \underline{\hspace{2cm}} \text{ Correct Initial Sounds Per Minute}$$

Fractions or decimals are rounded to the nearest whole number after the ISF score is calculated. (Any fraction less than ½ or any decimal less than 0.5 is rounded down to the nearest whole number. Any fraction ½ or higher or any decimal 0.5 or higher is rounded up to the nearest whole number.)

Here is an example of how to use the formula:

If the student has 12 correct responses and the cumulative time is 23.05 seconds, the calculation would be:

$$\frac{60 \times \boxed{12}\textit{correct responses}}{\boxed{23}\textit{seconds}} = \underline{\hspace{0.3cm}}③①\underline{\hspace{0.3cm}} \text{ Correct Initial Sounds Per Minute}$$

(Please note that the actual answer is 31.3, but we rounded down to the nearest whole number because the decimal in the answer—0.3—is less than 0.5.) In this case, the score of 31 would be recorded on the Summary of Scores page at the front of the Scoring Booklet.

DETERMINING CORRECT AND INCORRECT RESPONSES

Description of Correct Responses—First Three Questions in a Set

ISF has 16 questions, presented in four sets of 4 questions. Each of the first 3 questions in each set asks the student, "Which picture begins with [name sound]?" The student can point to a picture, name the picture, or point to a picture while naming the picture. For the first 3 questions in each set of 4 questions, a correct response is any of the following:

- Pointing to the correct picture
- Saying the name of the correct picture
- Pointing to and saying the name of the correct picture
- Pointing to an incorrect picture and renaming the picture with a word that begins with the target sound (An example might be when the four pictures are named *bump, insect, refrigerator,* and *skate.* When the question is "Which picture begins with /b/?", a student might point to the picture of an insect and say "bug." Because the student's oral answer "bug" begins with the sound /b/, his response is marked as correct. A more offbeat answer for the same four pictures might occur if the student points to the picture of the refrigerator and says "banana." Even though the word *banana* appears to have no relationship to refrigerator, the student's response would be correct because the word *banana,* which was the student's oral response, begins with the target sound /b/.[4])
- Saying any word that begins with the target sound, regardless of whether it relates to a picture, without pointing to any picture.

ISF is not a memory test; therefore, it does not matter if the student remembers the names of the pictures. The point is for the student to be able to demonstrate phonemic awareness by naming a word or identifying a picture that begins with the target sound. An example of a correct answer that does not relate to any of the pictures is when a student responds to the question "Which picture begins with the sound /b/?" with the word *balloon,* when no picture even remotely resembles a balloon. The answer "balloon" is correct because the student has demonstrated that he or she can produce a word that begins with the phoneme /b/.

---

[4] This was an actual answer from a kindergarten student being assessed by one of the authors. When asked to explain his answer, he said, "There might be bananas in the refrigerator." This proved to the author that one can never assume a student's answer is unrelated to the picture.

When the student points to a picture and says a word that is different from the picture's name, what the student says overrides the picture he or she points to.

Obviously, if the student points to the correct picture or gives the correct name of the picture, the answer is correct. However, if the student gives any word *that begins with the target sound* and either points to a different picture or doesn't point to a picture at all, the answer also is correct. In other words, *what the student says overrides what the student points to* when determining whether an answer is correct or not. This is because the purpose of the assessment is to measure whether the student can identify a word that begins with a target sound, not whether he or she can remember what the pictures were named.

Description of Correct Responses—Fourth Question in a Set

The fourth question in each set asks, "What sound does [name of picture] begin with?" The student articulates correct responses for the fourth question. A correct answer includes any part of the word that has the first sound but is not the entire word. For example, if the word is *bridge*, any of the following would be correct answers:

- /b/
- /br/
- /bri/.

In ISF, as in all DIBELS measures requiring production of phonemes, we accept a phoneme with *uh* added as correct. For example, if the student says the first sound in *milk* is *muh*, we count the answer as correct, even though the proper articulation of the sound /m/ would not have the sound *uh* added to it.

Description of Incorrect Responses

Each of the first three questions in each set asks the student, "Which picture begins with [name sound]?" Incorrect responses for the first three questions include the following:

- No response within five seconds
- Pointing to an incorrect picture
- Naming an incorrect picture
- Pointing to and naming an incorrect picture
- Pointing to the correct picture and naming a word that does not begin with the target sound
- Responding with any word that does not begin with the target sound
- Giving a letter name (the prompt "Remember to tell me a picture that begins with the sound [repeat stimulus sound]" can be given once when the student gives an incorrect answer if the student got the practice items correct).

The fourth question in each set asks, "What sound does [name of picture] begin with?" An incorrect response for the fourth question is any response in which a part of the word is named that does not include the first sound. Incorrect answers for the word *bridge* would include:

- /r/
- /j/
- /bro/, /bre/, etc.
- /ij/
- /bij/
- Any sound or word part that does not include a /b/.

PROGRESS MONITORING

DIBELS provides ISF Progress Monitoring Scoring Booklets for kindergarten. The progress monitoring booklets have 20 alternate assessment forms for ISF.

HELPING CHILDREN PREPARE FOR ISF DIRECTIONS

At the beginning of kindergarten, some children who are not used to school have difficulty with directions for all measures, including ISF. If the examiner thinks that a student may perform better on any measure, including ISF, a retest can be administered. In this case, the teacher or examiner might want to explain the directions before the retest is given.

After the beginning of kindergarten, directions for ISF are not a problem for most kindergarten students who have had instruction in phonemes, and there is little need to explain the directions to them. (An exception may be children with very low language skills or ELL students.) However, ISF directions may baffle some kindergarten students who have not yet been exposed to the concepts of phonemes and initial sounds. In this case, it is not the directions confusing the children, but the concept of an initial sound or phoneme. (A few kindergarten students proudly inform the examiner that the first sound in *flowers* is /f/ when they are told in ISF directions that *flowers* begins with the sound /fl/. These students are exhibiting excellent mastery of beginning sounds because they notice the difference between a blend and a single phoneme. This is not a problem!)

INTERPRETATION OF ISF SCORES

Children who score below benchmark scores on ISF may need immediate intervention in phonological awareness. Studies show that approximately 90% of students who struggle with reading have a phonological weakness (Shaywitz, 2003). Many children who score low on ISF need instruction in the lower-level phonological skills before phonemes are taught. This means that when a child scores below benchmark on ISF, the teacher needs to check whether the student understands how to identify, blend, and segment larger linguistic units, such as words, syllables, and onset and rime, before beginning instruction focused on identifying phonemes in words.

Students with scores below benchmark on ISF may have difficulties with either accuracy or fluency. A student who misses several answers obviously has accuracy issues, even if the student's score is relatively high because he or she answers quickly. For example, a student can get a score of 8 (benchmark at beginning of kindergarten) by answering only 4 questions correctly and missing 12 questions in 32 seconds. This student has accuracy issues, and the classroom teacher will need to focus on teaching this student to identify phonemes accurately before the next benchmark assessment. Another student who answers all 16 questions accurately but takes 64 seconds to do so (4 seconds per question) will have the same score of 8. However, this student has a fluency difficulty, and instruction will focus on helping the student identify phonemes faster.

In the middle of the year, a student's PSF score is often a better indicator of phonemic awareness than the ISF score.

FREQUENTLY OBSERVED MISTAKES MADE WHEN ADMINISTERING ISF

1. *Examiners do not ask all 16 questions, but stop when the cumulative time is one minute.* This measure is not given for one minute continuously. A formula is used to calculate the answer. Every student is asked all 16 questions, unless the discontinue rule is applied.

2. *Examiners record the correct number of questions answered on the Summary of Scores Page instead of using the formula to calculate the answer.* The correct number of answers, along with the time, is used in the formula at the bottom of the scoring page to calculate the student's score.

3. *Examiners record the number of seconds taken to answer questions on the Summary of Scores Page instead of using the formula to calculate the answer.* The cumulative number of seconds it takes the student to answer questions, along with the correct number of answers, is used in the formula at the bottom of the scoring page to calculate the student's score.

4. *When asking the first three questions in each set, examiners name the letter instead of the sound.* We find that some examiners name the letter instead of the sound. Some of these examiners also add the word *sound* at the end of the question, so that the question becomes, "Which picture begins with the *ch* sound?", naming the letters *c* and *h*. Questions are to be read exactly as written. The examiner should name the sound, not the letter, when reading the question.

5. *When reading the names of the pictures, the examiner inserts the article* a *or* an *before giving names of pictures and inserts and between the names of the last two*

pictures. The names of the pictures should be read exactly as written, without adding articles or conjunctions.

6. *Examiners clear their stopwatches before recording the cumulative time at the bottom of the scoring page.* It is very frustrating for examiners when they clear their stopwatches before they remember to record the time, because a retest will be need to be given. It is a good idea for examiners to pay conscious attention to recording the time at the bottom of the scoring page immediately after finishing the sixteenth question so they don't inadvertently clear their stopwatches before recording the time.

7. *Examiners look at the picture the student should point to.* Some students are able to determine the correct answer by following the examiner's eyes. Examiners should avoid any behaviors that might inadvertently give the student an indication of the correct answer.

FREQUENTLY ASKED QUESTIONS ABOUT ISF

1. Why are the pictures named so oddly? For example, why isn't the picture of an insect called a *bug*? Why isn't the picture of a cub called a *bear*?

First, the words are selected for ISF, then pictures are found to match the words. Sometimes it is difficult to find a picture for a selected word that is not a bit confusing. Avoiding confusion about picture names is one reason the examiner names the picture before asking the questions in ISF.

If the examiner thinks that a student's ISF score was affected because the pictures confused the student, the examiner can find alternate pictures of the target words and use them. (The target word should never be changed to match a picture.) Changing the picture is a DIBELS Approved Accommodation, and the "Tested with DIBELS Approved Accommodations" box should be checked when entering scoring data into the DIBELS Data System.

2. Why isn't there a prompt to remind students to give the letter sound, not the letter name? The prompt "Remember to tell me a picture that begins with the sound [repeat stimulus sound]" applies only to the first three questions and not to the fourth.

We don't know why there is no prompt for the fourth question. But we do want to remind examiners to resist the temptation to make up a prompt.

3. If you know your children are not familiar with the ISF vocabulary, can you teach it?

Yes, teaching the specific vocabulary used in ISF measures is a DIBELS Approved Accommodation. However, if the vocabulary words are taught explicitly, the teacher should be careful to teach only the pronunciation and meaning of the words, not what the first sounds in the words are. If the teacher explicitly teaches the child the first sound of words, the validity of the DIBELS score on ISF is compromised.

4. Do we round the ISF time that is shown on the stopwatch?

Yes, round the time on the stopwatch to the nearest second, using standard rounding rules. If the time on the stopwatch has a decimal of 0.5 or higher, round it to the next highest number of seconds. If the decimal is 0.49 or lower, drop the decimal. For example, if the stopwatch shows 27.89 seconds, the cumulative time recorded would be 28 seconds, and that number would be plugged into the formula used to calculate the score. When the calculation is completed, the answer to the formula would also be rounded to the nearest whole number. An ISF score without fractions or decimals is recorded on the Summary of Scores Page.

5. Do we round the ISF score that is calculated?

Yes. Use standard rounding rules. If the answer calculated by using the formula has a decimal of 0.5 or higher, round it to the next highest number. If the decimal is 0.49 or lower, drop the decimal. For example, a calculated score of 23.46 would be recorded as 23, whereas a calculated score of 23.62 would be recorded as 24.

6. Some words, like peanut and insect, can have the letter name as an initial sound. How do I score if the student gives a letter name for the first sound in these words?

Score a response of the letter name *p* for *peanut* or *n* for *insect* as correct because the letter name in these words is also a segment of the word that includes the first sound.

7. How do I pronounce the blend /fl/?

Blends can be difficult to isolate for articulation. It is important that examiners practice correct pronunciation of the blends in ISF, because examiner pronunciation can affect the reliability of the measure. The correct way to pronounce blends in isolation is to minimize the vowel sound as much as possible. This is easy to do for some blends that end in a continuant sound, such as /sm/ and /sn/. It is more difficult when the blend ends in a stop, such as /sk/ or /sp/. For blends such as /sk/ and /sp/, a minimal vowel sound will need to be added. (To minimize these two blends, it helps if the examiner whispers the blends because they both have two unvoiced sounds.) When isolating and articulating blends that end in /r/, such as /br/ and /pr/, some people are tempted to insert a vowel sound between the phonemes and say /ber/ or /per/. This is incorrect; /ber/ is the first part of the words *bird*, *birch*, and *burn*, but not the first sound in *bridge*. The blend /br/ is correctly pronounced with a minimal vowel sound after the blend: /brŭ/. The first syllable in the word *person* is /per/. The blend /pr/ is correctly pronounced with a minimal vowel sound after the blend: /prŭ/.

8. There are so many ways to articulate the /r/, /w/, and /y/ phonemes. How do I know if the student is using the correct one?

Any of the pronunciations for the phonemes /r/, /w/, or /y/ is counted as a correct answer.

9. **Why does DIBELS allow students to be sloppy in their pronunciation of phonemes, for example, allowing them to add the sound *uh* to the end of /m/ or /s/?**

The purpose of asking students to isolate phonemes is to learn whether they understand the concept that words are made of smaller parts. A student who names *muh* as the first sound in *mop* is demonstrating that he or she understands that there is a sound at the beginning of the word, even if the student doesn't know how to properly pronounce the phoneme. (Unfortunately, often the student who adds the sound *uh* to the end of phonemes is simply giving the pronunciation he or she has been taught in class.)

Phoneme Segmentation Fluency (PSF)

12

PSF Student Booklet Page, Benchmark Assessment Sample Page, First Grade, Middle of Year   **Figure 12-1**

There are no Student Materials for PSF because the student listens to the examiner say words and does not look at or read anything.

Benchmark 3
DIBELS® Phoneme Segmentation Fluency

but	/b/ /u/ /t/		yet	/y/ /e/ /t/	___/6
hat	/h/ /a/ /t/		eyes	/ie/ /z/	___/5
smart	/s/ /m/ /ar/ /t/		wheels	/w/ /ea/ /l/ /z/	___/8
right	/r/ /ie/ /t/		try	/t/ /r/ /ie/	___/6
lock	/l/ /o/ /k/		brings	/b/ /r/ /i/ /ng/ /z/	___/8
can	/k/ /a/ /n/		eat	/ea/ /t/	___/5
wife	/w/ /ie/ /f/		their	/TH/ /ai/ /r/	___/6
by	/b/ /ie/		was	/w/ /u/ /z/	___/5
lights	/l/ /ie/ /t/ /s/		fun	/f/ /u/ /n/	___/7
odd	/o/ /d/		less	/l/ /e/ /s/	___/5
leaned	/l/ /ea/ /n/ /d/		bee	/b/ /ea/	___/6
man	/m/ /a/ /n/		huge	/h/ /y/ /oo/ /j/	___/7

Error Pattern: Total: ____

Page 20   © 2003 All Rights Reserved.

BASIC INFORMATION

Purpose	Measures whether the student can segment one-syllable words with two to five phonemes into component parts. (The highest scores are obtained if the student segments words into its phonemes. However, the student will earn points by accurately naming any part of the word.)
Description	The student responds to a target word by breaking it into parts.
Relationship to the NRP's five essential components	Measures the ability to segment word parts, which is a component of phonemic awareness.
Approximate time to administer	2 minutes, depending on a student's response during the directions.

PSF BENCHMARK ASSESSMENT SCHEDULE AND RISK LEVELS

PSF is given as a benchmark assessment at the middle and end of kindergarten and in all three benchmark assessment periods in first grade. Students are expected to achieve the benchmark score of 35 by the end of kindergarten in order to be on track to meet the middle-of-year first grade NWF benchmark score and the end-of-year first grade ORF benchmark score.

Table 12-1													PSF Benchmark Scores
Phoneme segmentation fluency	**Kindergarten**			**First Grade**			**Second Grade**			**Third Grade**		
	B	M	E	B	M	E	B	M	E	B	M	E
Low Risk or Established		18+	35+	35+	35+	35+						
Some Risk or Emerging		7–17	10–34	10–34	10–34	10–34						
At Risk or Deficit		0–6	0–9	0–9	0–9	0–9						

Note: The letters **B**, **M**, and **E** stand for beginning, middle, and end of the school year.

PSF BENCHMARK SCORES DISCUSSION

Children who reach the PSF benchmark score of 35 by the end of kindergarten are on track to meet the NWF benchmark score by the middle of first grade. The established benchmark score of 35 can be applied as a target to students of any age who demonstrate weak phonemic awareness skills, including those in higher grades who score below benchmark for ORF and who are found, upon additional assessment, to have weak phonemic awareness skills.

DIRECTIONS

PSF directions require the student to respond by saying the sounds in the word *mop*. When giving directions for PSF, the examiner will read different wording, depending on whether the student responds correctly or incorrectly when asked to provide sounds for the word *mop*.

- *If the student provides the* correct *sounds*, the examiner will respond with the words in the box on the left ("Very good. The sounds in mop are /m/ /o/ /p/.") and then say the words beneath the boxes ("OK. Here is your first word.") before giving the student the first word from the scoring page.
- *If the student provides any* incorrect *sounds* or does not respond *after three seconds* have elapsed, the examiner will respond with the words in the box on the right ("The sounds in mop are /m/ /o/ /p/. Your turn. Tell me the sounds in *mop*.") and then give the student a second chance to respond. Whether the student's second response is correct, incorrect, or to say nothing, the examiner continues by saying the words beneath the boxes

("OK. Here is your first word.") and then gives the student the first word
from the scoring page.

The examiner will read these directions to the student:

PSF Directions   **Figure 12-2**

I am going to say a word. After I say it, you tell me all the sounds in the word. So, if I say, "sam," you would say /s/ /a/ /m/. Let's try one (one-second pause). *Tell me the sounds in "mop."*

CORRECT RESPONSE: If student says /m/ /o/ /p/, you say	INCORRECT RESPONSE: If student gives any other response, you say
Very good. The sounds in "mop" are /m/ /o/ /p/.	*The sounds in "mop" are /m/ /o/ /p/. Your turn. Tell me the sounds in mop."*

OK. Here is your first word.

Give the student the first word and start your stopwatch after saying the first word.

Please note that examiners should read the words going across the page. (Many examiners are tempted to read down the columns, which is incorrect.)

PSF ADMINISTRATION RULES

Timing	1 minute continuous
Stopwatch	Start immediately after giving the student the first word.
Hesitation time allotment	3 seconds
Hesitation prompt	When the student hesitates and does not give a response after three seconds, give him or her the next word. (Do not repeat the word or help him respond to the word. The word the examiner repeated is left unmarked and no score is given for that word.)
Discontinue rule	Stop giving the assessment if the student gives no correct sound segments in the first five words. (This rule applies only to the first five words, not to any subsequent five continuous words.)
Additional information	Read words on the scoring page going from left to right. Do not read words by column.

RECORDING STUDENT RESPONSES

Overview of Marking Student Responses

- Correct responses—Underline each sound segment that the student answers correctly. Use a separate underline for each sound segment.
- Incorrect responses—Mark with a slash (/) through the entire sound segment that is incorrectly named, and do not underline the segment. A sound segment is incorrect even if only one of the phonemes in the segment is incorrect and if the remaining phonemes are accurate.

157

- Omissions—Do not place any mark on segments of a word the student does not attempt to segment or say. Give no score for any segment omitted.
- Self-corrections—If a student self corrects an error within 3 seconds, write "sc" above the word, and do not count it as an error.
- Repeating the target word—Circle the word if the student repeats the target word. Give no score when the student repeats a word.
- Put a bracket ( ]) after the last phoneme, segment, or word the student attempts within the one-minute timeframe.

Figure 12–3 shows markings for a student's responses and his or her score. When scoring PSF, add the points (one point for each separate underline) for the two words in each row, and put that sum on the line to the right of the two words. To get the total score, add the numbers on the lines in the right column. Observe that you count the underlines, plus the self-corrections, to get the score for each line and then total the scores for each line to calculate the PSF score. The student's PSF score is recorded in the lower right corner of the scoring page and on the Summary of Scores Page.

Other conventions of DIBELS scoring for PSF include:

- Inserted word parts are ignored when scoring. (For example, if the word is *fog* and the student says /fr/ /o/ /g/, /fr/ is an incorrect word part and a

---

Figure 12-3   **PSF Scoring Booklet Page—Marked**

Benchmark 3
DIBELS® Phoneme Segmentation Fluency

but	/b/ /u/ /t/	yet	/y/ /e/ /t/	4 /6
hat	/h/ /a/ /t/	eyes	(/ie/ /z/) sc	2 /5
smart	/s/ /m/ /ar/ /t/	wheels	/w/ /ea/ /l/ /z/	6 /8
right	/r/ /ie/ /t/	try	/t/ /r/ /ie/	4 /6
lock	/l/ /o/ /k/	brings	/b/ /r/ /i/ /ng/ /z/	5 /8
can	/k/ /a/ /n/	eat	(/ea/ /t/)	3 /5
wife	/w/ /ie/ /f/	their	/TH/ /ai/ /r/	2 /6
by	(/b/ /ie/)	was	/w/ /u/ /z/	2 /5
lights	/l/ /ie/ /t/ /s/]	fun	/f/ /u/ /n/	2 /7
odd	/o/ /d/	less	/l/ /e/ /s/	___ /5
leaned	/l/ /ea/ /n/ /d/	bee	/b/ /ea/	___ /6
man	/m/ /a/ /n/	huge	/h/ /y/ /oo/ /j/	___ /7

Total: _30_

Error Pattern:

slash would be placed through the /f/ in the scoring booklet. However, if the student says /f/ /r/ /o/ /g/, the /r/ is considered an inserted word part and is not counted against the score. The examiner can make no mark, or the examiner can note that the student inserted the /r/ sound.)

- Phonemes articulated with a pronounced *uh*, such as *kuh*, *duh*, or *suh*, are accepted as correct answers. However, you may want to note in the Student Booklet that the student is adding the *uh* to the pronunciation of certain phonemes.

- Phonemes or word parts given out of order are incorrect.

- Elongating phonemes and running them together, rather than separating them, is accepted as a correct response. This is generally an issue only if the school uses one of several core reading programs that teach children to elongate phonemes and run them together, rather than separating the phonemes. For example, the student might say /mmmmmooooooop/ for *mop*. The phonemes /m/ and /o/, as continuants, must be held long enough to make it clear that the student intends to exaggerate the phoneme. The phoneme /p/ cannot be elongated because it is a stop, but it must be pronounced obviously or repeated several times in order to be counted as a correct response.

Marking and Counting Correct Responses

The "official" directions in the *DIBELS Administration and Scoring Guide* for obtaining the PSF score are to "count the number of different, correct sound segments produced." We have found that an easier way to understand scoring PSF is to think about counting the number of underlines. Because each underline is a segment for which the student gave a correct response, the score is obtained by counting the number of unique underlines plus any self-corrections.

The only underlines not counted are those that are exactly the same, meaning that the student repeated the same sound segment.[1] (A student gets credit for a complete sound segment only once.) For example, for the word *mind*, if the student says, /mī/ /mī/, the marks in the student booklet would be /m/ /ie/ /n/ /d/, and the student would get one point because the two underlines are exactly the same.

When a student correctly names two segments of the word, but they have an overlapping sound, both underlines are counted, and the student receives two points. For example, for the word *mind*, if the student says, /mi/ /ind/, the marks in the student booklet would be /m/ /ie/ /n/ /d/, and the student would get two points because the underlines are different.

When a student repeats the word, the examiner circles the word and the student gets no points for repeating the word.

> Count the number of underlines, plus self-corrections, to score PSF.

---

[1] Some examiners underline the word if the student repeats the word after giving segments. This would be another case in which the underscore—for the whole word—would not be counted.

> When scoring PSF, the entire sound segment must be correct in order for a response to be correct.

Scoring Correct Responses

When counting the score for PSF, a student gets credit for the following correct responses to the target word *best*:

- Saying all the separate phonemes
  - Student says, /b/ /e/ /s/ /t/ ; mark /b/ /e/ /s/ /t/ = 4 points
- Breaking the word into two parts
  - Student says, /b/ /ěst/; mark /b/ /e/ /s/ /t/ = 2 points
  - Student says, /bě/ /st/; mark /b/ /e/ /s/ /t/ = 2 points
  - Student says, /běs/ /t/); mark /b/ /e/ /s/ /t/ = 2 points
- Saying only one part of the word
  - Student says, /b/; mark /b/ /e/ /s/ /t/ = 1 point
  - Student says, /bě/; mark /b/ /e/ /s/ /t/ = 1 point
  - Student says, /běs/; mark /b/ /e/ /s/ /t/ = 1 point
  - Student says, /t/; mark /b/ /e/ /s/ /t/ = 1 point
  - Student says, /st/; mark /b/ /e/ /s/ /t/ = 1 point
  - Student says, /ěst/; mark /b/ /e/ /s/ /t/ = 1 point
  - Student says, /ě/; mark /b/ /e/ /s/ /t/ = 1 point
- Saying accurate phonemes or word parts but omitting one or more phonemes
  - Student says, /b/ /t/; mark /b/ /e/ /s/ /t/ = 2 points
  - Student says, /b/ /s/ /t/; mark /b/ /e/ /s/ /t/ = 3 points
  - Student says, /bě/ /t/; mark /b/ /e/ /s/ /t/ = 2 points
- Saying overlapping word parts
  - Student says, /běs/ /ěst/; mark /b/ /e/ /s/ /t/ = 2 points
  - Student says, /bě/ /ěst/; mark /b/ /e/ /s/ /t/ = 2 points (In this example, each segment uttered is different, even though each segment has the overlapping sound /e/. Because each segment is different, we give credit for each one, regardless of the overlapping part of the two segments.)
  - Student says, /b/ /běs/ /ěst/; mark /b/ /e/ /s/ /t/ = 3 points
  - Student says, /b/ /běs/ /běst/; mark /b/ /e/ /s/ /t/ = 2 points (In this example, the student gets credit for /b/ and /bes/ as correct segments, but does not get credit for naming the word.)

Scoring Incorrect Responses

Incorrect responses that are orally produced by the student are marked with a slash. Omissions are given no mark at all.

Scoring incorrect or partially incorrect answers is illustrated below for the target word *best*:

- Saying phonemes or word parts, some correct and some incorrect
  - Student says, /b/ /i/ /s/ /t/ ; mark /b/ /e/ /s/ /t/ = 3 points
  - Student says, /p/ /a/ /s/ /t/; mark /b/ /e/ /s/ /t/ = 2 points
  - Student says, /ba/ /st/; mark /b/ /e/ /s/ /t/ = 1 point
  - Student says, /bl/ /e/ /s/ /t/; mark /b/ /e/ /s/ /t/ = 3 points
  - Student says, /b/ /l/ /e/ /s/ /t/; mark /b/ /e/ /s/ /t/ = 4 points
    (There is no penalty for the extra sound added.)

- Repeating the word
  - Student repeats *best*; mark /b/ /e/ /s/ /t/

PROGRESS MONITORING

DIBELS provides progress monitoring materials for PSF. The PSF progress monitoring Scoring Booklet has 20 alternate forms that can be used throughout the year. (There are no Student Materials for PSF progress monitoring because the assessment is oral and students do not need to look at any words.)

Although the PSF progress monitoring materials are labeled for kindergarten, PSF words are not "grade leveled" and can be used for progress monitoring students of any age who are receiving intervention instruction in phonemic awareness. We recommend marking out the word *kindergarten* on the progress monitoring materials when they are used for students in first grade or later.

The charting page on the DIBELS progress monitoring booklets is designed for use in the middle of kindergarten, beginning in December. In the Appendix we have provided a PSF progress monitoring chart that can be used for any six-month period by students in any grade. The chart can be customized for any time period up to six months by writing in the names of the months below the horizontal axis on the chart.

HELPING CHILDREN PREPARE FOR PSF DIRECTIONS

The directions for PSF can be confusing to some young children, even those who are used to segmenting words as part of their core reading program. Several excellent core reading programs use specific words as directions to instruct students to segment a word into phonemes, and the children using these programs often expect to hear these words when they are asked to segment words into phonemes. (These instructions are generally something like, "Break it down," "Say it slowly," "Name each sound," or "Say it the hard way.") Therefore, although children know how to segment words, they sometimes do not understand what they are being asked to do when they are given the DIBELS instructions for PSF.

We have seen a few children fail to demonstrate their abilities to segment phonemes because they did not understand the PSF directions, especially kindergarten students and first grade students with limited vocabularies. If an examiner thinks that a student's performance on PSF was hindered because the student did not understand the directions and if the student scored below benchmark, the examiner can recommend that the student be retested in PSF. Before the retest, the teacher or examiner may review the directions for PSF, explaining that there are different words that can be used to ask them to name the sounds in a word. The teacher may want to ask the student to segment a few words (not words taken from DIBELS benchmark or progress monitoring assessments) before giving the actual DIBELS directions and assessment.

PSF PRONUNCIATION GUIDE

DIBELS Scoring Booklets for PSF do not use conventional diacritical marks or letters to indicate some of the phonemes, especially the vowels. Initially, this is confusing for some DIBELS examiners. However, nearly all examiners are quick to decipher the DIBELS conventions for indicating sounds because all sounds are matched to a word in the PSF Scoring Booklet. For example, the phonemes in the word *good* are given as /g/ /uu/ /d/. Although /uu/ is not a typical representation for the vowel sound in *good*, examiners can determine that /uu/ represents the phoneme /ŏŏ/ as in *book*, *put*, *pull*, or *hood* because /uu/ obviously represents the middle phoneme in the target word *good*.

The DIBELS Pronunciation Guide for vowel and consonant phonemes is shown in *Table 12–2*. DIBELS doesn't use diacritical marks, but represents vowel sounds with spelling combinations between slashes. In *Table 12–2*, the more unusual DIBELS representations for vowel phonemes are marked with an asterisk (*), and a more typical sound representation is shown to the right.

Most consonant phonemes are marked conventionally in DIBELS. Noticeably missing from the list of DIBELS consonants is the /wh/ phoneme. This is because in almost all regions of the United States, the /wh/ phoneme has disappeared and been replaced with the /w/ phoneme. (For example, few children in the United States make a distinction when pronouncing *which* and *witch*, whereas in England these are obviously different words with obviously different initial phonemes.) In *Table 12–2*, the two more unusual DIBELS representations for consonant phonemes are marked with an asterisk (*) and a more common representation is shown to the right.

DIBELS Vowel and Consonant Phoneme Representations Compared With Conventional Representations

Phoneme Pronunciation Representations   Table 12-2

Vowels			Consonants		
DIBELS Phoneme Representation	Word With DIBELS Phoneme Representation Spelling	More Typical Phoneme Representation	DIBELS Phoneme Representation	Word With DIBELS Phoneme Representation Spelling	More Typical Phoneme Representation
/ai/*	bait	/ā/	/th/	thin	/th/
/ea/*	bead	/ē/	/TH/*	then	/t͟h/
/ie/*	tie	/ī/	/sh/	shed	/sh/
/oa/*	boat	/ō/	/SH/*	measure or beige	/zh/
/oo/*	food	/ōō/	/ch/	chin	/ch/
/a/*	bad	/ă/	/j/	jam or edge	/j/
/e/*	bed	/ĕ/	/p/	pen	/p/
/i/*	bid	/ĭ/	/t/	tap	/t/
/o/*	cod or law[2]	/ŏ/ or /aw/	/k/	can	/k/
/u/*	bud	/ŭ/	/b/	bat	/b/
/uu/*	good	/ŏŏ/	/d/	dad	/d/
/ow/	cow	/ow/ or /ou/	/g/	gun or frog	/g/
/oi/	noise or point	/oi/ or /oy/	/m/	man or jam	/m/
/ar/	car	/ar/	/n/	nap	/n/
/ir/*	bird	/er/ or /ur/	/ng/	sing	/ng/
/or/	for	/or/	/f/	fat	/f/
			/v/	van	/v/
			/s/	sit	/s/
			/z/	zoo	/z/
			/r/	rat or frog	/r/
			/l/	lap	/l/
			/w/	wet	/w/
			/h/	hot	/h/
			/y/	yell	/y/

USING PSF SCORES FOR OLDER STUDENTS

Although PSF is given as a benchmark assessment and has benchmark scores only for kindergarten and first grade, it can be used to screen and progress monitor phonemic awareness skills for students of any age. Any of the PSF progress monitoring forms can be used for screening older students. (PSF word

---

[2] In DIBELS, the /o/ symbol represents both /ŏ/ and /aw/ phonemes. This may be because the /aw/ phoneme is not often used in Oregon's regional speech and in many areas of the West and South.

lists in benchmark assessments and progress monitoring booklets are not grade leveled.) Any student of any age who struggles with reading and cannot achieve the established benchmark score of 35 is likely to need instruction in phonemic awareness.

Once an older student is deemed to need instruction in phonemic awareness, the DIBELS PSF progress monitoring materials can be used to measure the effectiveness of phonemic awareness instruction for students of any age. The goal for these students would be to reach or exceed the established benchmark score of 35 for PSF. The PSF progress monitoring chart in the Appendix can be used for charting progress monitoring for older students.

INTERPRETATION OF PSF SCORES

Students who cannot segment words into phonemes may have difficulty matching phonemes with graphemes (a letter or letter combination that represent sounds). These students are likely to have difficulty recoding (blending) the sounds in written words, even if they can accurately identify the letter sounds. (The lack of the ability to recode will show up when a student cannot blend the sounds for nonsense words in NWF to form complete words.) A student who cannot correctly segment words on PSF lists into at least 35 parts in one minute by the end of kindergarten is at risk for not meeting the NWF benchmark by the middle of first grade and the ORF benchmark by the end of first grade. Students who do not meet the PSF established benchmark score of 35 after the end of kindergarten are likely to need instructional intervention to help them develop phonemic awareness.

PSF scores below benchmark can indicate either accuracy or fluency difficulties, or both. A student who guesses at sounds quickly could conceivably get a relatively high score because he or she guesses fast and happens to guess some phonemes or word segments correctly. A student who correctly names every sound attempted but fails to score 35 exhibits a fluency difficulty. Two examples are given for students at the end of kindergarten who have the same score but different instructional needs:

- Student A attempts 60 sounds on a sound-by-sound basis and names one half of the sounds correctly. He would have a score of 30, which is in the Emerging risk category. Student A has difficulty with accuracy, not difficulty with speed. Intervention for Student A would need to focus on segmenting words into phonemes accurately, perhaps slowing down as he or she practices, and then teaching Student A to blend sounds into words.
- Student B attempts only 30 sounds and gets them all correct, achieving the same score as Student A. Student B is also in the Emerging risk category. Student B has no difficulty with accuracy, but needs to improve speed. Intervention would focus on getting Student B to segment sounds faster and then teaching Student B to blend sounds into words. (Although DIBELS

assesses only sound segmentation, blending sounds into words is another phonemic awareness skill that is critical to reading.)

Studies show that approximately 90% of struggling readers have poor phonemic awareness (Shaywitz, 2003). That means that they have difficulty understanding that words can be broken into smaller parts, called phonemes. These students also may have difficulty discriminating or manipulating phonemes in words. Students with weak phonemic awareness need explicit instruction to be able to isolate the phonemes in words accurately so that they can later match them with graphemes as they read and spell.

Students with poor phonemic awareness often struggle with other, simpler components of phonological awareness, such as identifying syllables and onset and rime[3] in words. Some younger children even have difficulty understanding that words in a sentence are separate units. Therefore, it is always a good idea to check whether students with low PSF scores can accurately segment and blend syllables and onset and rime before attempting to teach them phonemes.

One interesting note about PSF scores is that, for many children, PSF scores fall once they begin reading. Therefore, if a student has ORF and NWF scores above benchmark and is reading NWF whole words (rather than sound by sound), but scores in the Emerging category for PSF, we do not recommend intervention instruction in PSF. This is especially true if the student has scored above benchmark for PSF in previous assessments. We believe that students with this profile (ORF and NWF above benchmark with PSF Emerging) are concentrating on letter–sound relationships and do not need to rely on specific phonemic awareness knowledge to become good readers. (Remember that achieving phonemic awareness is a means to an end—which is reading—not an end in itself.)

FREQUENTLY OBSERVED MISTAKES MADE WHEN ADMINISTERING PSF

The most common mistakes we observe in PSF scoring are:

1. *Giving words in columns, not reading the words across the row.* For PSF, we always read the two words going across the page, even though the words are in two columns. The scoring page is set up so that the score for two words is added across the page and recorded on the line on the right side of the two words. The numbers on the lines are then totaled to get the PSF score. (See *Figure 12–3*, page 156).

---

[3] Onset is the part of the word before the vowel, and rime is the part of the word including the vowel and everything after it. For example, in the word *shirt*, the onset is /sh/ and the rime is /irt/; in the word *lake*, the onset is /l/ and the rime is /ake/; and in the word *smile*, the onset is /sm/ and the rime is /ile/.

2. *Not underlining each separate sound segment the student produces, but instead underlining the entire word.* We have seen Scoring Booklets that have one underline for the entire word, with the maximum number of points given for that word. When reviewing the Scoring Booklets to determine error patterns, we can only assume that the student named each individual sound in this case. The correct marking for a response that separately produces each phoneme in a word is to underline each phoneme separately. The correct marking for a student who repeats the word is to circle the word.

3. *Underlining each separate sound segment when the student says a word part with two or more phonemes, instead of underlining the entire word part.* This is not as common as No. 2, above, but is nevertheless a common mistake. In this case, when we review Scoring Booklets to determine error patterns when planning instruction, we can only assume that the student named each separate sound instead of combining sounds in a word part. The correct marking for a response that produces an entire word part is to underline the entire word part.

4. *Underline a word the student repeats instead of circling it.* The correct marking when a student repeats a word is to circle the word. The student receives no points for repeating the word.

5. *Giving one point for repeating the word.* Repeated words are circled and not counted as correct. A student gets no points for repeating the word because he or she has not indicated that he understands that words are made of parts.

6. *Not underlining correct answers, but instead leaving correct answers unmarked.* When examiners give points for a word that is not underlined, we can only assume that the student read the number of sounds equal to the number of points given. The correct marking for a response that separately names each phoneme in a word is to underline each phoneme separately.

7. *Overemphasizing the phonemes when giving the words.* For some examiners, it is difficult to take off the "teacher hat" and put on the "examiner hat." Sometimes examiners want to help the children succeed, and, in their efforts to do so, they sometimes unconsciously provide children with hints by elongating or emphasizing the sounds as they give PSF words to children. Examiners should pronounce words precisely, but they should not "overpronounce" the word.

8. *Giving credit when a student utters a word part that is only partially accurate.* The entire word part must be accurate in order for the student to receive credit. For example, when a student gives the word parts /br/ /a/ /g/ for the word *bag*, the first word part, /br/, is incorrect, even though the student included the first sound of the word in this part. The entire sound segment has to be correct in order to give credit for the word part.

FREQUENTLY ASKED QUESTIONS ABOUT PSF

1. **Scoring for PSF seems very confusing, especially when a student names a phoneme twice, but the phoneme is in two different word parts. An example is for the word *hall*, the student says /h/ /ol/ /l/. Does the student get a point for saying the sound /l/ twice? How would I score this?**

   To mark the student's answer, underline each word part that he or she names:
   /h/ /o/ /l/

   It is much easier to understand scoring PSF if the examiner simply counts the underlines and does not try to find a reason for the number of points earned. By employing this strategy, the above example has three underlines, so the score would be 3. Counting the underlines eliminates the need to think about "overlapping" sounds.

   In the scoring for the word *hall* above, the student gets 3 points because he or she named three separate, distinct, and correct word parts. The word parts /ol/ and /l/ both earn a point because they are separate and correct word parts, even though one sound overlaps.

2. **There seem to be inconsistencies in PSF scoring directions in the Sopris West DIBELS implementation video with regard to when to circle the word if the student repeats it. In the video, the examiner underlines the word *smile* after the student first says /sm/ as a word part and then says *smile*. Why doesn't the examiner circle the word *smile* when the student repeats it?**

   In general, circling a word is used to indicate that the child repeated the word, no matter the circumstances. However, if the child repeats the word first and then gives sound segments or if the child gives sound segments and then repeats the word, the important scoring is to underline the sound segments that the student names correctly so that he or she is given points for those segments. When the student repeats the word *and* gives sound segments, circling the word indicates that the student used time when repeating the word, which may be valuable diagnostic information. In the video, the examiner underlines the word when it is repeated, which is not in accordance with conventional scoring rules but is marked well enough for us to understand the student's response. If you are counting the underlines to score PSF and you underline an entire word, as in the video, you need to be careful not to count any underline that is beneath an entire word.

3. **Some of my students repeat every word before segmenting the sounds. Do I have to circle the word every time the student repeats the word, even though I know that he or she is going to segment the sounds after repeating the word?**

   When a teacher notices this pattern in a student's responses, the teacher can note on the scoring page that the student first repeated each word before segmenting the sounds, eliminating the need to circle every word. The note will help to explain that the student used time by repeating each word if anyone questions why the student scored lower than expected.

4. If a student repeats the word before segmenting the sounds for every word and he or she scores only slightly below the benchmark score, may I retest the student?

Yes, you may retest the student in this case. Before you retest, you may want to remind the student, before you give the directions, that he or she does not have to repeat the word aloud before saying the sounds.

5. How do I know whether phonemes articulated by the student that sound "different" are due to a regional dialect, and thus acceptable, or whether they are incorrect?

Part of making this decision depends on the examiner's knowledge of the student's regional dialect. Deciding whether to accept a nonstandard pronunciation that might be due to a regional dialect is somewhat subjective. However, we can give two examples of regional dialects that would produce acceptable answers. These examples may help examiners understand this issue better.

- Example #1. In most areas of the country, the word *park* has an *r*-controlled vowel sound, and the phonemes would be correctly articulated as /p/ /ar/ /k/. However, in Boston, many people pronounce the word *park* using a short *o* vowel sound: /p/ /o/ /k/. The student in Boston who names the vowel in *park* as short *o* or /aw/ should be considered to have given a correct response.

- Example #2. In most areas of the country, the word *oil* is articulated as /oi/ /l/. However, in regions of several southern states, the word *oil* is pronounced the same as the word *all*. The student in any of these areas who names the vowel in *oil* as short *o* should be considered to have given a correct response.

6. If the child does not respond within three seconds and I have to give the next word before he answers, how is that word marked?

Any segments that are not attempted should be left unmarked, including when a child hesitates for three seconds and the examiner provides the next word.

7. My students are taught to elongate the sounds in words as they run the sounds together. They are not taught to break the sounds into separate and isolated segments. Will my students get credit if they elongate the sounds?

Students who *obviously* elongate the sounds in a word are given credit. Students who have been taught to elongate sounds are demonstrating knowledge that words are made of phonemes according to the way they have been instructed. The purpose of PSF is to measure whether students understand that words have phonemes and can articulate the phonemes. A child who is taught to *obviously* elongate sounds demonstrates this knowledge. One caution for examiners who are not used to hearing students elongate sounds is that sounds that are stops (see the Glossary for a definition) cannot be elongated. For example, in the word *mop*, the phonemes /m/ and /o/ are continuants and can be elongated, but /p/ is a stop and cannot be elongated. The student who articulates /mmmmmmmmooooooooooop/ is given credit for all three phonemes, as long as the /p/ phoneme is obviously articulated. If the reading program used in your school teaches children to elongate sounds rather than to segment them, you may want to remind the examiners that elongated sounds are acceptable answers for PSF.

8. **If the student obviously elongates the sounds in *mop* during the directions, rather than segmenting them, can I elongate the sounds when I respond with the rest of the directions?**

No. You need to fully segment the sounds when giving DIBELS directions. DIBELS directions for benchmark assessments are standardized and must be given exactly as written unless a change is allowed as an Approved Accommodation. (See Chapter 6 for a discussion of DIBELS Approved Accommodations. There is no accommodation for elongating the sounds in the sample word in the PSF directions.)

9. **Why did the DIBELS creators use an assessment that measures segmenting sounds when blending sounds is the skill used for reading, and segmenting sounds is the skill used for spelling?**

Researchers piloted both blending and segmenting sounds, and they found that segmenting sounds is a better indicator of phonemic awareness than blending sounds. Because one of the goals of DIBELS is to offer an efficient way to identify students who are at risk for reading difficulties, the researchers selected segmenting skills, rather than blending skills, as the DIBELS measure for phonemic awareness because segmenting is the stronger predictor.

10. **In PSF, why does DIBELS give students words with as many as five sounds and with short, long, and *r*-controlled vowels, when they may be learning to read only three-sound words with short vowels?**

PSF is an exercise in *hearing* the sounds that make up words, not in reading words. A person's ability to hear sounds is independent of his or her knowledge of letter names and letter sounds or of his or her ability to read. Therefore, a student can segment sounds in words that he or she cannot read yet. PSF measures the student's ability to hear the sounds in words, regardless of how the word is spelled. (NWF is the DIBELS measure for determining whether a student can match sounds and letters. NWF includes only one-syllable words with two and three sounds and only short vowels.)

13

Nonsense Word Fluency (NWF)

NWF Student Materials Page and Scoring Booklet Page
Benchmark Assessment, Second Grade, Beginning of Year

Figure 13-1

vog	tel	ut	vov	lac
zek	rok	en	zub	pez
iv	lig	faf	wel	koz
wom	jop	dav	eg	laf
kiz	fom	im	fos	kuj
zab	yom	wuj	sed	kib
tam	wab	juz	az	zul
vep	nej	yeg	bok	bov
ap	bej	yaz	liv	pem
lek	dun	soj	eb	meb

Benchmark 1
Page 2

DIBELS® Nonsense Word Fluency
© 2003 All Rights Reserved

Figure 13-2

Benchmark 1
DIBELS® Nonsense Word Fluency

vog	tel	ut	vov	lac	__/14
zek	rok	en	zub	pez	__/14
iv	lig	faf	wel	koz	__/14
wom	jop	dav	eg	laf	__/14
kiz	fom	im	fos	kuj	__/14
zab	yom	wuj	sed	kib	__/15
tam	wab	juz	az	zul	__/14
vep	nej	yeg	bok	bov	__/15
ap	bej	yaz	liv	pem	__/14
lek	dun	soj	eb	meb	__/14
				Total:	_____

Error Pattern:

Page 2

© 2003 All Rights Reserved.

BASIC INFORMATION

Purpose	Measures two skills: (1) whether students can name letter sounds; and (2) whether students can blend sounds to read unfamiliar words with short vowels in CVC or VC syllable patterns.
Description	The student reads nonsense words spelled with two or three letters with a CVC or VC letter configuration.
Relationship to the NRP's five essential components	Measures knowledge of and ability to apply letter–sound relationships, which is *phonics*.
Approximate time to administer per student	2.5 minutes

NWF BENCHMARK ASSESSMENT SCHEDULE AND RISK LEVELS

NWF is given as a benchmark assessment at the middle and end of kindergarten, for all three assessment periods in first grade, and at the beginning of second grade. Students who achieve the benchmark score of 50 and read 15 words as whole words by the middle of first grade are on track to meet the benchmark ORF score at the end of first grade.

| Table 13-1 | | | | | | | | | | | NWF Benchmark Scores |

Nonsense Word Fluency	Kindergarten			First Grade			Second Grade			Third Grade		
	B	M	E	B	M	E	B	M	E	B	M	E
Low Risk		13+	25+	24+								
Established					50+	50+	50+					
Some Risk		5–12	15–24	13–23								
Emerging					30–49	30–49	30–49					
At Risk		0–4	0–14	0–12								
Deficit					0–29	0–29	0–29					

Note: The letters **B**, **M**, and **E** stand for beginning, middle, and end of the school year.

NONSENSE WORD FLUENCY BENCHMARK SCORES

> The NWF milepost at the middle of first grade requires that students achieve a benchmark score of 50 and that the score is achieved by reading words as whole entities. Students who read sound by sound and achieve a score of 50 do not show mastery of early phonics skills.

Children who are on track to reach the end-of-year ORF benchmark score will have reached the NWF benchmark score of 50 by the middle of first grade and be able to blend the sounds into words.[1] (Students who achieve a score of 50 by reading sound by sound or reading word parts, such as onset and rime, are not demonstrating mastery of beginning phonics skills.) The NWF benchmark score of 50 while recoding (blending) sounds into words can be applied to students of any age who demonstrate weak phonics skills, including those in Grades 2–6 who score below benchmark on ORF and who are found, upon additional assessment, to have weak beginning phonics skills.

The DIBELS NWF measure is designed to assess two early reading skills related to letters and phonics. The lower-level skill is the knowledge that letters represent sounds and the knowledge of the most common sounds for each letter. Students who accurately name the sounds for letters in NWF words demonstrate that they know letter sounds, but they do not demonstrate the ability to recode (blend) the letter sounds into words. (It is possible for some students to name letter sounds so fast that they achieve a score of 50 or higher on NWF. These students do not meet the benchmark score for NWF because they do not demonstrate the ability to

---

[1] At the DIBELS Summit in February 2005, Roland Good and Ruth Kaminski announced that a new guideline requiring a NWF score of 50 and 15 words recoded will be included in the DIBELS 7th edition *Administration and Scoring Guide*, scheduled for Fall 2006.

read the words as whole entities. They will need to receive instruction in blending sounds into words in their intervention.)

The more advanced skill measured by NWF is the ability to recode (blend) letter sounds into unfamiliar words that cannot be recognized by sight. Students who accurately read the words in NWF as whole entities demonstrate early phonics skills. It is necessary to achieve a NWF score of 50 while recoding (blending) the sounds into words in order to achieve a benchmark score for NWF.

DIRECTIONS

Overview of NWF Directions

Nonsense Word Fluency directions are designed to demonstrate to the student that he or she can either name the sounds for the letters or read the whole word. In order to shorten the time it takes to give the NWF directions, the directions can be shortened for progress monitoring. However, examiners are cautioned to use the shortened version only after students have demonstrated that they understand the full directions and procedure. The shortened version of the directions is explained in the section called "Shortened Version of NWF Directions."

Full Version of NWF Directions

The first part of NWF directions explains that the words are make-believe, with *sim* as the example. The directions then require the student to respond by reading the nonsense word *lut*. When giving the student directions for NWF, the examiner will read different wording, depending on whether the student responds to the word *lut* correctly or incorrectly.

- If the student provides the correct sounds or reads the word correctly, the examiner responds with the words in the box on the left ("That's right. The sounds are /l/ /ŭ/ /t/ or *lut*.") and then reads the words beneath the boxes (beginning with, "Here are some make-believe words . . .").
- If the student provides any incorrect sounds when attempting to read *lut*, reads the word incorrectly, or does not respond at all, the examiner will respond with the words in the box on the right ("Remember, you can say the sounds or you can read the whole word. Watch me: the sounds are /l/ /u/ /t/ or *lut*. Let's try again. Read this word the best you can.") Whether the student's response is correct, incorrect, or to say nothing, the examiner continues by saying the words beneath the boxes (beginning with, "Here are some make-believe words . . .").

It is very important for examiners to understand that, when a student reads *lut* incorrectly, they give the directions in the right box *only once*. We have seen several examiners continue to give the directions in the right box a second, third, and even fourth time because the student did not answer correctly or was silent. The DIBELS instructions are not an infinite loop to allow the student multiple opportunities to respond with a correct answer. Although it is at first awkward for many examiners, we all must learn that, no matter what the student responds the second time he or she is given a chance to read the word *lut*, we continue with the rest of the directions. (Notice that the directions are carefully worded not to indicate that the student's response was correct.)

The examiner will place the page from the Student Materials that has the words *sim* and *lut* and read these directions to the student:

| **Figure 13-3** | **NWF Directions—Full Version** |

Look at this word (point to first word on practice page). **It's a make-believe word. Watch me read the word: /s/ /i/ /m/ "sim"** (point to each letter, then run your finger fast beneath the whole word). **I can say the sound of the letters, /s/ /i/ /m/** (point to each letter) **or I can read the whole word, "sim"** (run your finger fast beneath the whole word). **Your turn to read a make-believe word. Read this word the best you can** (point to the word "lut"). **Make sure you say any sounds you know.**

CORRECT RESPONSE:	INCORRECT RESPONSE:
If the student responds with "lut" or all the correct sounds, say	If the student does not respond within 3 seconds or responds incorrectly, say
That's right. The sounds are /l/ /u/ /t/ or "lut."	**Remember, you can say the sounds or you can say the whole word. Watch me: The sounds are /l/ /u/ /t/** (point to each letter) **or "lut"** (run your finger fast beneath the whole word). **Let's try again. Read this word the best you can** (point to the word "lut").

Place the student copy of the nonsense words in front of the student.

Here are some more make-believe words (point to page the student will read). **Start here** (point to the first word) **and go across the page** (run your finger under the first row). **When I say, "Begin," read the words the best you can. Point to each letter and tell me the sound or read the whole word. Read the words the best you can. Put your finger on the first word. Ready, begin.**

Start your stopwatch after saying "begin."

Shortened Version of NWF Directions

After a student has demonstrated that he or she clearly understands the directions and procedures for NWF, the directions can be shortened to the final paragraph.

A recommendation is to use the shortened version of NWF directions only for progress monitoring and that examiners read the full directions for benchmark assessments for all students.

Place the student copy of the nonsense words in front of the student.

Here are some more make-believe words (point to page the student will read)***. Start here*** (point to the first word) ***and go across the page*** (run your finger under the first row)***. When I say, "Begin," read the words the best you can. Point to each letter and tell me the sound or read the whole word. Read the words the best you can. Put your finger on the first word. Ready, begin.***

Start your stopwatch after saying "begin."

NWF ADMINISTRATION RULES

Timing	1 minute continuous
Stopwatch	Start the stopwatch immediately after saying, "begin."
Hesitation time allotment	3 seconds
Hesitation prompt	When the student hesitates in giving a response for 3 seconds or is still trying to figure out a response after 3 seconds, the examiner's response depends on whether the student has been reading sound by sound, whole words, or a combination of both.
The student is reading sound by sound.	The examiner provides the sound, points to the next sound, and asks, "What sound?"
The student is reading words.	The examiner provides the word, points to the next word, and asks, "What word?"
The student is reading a combination of sounds and words.	Sometimes a student will be reading some words as whole words and some words sound by sound. In that case, use the prompt for the most common pattern the student is using or use your judgment to prompt what seems to be difficult for the student. When in doubt, prompt for the sound.
Discontinue rule	Stop giving the assessment if the student gives no correct sound segments in the first five words. (This rule applies only to the first five words, not to any subsequent five continuous words.)

RECORDING STUDENT RESPONSES

- Correct responses—Underline each sound segment that the student answers. Use a separate underline for each segment. For example, if the word is *nop*, the student could respond correctly in any of the following ways:

  – Student reads, *nop*; mark <u>n o p</u>

  – Student reads, /n/ /o/ /p/; mark <u>n</u> <u>o</u> <u>p</u>

  – Student reads, /n/ /op/; mark <u>n o p</u>

  – Student reads, /no/ /p/; mark <u>n o</u> <u>p</u>

  – Student reads, /n/ /o/ /p/ *nop*; mark <u>n</u> <u>o</u> <u>p</u>

  – Student reads, nop /n/ /o/ /p/; mark <u>n</u> <u>o</u> <u>p</u>

- Incorrect responses—Underline all letters the student attempts to pronounce and put a slash (/) through any letter the student does not pronounce correctly, whether that letter is read as part of the whole word or sound by sound.

    – Student reads, *nap*; mark n̲ ø̸ p

    – Student reads, /n/ /ot/; mark n̲ o̲ p̸

- The student does not get credit for responding with letter names.
- Omissions—Do not place any mark on letters for which the student does not attempt a sound.
- Self-corrections—If a student self-corrects an error within 3 seconds, write "sc" above the word, and do not count it as an error.
- Reading the entire word—Underline the entire word if the student reads the whole word. If the student reads an incorrect sound for one or more of the letters, put a slash through the letters for which sounds are incorrect.
- Put a bracket ( ]) after the last word or sound the student attempts.

Figure 13–5 is an NWF scoring page, with the student responses marked and the score totaled. Note that a point is given for every letter that is underlined and does not have a slash through it. Points are also given for self-corrections. When scoring NWF, count the points for the five words in each row, and put that sum on the line to the right of the five words, as shown in *Figure 13–5*. (The number to the right of the slash at the end of each line is the maximum number of points that can be earned for the five words in that line.) To calculate the total score, add the numbers on the lines in the right column, and write the sum on the line

> Count the number of underlined letters that don't have slashes through them, plus self-corrections, to score NWF.

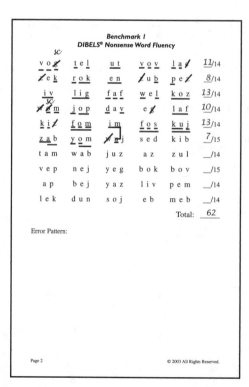

at the bottom of the page, as shown in *Figure 13–5*. This score is recorded on the Summary of Scores Page at the beginning of the Scoring Booklet.

Other conventions of DIBELS scoring for NWF include:

- Inserted sounds are ignored when scoring. The student uses time when inserting sounds, which is how his or her score is affected.
- Letter sounds articulated with a pronounced *uh*, such as *kuh*, *duh*, or *suh*, are accepted as correct answers. However, you may want to note in the Student Booklet that the student is adding the *uh* to the pronunciation of certain phonemes.

Counting Correct Responses

The student is given a point for each letter read or named with the correct sound. The student receives credit whether the letter is read correctly as an individual sound or is blended into a word or word part. The maximum number of points a student can receive is the number of letters in the word. To obtain the score, count the number of underlined letters that do not have slashes through them.

Examples are given below for scoring correct answers in NWF when the word is *nop*:

- Reading the word correctly as a whole word

  – Student reads, *nop*; mark <u>n o p</u> = 3 points

- Reading sound by sound, with the sound for each letter read correctly

  – Student reads, /n/ /o/ /p/; mark <u>n</u> <u>o</u> <u>p</u> = 3 points

- Breaking the word into two parts

  – Student reads, /n/ /op/; mark <u>n o p</u> = 3 points

  – Student reads, /no/ /p/; mark <u>n o p</u> = 3 points

- Reading one part of the word, but omitting other parts (omitted parts are left unmarked)

  – Student reads, /n/; mark <u>n</u> o p = 1 point

  – Student reads, /o/; mark n <u>o</u> p = 1 point

  – Student reads, /p/; mark n o <u>p</u> = 1 point

  – Student reads, /no/; mark <u>n o</u> p = 2 points

  – Student reads, /op/; mark n <u>o p</u> = 2 points

- Reading overlapping word parts

  – Student reads, /no/ /op/; mark <u>n o p</u> = 3 points

  – Student reads, /n/ /no/ /nop/; mark <u><u>n</u> o p</u> = 3 points

  – Student reads, /no/ /o/ /op/; mark <u>n <u>o</u> p</u> = 3 points

  – Student reads, /no/ /o/; mark <u>n <u>o</u></u> p = 2 points

Examples are given below for NWF scoring of answers that are partially or fully incorrect when the word is *nop*:

- Reading the whole word with one sound incorrect

    - Student reads, *mop*; mark m̸ o p = 2 points

    - Student reads, *nap*; mark n ø̸ p = 2 points

    - Student reads, *nod*; mark n o p̸ = 2 points

- Reading the whole word with two sounds incorrect[1]

    - Student reads, *map*; mark n̶o̶p = 1 point

- Reading the whole word with all three sounds incorrect

    - Student reads, *mad*; mark n̶o̶p̶ = 0 points

- Reading sound by sound, missing one or more sounds

    - Student reads, /m/ /o/ /p/; mark m̸ o̲ p = 2 points

    - Student reads, /m/ /a/ /p/; mark m̸ ø̸ p = 2 points

    - Student reads, /n/ /o/ /t/; mark n̲ o̲ p̸ = 2 points

If a student gives the correct sound for a letter or reads the correct word but then changes his or her mind and rereads the letter or word incorrectly within three seconds, give the student credit for the correct answer. His or her score is penalized by using time when first naming the incorrect sound.

Importance of Sound Order

A DIBELS scoring rule for NWF states that when students read nonsense words sound by sound, they get credit for correct sounds, no matter the order in which the sounds are read, *as long as the student is pointing at the correct letter as he or she names the sound.* However, when a student reads the nonsense words as whole words, the student does not get credit if the sounds are reversed. The reason for this rule is that NWF measures two skills: (1) whether the student can name the letter sounds; and (2) whether the student can recode (blend) the sounds into words.

The earliest developmental skill measured is the student's knowledge of letter–sound correspondences. When students demonstrate mastery of this skill, they provide the names of letters, and it is not necessary for them to name the letters in order. It is adequate for them to point to a letter and give its sound. Students

---

[1] This scoring procedure differs slightly from that shown in the *DIBELS Administration and Scoring Guide.* We recommend underlining the whole word when the student attempts to read the whole word but incorrectly names the sounds for one or more letters. The *DIBELS Administration and Scoring Guide* instructs examiners to underline only the letters that are pronounced with the correct sound and to put slashes through letters that are incorrectly pronounced. We have found that underlining the entire word and putting slashes through the incorrectly pronounced letters allows us to more accurately recreate what the student answered. (Using the *DIBELS Administration and Scoring Guide* recommendation provides no differentiation as to whether the student read the word sound by sound or as a whole word.)

who are on track to become grade-level readers may know only letter sounds in kindergarten and at the beginning of first grade. At this point they may not be able to recode (blend) the sounds into a word. The benchmark scores for NWF can be met at these stages by simply naming the sounds for letters, and it is not mandatory that the sounds are given in sequence. *It is, however, mandatory that the student point to any letter when giving sounds out of sequence so that the examiner can be certain that he or she is accurately naming the sound for the letter.* (If the student does not point to the letter, the examiner cannot be certain that the student has given the sound out of sequence.)

A higher-level developmental skill is evidenced when the student recodes (blends) the letter sounds together and reads the nonsense word. In this case, if the student gets the sounds out of order, he or she has not demonstrated the ability to properly recode words, and any sounds not in the correct order are counted as incorrect.

PROGRESS MONITORING

DIBELS provides progress monitoring materials for NWF. The NWF progress monitoring Scoring Booklet has 20 alternate forms that can be used throughout the year.

Teachers occasionally report that students are opposed to reading any word that is not "real" (familiar to them). We find that it helps to show these students: (1) that bigger words such as *accomplishment* are easy to read if you consider that they are just several small nonsense words put together; and (2) that some real words might be unknown to the student, in which case he or she has to be able to read what seems like a nonsense word in order to attempt a pronunciation. Examples might be the words *jab* or *fez*, both words that might not be in the vocabularies of even precocious young children.

Once children accurately read the letter sounds, intervention lessons should be oriented toward teaching and encouraging these children to blend the sounds into words before reading the words orally. Progress monitoring assessments afford an excellent opportunity to measure the progress of the child who is moving from accurate sound-by-sound reading to reading words as a whole. (We find that a few children will get stuck in the phase where they always read sound by sound and are very accurate when reading letter sounds. Our recommendation is that during progress monitoring, teachers encourage these students to read the whole word during progress monitoring assessments *if they are ready to take that step.*)

Although the NWF progress monitoring materials are labeled for first grade, NWF words are not grade leveled and can be used for progress monitoring students of any age, beginning in kindergarten, who are receiving instruction in beginning phonics. We recommend covering or marking over the words "First Grade" on the progress monitoring materials when they are used for students in second grade or later.

The DIBELS progress monitoring chart at the front of the student booklet is designed for the months September–February only and has the words "First Grade" on it. Many teachers use NWF progress monitoring charts for time periods other than September–February and for grades other than first. The NWF progress monitoring chart in the Appendix is designed for use during any six-month time period and does not have a grade level on it. It can be customized for any grade and any time period up to five months by writing in the names of the months below the horizontal axis on the chart.

HELPING CHILDREN PREPARE FOR NWF DIRECTIONS

The directions for NWF can be confusing to young children, even those who are used to reading nonsense words as part of their core reading program. The NWF directions include 16 sentences (116 words) if the student reads the nonsense word *lut* correctly during the directions, and they include 18 sentences (139 words) if the student reads *lut* incorrectly. These are very long directions for anyone to follow, but especially for children in kindergarten and first grade who often have short attention spans and may not even know what a make-believe word is.

Sometimes, an examiner will observe that a student's NWF score was negatively affected because the student did not understand the directions. If this is the case and the student's score is below benchmark, the examiner can recommend a reassessment for NWF. Before the reassessment, the examiner or teacher may want to prepare students by explaining what a "make believe" word is and having them practice reading a few nonsense words, following directions that are given in the examiner or teacher's own words. To maintain the validity of the DIBELS benchmark assessment scores, *it is imperative that teachers do not use words from the DIBELS materials to practice reading nonsense words.*

Another reason not to use DIBELS nonsense words for teaching practice is that many of the DIBELS nonsense words do not use spelling patterns common in the English language. Examples are shown below:

- Virtually no word in the English language ends in *v* or *j*. Many DIBELS NWF words end in these letters (examples of DIBELS nonsense words are *foj* and *tev*).
- In a one-syllable word, the sound /k/ after a single vowel is almost always spelled *ck* (*back*, *peck*, *sick*, *flock*, *tuck*, etc.). DIBELS nonsense words do not follow this pattern, and often the sound /k/ in a CVC word is spelled with the letters *c* or *k* (examples of DIBELS nonsense words are *kec* and *sok*).
- The "floss rule" is not followed for DIBELS nonsense words. The floss rule is the spelling convention that the letters *f*, *l*, and *s* are doubled when they immediately follow a single short vowel in a one-syllable word. Examples of DIBELS nonsense words that do not follow this rule are *wif*, *ril*, and *vos*. (English words with these pronunciations would typically be spelled with the last letter doubled.)

- A number of DIBELS nonsense words sound like real words when they are read aloud. We do not want children to practice reading words that sound like real words and may look to the student as if they are spelled incorrectly. Examples of DIBELS nonsense words that sound like real words when they are read aloud are *kic* (kick), *pac* (pack), *lej* (ledge), *iz* (is), and *ol* (all).

Teachers need to avoid using words that do not have conventional spelling patterns if they have students read nonsense words for practice, even though using DIBELS nonsense words that do not have conventional orthographic spelling patterns occasionally for assessment is not a problem.

Some SBRR (Scientifically Based Reading Research)-aligned core and intervention reading programs include practice reading nonsense words, whereas others do not. Although we do not espouse teaching to any test, we find that, because NWF is a DIBELS measure, many teachers want to include reading nonsense words as part of their reading lessons from time to time. Unfortunately, we occasionally observe teachers who select nonsense words from DIBELS materials to use for instruction, especially when they have no other source for nonsense words. *In no case should any teacher ever use DIBELS nonsense words from benchmark or progress monitoring assessments as the source for nonsense words that are used in instruction.* Teachers who are looking for ways to include nonsense words in their intervention instruction can find ideas and activities in several sources, including a number of packaged reading intervention programs.

NWF PRONUNCIATION GUIDE

All DIBELS nonsense words are pronounced with short vowel sounds. When children encounter an unknown word, we want them to read the most common pronunciation as their "first try." In the English language, the short vowel sound is the most common pronunciation for VC and CVC words. The only exception is when a VC or CVC word ends with the letter *r*, creating an *r*-controlled vowel.[2] None of the DIBELS nonsense words end with the letter *r*, so there are no words with *r*-controlled vowels in NWF.

Some teachers in workshops ask for a review of the short vowel sounds. Therefore, following is a list of words that begin with each of the short vowel sounds:

Short *a—apple*
Short *e—edge*
Short *i—itch*
Short *o—octopus*
Short *u—up*

---

[2] An *r*-controlled vowel sound occurs when some vowels are followed by the /r/ sound. The letter combinations *ar*, *or*, and *ir* in VC and CVC words (as in *car*, *for*, and *sir*, respectively) do not have short vowel sounds.

In DIBELS NWF words, the letters *c* and *g* always represent the hard sounds /k/ and /g/, respectively, because these two letters are always at the end of DIBELS nonsense words and are not followed by *e*, *i*, or *y*.[3]

Teachers sometimes are tempted to pronounce the letter *a* in some DIBELS nonsense words as the short *o* sound because the letter *a* does sometimes represent /ŏ/ (short *o*) (or a very similar sound), especially when the letter *a* follows the letter *w* (*water*, *wash*, *wad*, *wand*, *watch*, *want*, and *wasp*) and occasionally in words of German or Anglo-Saxon derivation (*dachshund*, *Bach*, and *father*). However, the most common pronunciation for the letter *a* in VC and CVC words is /ă/ (short *a*), as in *ad*, *at*, *ax*, *bat*, *cap*, *dab*, *gap*, *hat*, *lab*, *nap*, *pat*, *sat*, *tab*, *wax*, *wag*, and *zap*. Therefore, the letter *a* is scored as correct in NWF only when it is pronounced with the short *a* sound.

The letters *x* and *q* are never used in DIBELS nonsense words. This is because in the English language, *q* is almost always followed by *u* (*u* representing the sound /w/), and words with *qu* would not fit into the VC or CVC pattern required in DIBELS nonsense words. In its most common pronunciation, *x* represents two phonemes—/ks/—when it is at the end of a syllable, and using the letter *x* would require having a CVC or VC word with more sounds than letters.

USING NWF SCORES FOR OLDER STUDENTS

NWF is given as a benchmark assessment from the middle of kindergarten through the beginning of first grade. However, NWF can be used to screen phonics skills for students of any age. We suggest using NWF progress monitoring for older students who score below benchmark on the ORF benchmark assessment if their difficulty is in decoding words. (NWF progress monitoring words are not grade leveled.) Any older student who struggles with reading and cannot achieve the established benchmark score of 50 while blending the sounds into words and reading at least 15 words correctly is likely to need instruction in letter–sound relationships or beginning phonics. (A student of any age who scores below benchmark in both PSF and NWF is likely to need instruction in both phonemic awareness and phonics.)

DIBELS progress monitoring materials can be used to measure the effectiveness of phonics instruction for students of any age. The goal for all students in intervention for beginning phonics, no matter what their age, would be to reach the benchmark score of 50 for NWF while reading at least 15 words as single units, with no sound-by-sound reading. The NWF progress monitoring chart in the Appendix can be used for monitoring older students' progress in understanding and applying the alphabetic principle.

---

[3] The hard sound for *c* is /k/ as in *cat*. The hard sound for *g* is /g/ as in *rag*. The soft sound for *c* is /s/ as in *city*. The soft sound for *g* is /j/ as in *giraffe*. In the English language, the letters *c* and *g* are soft only when they are followed by the letters *e*, *i*, or *y*.

INTERPRETATION OF NWF SCORES

NWF measures the student's understanding of two early reading principles: that letters represent sounds and that letter sounds can be blended into words. Kindergarteners would be expected to achieve an NWF score only by naming letter sounds and not by blending letter sounds into words. By the middle of first grade, when the NWF benchmark is labeled Established, students are expected to recode (blend) the letter sounds into words and not to read sound by sound. The student who cannot provide the correct sound for at least 50 letters in one minute and recode (blend) the letter sounds for at least 15 words by the middle of first grade is at risk for not reading at grade level by the end of third grade. Students who do not meet the NWF established benchmark score of 50 while reading words as whole entities by the middle of first grade need intervention in phonics to help them develop rapid processing of letter–sound relationships and the ability to recode letter sounds into words.

Students who do not process words by relying on sound–symbol relationships often use more inefficient strategies, such as relying on a few letters combined with context, to read the words they do not know by sight. This strategy often leads to misreading key words in text, especially as the child gets older and encounters more difficult text. When students read *real* words, it is unclear whether they have read the word by memorizing it or whether they understand the alphabetic principle. When students read *nonsense* words they are demonstrating they understand that letters represent sounds and that they can read words that are unfamiliar to them.

Children who have both PSF and NWF scores below benchmark need to demonstrate that they have achieved good phonemic awareness skills before their intervention instruction focuses primarily on phonics. This is because a child who cannot accurately and fluently segment and blend the phonemes in words without relying on letters will generally not be able to recode letter sounds into words. (The classic case is the student who can accurately name letter sounds in NWF but cannot blend the letter sounds into words.) Phonics is a higher-level basic reading skill than phonemic awareness. The student needs phonemic awareness (specifically the ability to blend sounds into words) in order to recode letter sounds into words. Without phonemic awareness, phonics makes no sense to the struggling reader.

Some children may score below benchmark on NWF, yet achieve benchmark on ORF. Assuming the child understood the NWF task, this profile may indicate that the child has a large base of sight words, is using context clues with relative success when reading the ORF passage, or both. This DIBELS scoring pattern is most often found in children who have high intelligence and mildly to moderately weak decoding skills. The low NWF score indicates that the child does not fully understand the alphabetic principle. This child will need intervention instruction in phonics, perhaps only for a short time, to learn that we use letter sounds to pronounce words we do not know. In intervention groups, the child will need to

183

learn to look at all the letters in the word as he or she reads, not just the first few letters or the shape of the word. The student will need to read many nonsense words and lists of words that look similar such as *wet* and *wit*, *fun* and *fan*, *lot* and *lit*, *first* and *final*, *lost* and *last*, or *love* and *live*. He or she also will need to read independent-level[4] connected text in sentences and passages orally, with the focus on reading every word accurately. This intervention instruction will ensure that the child learns good word-attack skills that will work even on those words that are not in his or her vocabulary or repertoire of sight words. Such intervention instruction also will ensure that the student reads every word accurately, not mistaking similar words such as *mast* and *most*, *thirst* and *third*, *bend* and *band*, *even* and *ever* and *every*, etc.

Students who score below the benchmark score on NWF are demonstrating that they have an accuracy problem, a fluency problem, or both. Accuracy problems are identified when the student makes errors on the words or sounds attempted. Fluency problems are identified when the student reads words or sounds accurately but achieves a low score. *Accuracy difficulties should always be remedied before fluency instruction becomes the focus of instruction.*

One caution is warranted for students who score above benchmark but are reading sound by sound or reading word parts and not blending the sounds or word parts into words. It is possible for children to be very fast at reading word parts but to lack the skill of blending the parts into whole words as they read. These children often will need intervention instruction to help them learn to move from reading words in parts to reading the whole word. It is the responsibility of DIBELS examiners to note children with this pattern, even if they achieve the benchmark score, and discuss their instructional needs with the teacher.

COMMON MISTAKES MADE WHEN ADMINISTERING NWF

The most common mistakes we observe in NWF scoring are:

1. *Giving students credit for reading the nonsense words with long vowel sounds, when credit should be given only for letters or words read with short vowel sounds.* We often observe teachers who do not mark the vowel as incorrect when the student uses a long vowel sound. All DIBELS nonsense words are correct only if they are pronounced with the short vowel sound.

2. *Giving students credit for reading the letters* c *and* g *with their soft sounds.* We often observe teachers who do not mark the letters *c* or *g* as incorrect when the student reads the sound /s/ for *c* or /j/ for *g*. The letters *c* and *g* always occur at the end of the word in DIBELS nonsense words and represent their hard

---

[4] Independent reading occurs with material in which the child can read at least 97% of the words accurately without any instruction or help. Instructional-reading-level material is defined as that in which the child can read 90%–97% of the words accurately. Material in which the student struggles with more than 10% of the words is considered frustration level (Leslie & Caldwell, 2001).

sounds (/k/ for *c* and /g/ for *g*). This is because the letters *e*, *i*, or *y* must follow a *c* or *g* in order for those letters to have the soft sound. When the letters *c* and *g* are at the end of a word, they must have their hard sounds.

3. *Allowing students more than three seconds to try to sound out a word.* We often observe teachers not using the three-second hesitation rule because they do not want to interrupt the student as he is trying to sound out the word. Teachers who do this may be lowering the student's score by allowing him or her to spend extra time on a word at the expense of having the opportunity to read other words that would be easier for the student. In DIBELS NWF, we allow students only three seconds on any sound or word, even if the student is still trying to sound out a word after three seconds.

4. *Using the prompting rule incorrectly.* We observe teachers who lead their students to the correct answer by saying "Try another sound" or by giving the prompt "That's a letter name. What is the sound?" There is no prompt for giving letter names or if the student gives an incorrect sound. The only time to give a prompt is when the student hesitates for three seconds.

FREQUENTLY ASKED QUESTIONS ABOUT NWF

1. Why aren't real words used in the DIBELS assessment instead of nonsense words?

Some students can read many real VC and CVC words using sight word recognition skills. By using nonsense words, DIBELS more accurately assesses the student's ability to use knowledge of phonics to decode unknown words.

2. When some of the nonsense words are read, they sound like real words. Why?

NWF measures the student's knowledge of and speed when identifying and blending sound–letter correspondences. For purposes of the DIBELS NWF measure, a nonsense word is any word that does not have a recognized spelling. For example, the nonsense word *kic* sounds the same as the real word *kick*. "Kic" is considered a nonsense word because of its spelling. Similarly, the nonsense word *uv* sounds like the real word *of*. A child may be able to read the real word *of* because it is a memorized sight word. However, the child must use known letter–sound correspondences to articulate the same word from the spelling of the nonsense word *uv*. As an aside, we want to remind teachers not to use these types of nonsense words for instruction. Words that sound like real words but are spelled differently should be avoided in all situations that are not occasional assessments.

3. Why is the answer correct when students read the words sound-by-sound?

One of the components of early reading skills that DIBELS NWF measures is whether the student understands that letters represent sounds. When students are first learning to sound out individual letters, we are not as concerned about whether they can blend the sounds into a word or not. If the student can blend the sounds into a word without reading the letters sound by sound, he or she will generally achieve a higher score than the student who reads the letters sound by sound. (The benchmark score of 50 at the middle of first grade is considered to be achieved only if the student is reading the words and not reading sound by sound.)

4. Why does the *DIBELS Administration and Scoring Guide* state that the answers for NWF are scored as correct if the student reads sound by sound but reads the sounds out of order?

This is probably the most controversial DIBELS scoring rule. The part of the rule that most people miss, because it is not explicitly stated in the guide, is that the student must point to the letters in the order that he or she reads the sounds to get credit for reading the sounds out of order. The authors' experience is that this almost never happens.

5. Why are all vowels short in DIBELS nonsense words?

All vowels in NWF are short because in VC and CVC words, the most common pronunciation for the vowel is the short sound. NWF measures whether students read unfamiliar words first using the most common sound–letter correspondences.

6. Why do I count *c* and *g* as incorrect when the student reads them with their soft sounds (/s/ and /j/) when both these letters can also represent the soft sounds?

In NWF, *c* and *g* are always at the end of the word. In the English language, the only time *c* and *g* are pronounced with their soft sounds is when they are followed by the vowels *e*, *i*, and *y*. Because in NWF, the letters *c* and *g* are always at the end of the word, they are never followed by an *e*, *i*, or *y*. Therefore, the letters *c* and *g* always represent the hard sounds /k/ and /g/, respectively, in NWF words.

7. Why are the letters *r*, *y*, *h*, and *w* used only at the beginning of nonsense words in NWF and never at the end?

Generally, if the letter *r* follows a vowel in a CVC word, the vowel does not represent its short sound (*her*, *car*, and *for*). In the English language, when *y*, *h*, and *w* end a CVC word, they are always part of the spelling representing the vowel sound (*say*, *oh*, and *raw*). Not including words that end with the letters *r*, *y*, *h*, or *w* allows all vowels in NWF words to have their short sound as the most common pronunciation.

8. Why aren't the letters *x* and *q* used in nonsense words in NWF?

The most common pronunciation for *x* is /ks/, and that pronunciation occurs only when the letter is at the end of a word or syllable (*tax*, *jinx*, and *six*). When *x* is at the beginning of a word, its most common sound is /z/ (*xylophone*). The letter *x* in the middle of word can also represent the sound /gs/ (*exotic, exigent, exile,* and *exhilarate*) as well as the sound /ks/ (*exhibition, exodus,* and *expanse*). Not including the letter *x* in nonsense words eliminates any confusion that might occur because of these multiple pronunciations for the letter *x*.

In the English language, the letter *q* is almost always followed by the letter *u*, with the letter *u* representing the /w/ phoneme. Because a vowel must follow the *qu* letter combination, the CVC pattern does not occur in words that begin with the letter *q*.

9. If the student reads both words and phonemes, which prompt do I use?

Examiners can use their judgment and select the prompt for the most common pattern the student is using. When in doubt, select the prompt based on sound.

10. How do you score when a child gives each individual sound correctly but goes back and reads the whole word incorrectly?

Whenever the student gives a correct letter sound response in NWF, the student receives a point. If the student goes back and reads the whole word incorrectly, that is counted as an addition and ignored in scoring. The student's score will be affected, however, because the student used time when saying the incorrect blended sounds. An example is a student who reads *pev* as "/p/ /e/ /v/" and then says, "pav." The score would be three points because the letter sounds were read correctly. When the student reads the entire word and uses the incorrect vowel sound, it negatively affects the score by taking up time to say the whole word, but no points are subtracted.

Marking and scoring for the student who reads *pev* as three separate phonemes, "/p/ /e/ /v/," and then blends the sounds into "pav" would be the same as if the student read the three sounds: p e v = 3 points. The reading of "pav" is ignored when scoring. If this is a consistent pattern, the examiner should note this student response pattern in the Scoring Booklet.

11. How do you score when a child reads the word sound by sound, giving one or more incorrect sounds, but reads the whole word correctly? (This is the opposite of question No. 10 above.)

If the word is *pev*, and the student were to say "/p/ /a/ /v/" and then say, "pev," the score would be three points because the word was ultimately read correctly, even though the phoneme given for the /e/ sound was incorrect when the student read sound by sound. The examiner should note this student response pattern if it is consistent. Marking and scoring for the student who reads pev as "/p/ /a/ /v/" and then says, "pev," would be as follows:

$\underline{p\cancel{a}v}^{sc}$ = 3 points

12. Why are there no progress monitoring materials for NWF in kindergarten or second grade, even though the benchmark assessment includes NWF as a measure in those grades?

Kindergarten and second grade children who need progress monitoring for NWF can use the first grade DIBELS progress monitoring materials. Indeed, NWF progress monitoring materials can be used with students of any age who are receiving basic phonics instruction and learning to apply the alphabetic principle. (NWF word lists are not grade leveled.) We recommend that teachers mark out the words "First Grade" when using the materials for students in grades higher than first grade. Teachers may want to use the NWF progress monitoring chart in the Appendix because they can write in the appropriate months on that chart, and the words "First Grade" are not included.

13. Why are the benchmarks for second grade NWF at the beginning of the year not posted on the DIBELS Web site?

As of July 2005, NWF scores for various risk categories for the beginning of second grade were not posted on the dibels.uoregon.edu/benchmark.php Web site, but they are included on the dibels.uoregon.edu/benchmarkgoals.pdf Web site. However, risk category scores for NWF at the beginning of second grade are the same as risk categories at the middle and end of first grade, because the NWF benchmark score is Established by the middle of first grade. NWF risk category scores for the beginning of second grade are included on the DIBELS Benchmark Scores Table in the Appendix.

14. Can students use a ruler or other marker to track words for NWF?

If the use of a marker such as a ruler or an index card is required in order to get the most accurate measure of what the student knows, then it can be used. However, using a marker is an Approved Accommodation, which must be indicated when scores are entered into the DIBELS Web site. (See Chapter 6 for a discussion of Approved Accommodations.) We recommend providing students with any Approved Accommodations, including a ruler or marker, only after the student has taken the assessment without the ruler or marker and scored below benchmark.

14

Oral Reading Fluency (ORF)

NWF Student Materials Page and Scoring Booklet Page
Benchmark Assessment, Second Grade, Beginning of Year

Figure 14-1

Having a Checkup

I don't mind going to my doctor's office. There are lots of things to do while we wait. My doctor has puzzles I like to put together. There is a big fish tank in the waiting room. It has yellow and black angel fish and a pretty blue fish. When I stare at the fish they stare back at me.

Every door has an animal painted on it. Inside there are chairs that look like zebras, tigers, or lions. Even the nurse wears a jacket with animals on it. They must like animals.

Then I have my checkup. First I stand on the scale. Then the nurse measures me. She looks in my ears. Then she asks questions about how I feel. My mother helps me with the answers if I'm not sure.

My doctor has taken care of me since I was a baby. She comes in when the nurse is done. She asks more questions. She says I look very healthy and won't need to come back until next year.

I like having a checkup when I'm not sick. I didn't even have to have a shot. And the nurse gave me some cool animal stickers.

Figure 14-2

Benchmark 2.3
DIBELS® Oral Reading Fluency

Having a Checkup

I don't mind going to my doctor's office. There are lots of	12
things to do while we wait. My doctor has puzzles I like to put	26
together. There is a big fish tank in the waiting room. It has	39
yellow and black angel fish and a pretty blue fish. When I stare	52
at the fish they stare back at me.	60
Every door has an animal painted on it. Inside there are	71
chairs that look like zebras, tigers, or lions. Even the nurse wears	83
a jacket with animals on it. They must like animals.	93
Then I have my checkup. First I stand on the scale. Then the	106
nurse measures me. She looks in my ears. Then she asks	117
questions about how I feel. My mother helps me with the	128
answers if I'm not sure.	133
My doctor has taken care of me since I was a baby. She	146
comes in when the nurse is done. She asks more questions. She	158
says I look very healthy and won't need to come back until next	171
year.	172
I like having a checkup when I'm not sick. I didn't even have	185
to have a shot. And the nurse gave me some cool animal tickers.	198

Retell:_____   ORF Total:_____

⊛ • ⊛	30
⊛ • ⊛	60
⊛ • ⊛	90
⊛ • ⊛	120
⊛ • ⊛	150
⊛ • ⊛	180

Retell Total:_____

BASIC INFORMATION

Purpose	Measures whether the student can read connected text accurately and fluently.
Description	The student reads three passages, each for one minute.[1] (The student's DIBELS score is the middle numerical score from the three passages.)
Relationship to the NRP's five essential components	Measures student's ability to read text with *fluency*.
Approximate time to administer per student	4 minutes (time for reading three passages).

[1] Although it is not recommended, some schools elect to give only one passage for the ORF benchmark assessment. This choice lowers the reliability of DIBELS ORF as a predictor. We highly recommend giving three ORF passages because the score provides a higher level of predictability as to the student's progress toward reading at or above grade level by the end of third grade.

ORF BENCHMARK ASSESSMENT SCHEDULE AND RISK LEVELS

ORF is given as a benchmark assessment beginning in the middle of first grade and continuing through the end of third grade. (It is also given in Grades 4–6.) Students who meet each ORF benchmark are on track to meet the next ORF benchmark score.

Table 14-1											ORF Benchmark Scores
	Kindergarten			First Grade			Second Grade			Third Grade		
Oral Reading Fluency	B	M	E	B	M	E	B	M	E	B	M	E
Low Risk					20+	40+	44+	68+	90+	77+	92+	110+
Some Risk					8–19	20–39	26–43	52–67	70–89	53–76	67–91	80–109
At Risk					0–7	0–19	0–25	0–51	0–69	0–52	0–66	0–79

Note: The letters **B**, **M**, and **E** stand for beginning, middle, and end of the school year.

ORAL READING FLUENCY BENCHMARK SCORES

The most important mileposts for ORF are the end-of-year benchmarks, which increase every year. Achieving the middle-of-year benchmarks will help ensure that students reach the end-of-year ORF mileposts.

All of the ORF mileposts are scores labeled Low Risk, Some Risk, or At Risk. The reason that none of the of the ORF scores for Grades 1–6 are labeled Established, Emerging, or Deficit and that none are considered final benchmarks is that students in those grades are expected to continue improving their Oral Reading Fluency rates until middle school or beyond.

A number of teachers and examiners question the decrease in the benchmark score from 90 at the end of second grade to 77 at the beginning of third grade. This decrease is because the difficulty of passages increases from end of second to end of third grade, and, because passages are significantly more difficult, many students have more difficulty reading them. A summer lag may also play a part in the decrease of the benchmark score between the end of first grade and the beginning of second grade.

DIRECTIONS FOR STUDENT

The student reads three passages for ORF. Before each passage, the examiner will read these directions to the student:

ORF Directions   Figure 14-3

Please read this (point) *out loud. If you get stuck, I will tell you the word so you can keep reading. When I say "Stop," I may ask you to tell me about what you read, so do your best reading. Start here* (point to the first word of the passage)*. Begin.*

Start your stopwatch when the student says the first word of the passage.

Let's try another one. Start here (point to the first word of the passage)*. Begin.*

ORF ADMINISTRATION RULES

Timing	1 minute continuous
Stopwatch	Start the stopwatch immediately after the student reads the first word.
	If the student reads the title, wait until he or she reads the first word of the passage before starting the stopwatch.
Hesitation time allotment	3 seconds
Hesitation prompt	If the student says nothing for 3 seconds or is trying unsuccessfully to sound out a word for 3 seconds, say the word.
	If the student doesn't immediately begin reading the next word, point to the next word and say, "Keep reading."
Discontinue rule	Stop administering the assessment if the student gets none of words in the first line correct. (The student could read all words incorrectly, you would have given a prompt for every word, or a combination of both.)
Additional information	If the student reads fewer than 10 words accurately in the first passage, stop and record the score for that passage. Do not administer the second or third passages. (If the student reads fewer than 10 words correctly in the second passage, continue with the third passage, but do not ask the student to retell the story.)
	Do not administer RTF for any passage if the student reads fewer than 10 words correctly.

RECORDING STUDENT RESPONSES

- Correct answers—Do not mark.
- Incorrect answers—Mark with a slash (/) through the word and count as an error. (Once an examiner is fluent with scoring, the child's specific error may be recorded. In no case should examiners take the chance of misscoring DIBELS, nor should examiners slow the student's reading in order to record the child's errors.)
- Skipped lines—Draw a line through any line that is skipped. (Do not count these words when totaling the score.)
- Self-corrections—If a student self-corrects an error within three seconds, write "sc" above the word, and do not count it as an error.

Other conventions of DIBELS scoring for ORF include:

- The same word read incorrectly more than once is counted as incorrect every time.
- A word with two pronunciations must be read with the correct pronunciation based on context.
- Words read out of order are incorrect.
- Words not read exactly as written are incorrect.
- If two separate words are read as one contraction, both words are incorrect.
- If a contraction is read as two separate words, the misreading of the contraction is counted as one error.
- Words the student inserts or adds are ignored and not counted as errors. (When the student inserts words, it uses his or her time, which will negatively affect his or her score.)

Counting Correct Answers in One Passage

Count the number of words the student reads correctly. This is made easier because at the end of each line is a number that represents the cumulative number of words through that line. Therefore, the examiner can use the formula in *Figure 14–5* to determine the student's score. (Some examiners make copies of this formula and use it when calculating ORF scores. They find that they make fewer errors when they use a calculator to add and subtract numbers.)

Figure 14-4   **PSF Scoring Booklet Page—Marked**

Benchmark 2.3
DIBELS® Oral Reading Fluency

Having a Checkup

I don't mind going to my doctor's office. There are lots of	12
things to do while we wait. My doctor has puzzles I like to put	26
~~together. There is a big fish tank in the waiting room. It has~~	39
yellow and black angel fish and a pretty blue fish. When I stare	52
at the fish they stare back at me.	60
Every door has an animal painted on it. Inside there are	71
chairs that look like zebras, tigers, or lions. Even the nurse wears	83
a jacket with animals on it. They must like animals.	93
Then I have my checkup. First I stand on the scale. Then the	106
nurse measures me. She looks in my ears. Then she asks	117
questions about how I feel. My mother helps me with the	128
answers if I'm not sure.	133
My doctor has taken care of me since I was a baby. She	146
comes in when the nurse is done. She asks more questions. She	158
says I look very healthy and won't need to come back until next	171
year.	172
I like having a checkup when I'm not sick. I didn't even have	185
to have a shot. And the nurse gave me some cool animal tickers.	198

Retell: _____   ORF Total: __62__

Page 16   © 2003 All Rights Reserved.

93 - *words at end of final line*
_-9_ - *words not attempted in final line*
84 - *words at bracket*
_-13_ - *words in skipped line*
71 - *words attempted*
_-9_ - *words missed (don't count self-correct as error)*
62 - *correct*

Formula to Calculate ORF Score for One Passage   Figure 14-5

Total number of words at end of last line read.   _____

Less: Number of words after the bracket that the student did not read.   _____

Equals: Number of words up to last word attempted.

Less: Number of words in any skipped lines.   _____

Equals: Total attempted.

Less: Number of words with slashes through them (except self-corrections). _____

Equals: Total number of words read correctly.

For example, the student's score in *Figure 14–4* would be calculated as:

Calculation of ORF Score for Passage in Figure 14-4   Figure 14-6

Total number of words at end of last line read.   __93__

Less: Number of words after the bracket that the student did not read.   - 9

Equals: Number of words up to last word attempted.   84

Less: Number of words in any skipped lines.   - 13

Equals: Total attempted.   71

Less: Number of words with slashes through them (except self-corrections). - 9

Equals: Total number of words read correctly.   62

SELECTING THE MIDDLE SCORE

To select the middle score from the three ORF passages the student reads, eliminate both the highest and lowest scores. Record the score that remains after eliminating the highest and lowest scores on the front of the DIBELS booklet. (A mathematical implication of selecting the middle score is that when a student's scores on two passages are the same, the repeated score is recorded.)

Examples of middle ORF scores for three students are shown below.

Student A	Student B	Student C
Passage 1—32	Passage 1—26	Passage 1—127
Passage 2—40	Passage 2—26	Passage 2—142
Passage 3—37	Passage 3—13	Passage 3—196
Middle Score = 37	**Middle Score = 26**	**Middle Score = 142**

We find that some examiners incorrectly average the three ORF scores, and others incorrectly record the score from the middle passage. Neither of these is correct. The median score is used because it is the most robust score, meaning very high or very low scores do not influence it. Therefore, statistically, the median score is the most technically sound score to use.

PROGRESS MONITORING

DIBELS provides ORF progress monitoring materials for first- through sixth-grade levels. Each level of ORF progress monitoring materials has 20 alternate forms that can be used throughout the year.

Only one ORF passage needs to be given for progress monitoring, as opposed to three during the benchmark assessment. (However, DIBELS researchers recommend making changes in intervention when three consecutive progress monitoring scores are below the aimline).

HELPING CHILDREN PREPARE FOR ORF DIRECTIONS

The directions for ORF are straightforward. Because ORF is not administered until the middle of first grade, most children have no difficulty understanding and following the directions.

Some teachers like to prepare the children for DIBELS ORF assessment by timing their reading of connected text used in classroom instruction for one minute. This helps children not be intimidated by the use of the stopwatch for ORF. Indeed, timing repeated readings is a good way to build fluency in young readers as part of regular or intervention reading instruction (National Institute of Child Health and Human Development, 2000). However, when conducting fluency instruction, teachers need to make sure that students are reading words accurately and paying attention to meaning, as well as fluency, as they read. Techniques to ensure that meaning is always part of fluency exercises might include asking the students questions about what they read or asking them to retell or summarize a passage after they are timed. Teachers who are teaching students to summarize also might include teaching the difference between retelling and summarizing.

INTERPRETATIONS OF ORF SCORES

Because ORF is one of only three DIBELS benchmark assessment measures given after the beginning of second grade,[2] many teachers assume that they should begin intervention with fluency instruction when a student does not meet the benchmark score for ORF. Many students in Grades 2–6 who do not meet benchmark scores for the ORF benchmark assessment have problems with phonics or phonological awareness. By looking at error patterns in the ORF passage in the student booklet, the teacher may get a feel for the student's particular weakness. A student who misses many words may have underlying issues with phonics or phonological awareness. A student who reads accurately but does not meet the benchmark score may need to work on fluency. A general rule is that students who score lower than 20 on ORF at any age most likely have a strong need for basic phonics instruction. Students who score higher than 40 with at least 95% accuracy most likely need fluency instruction. Students who read more than 5% of the words inaccurately, no matter what their score, most likely need help with either decoding skills or slowing their reading pace so that they read more accurately.

We recommend that all students in Grades 2–6 who have scores in the At Risk or Some Risk categories for ORF also take the NWF and PSF DIBELS measures to determine whether they have achieved Established benchmark scores for those skills.[3]

Any student in Grades 2–6 who is below the Established benchmark score of 50 and cannot read at least 15 nonsense words as whole entities accurately on NWF should begin intervention at the phonics level. Demonstration of fluent recoding of nonsense words is very important because it shows that the student has an easy facility with the ability to read unfamiliar words that are not in his sight vocabulary.

If a student with a low ORF score has a PSF score lower than 35, his or her intervention instruction should include both phonemic awareness and phonics. (Some students with extremely poor phonemic awareness need to have instruction in only sounds before they can begin to understand phonics, which is the relationship between sounds and letters.) Progress monitoring materials for

---

[2] The other two assessments are Retell Fluency and Word Use Fluency, both of which are optional, and some schools may elect not to give them.

[3] Some schools offer other diagnostic assessments to determine whether basic phonics skills or phonological skills are weak in students with low ORF scores. If other assessments are used for informal diagnosis of these skills, it is not necessary to give NWF or PSF.

PSF[4] or NWF[5] should be used until benchmark scores are achieved in phonemic awareness and beginning phonics, respectively.

Instruction in fluency with grade-level connected text and progress monitoring with ORF should begin only after students are proficient in phonemic awareness and with basic phonics skills, meaning that they are both accurate and fluent with those skills. Teachers should give periodic ORF progress monitoring even when they are emphasizing lower-level skills to learn whether the skills being taught are generalizing into improvement in the ORF scores. For children who are below grade level in reading skills, lower-grade-level ORF passages can be used initially for progress monitoring (but not for benchmark assessments), working up to passages at the student's grade level as skills progress. In order to be considered reading at the desired level, the student must achieve the benchmark score for his or her grade level using ORF materials at that grade level.

MISTAKES MADE WHEN ADMINISTERING ORF

The most common mistakes we observe in ORF administration and scoring are as follows:

1. *When scoring, not subtracting the unread words after the bracket in the last line read.* This causes inflated scores.

2. *The examiner corrects the word when a child reads a word incorrectly.* In DIBELS ORF, the examiner supplies the student with a word *only* if the student does not read the word at all or tries to sound out the word but does not complete the sounding-out process within three seconds. If the student reads a word incorrectly, the examiner does not correct him or supply him with the correct word. This convention is a DIBELS assessment technique only and is not recommended for instruction.

3. *Allowing the student more than three seconds to sound out a word.* The three-second rule applies whether the student is silent for three seconds or whether he is still trying to sound out a word after three seconds.

4. *Incorrectly putting a check or other mark above words the student reads correctly.* Sometimes teachers put a check mark above words read correctly and omit any mark from words skipped or read incorrectly. (We believe this is because these teachers are used to scoring running records in this way.) It is very important to use the DIBELS standard marking and scoring procedures on all DIBELS measures.

---

[4] All PSF progress monitoring materials are labeled "Kindergarten." Because we often use these materials for children in Grades 1–6, we mark out the "Kindergarten" label so that children will not be sensitive that they are being given kindergarten materials.

[5] All NWF progress monitoring materials are labeled "First Grade." Because we often use these materials for children in Grades 2–6, we mark out the "First Grade" label so that children will not be sensitive that they are being given first grade materials.

5. *Not clearly marking the words that the student misses.* Teachers sometimes do not put a slash through words read incorrectly or omitted and instead simply write the error above the word without using a slash. DIBELS scoring requires a slash through all words that are read incorrectly or omitted when reading.

6. *Starting the timer before the student reads the first word.* Teachers sometimes start the stopwatch immediately when they say "begin" instead of waiting for the student to read the first word. This can take two or three seconds of time away from some students who do not begin to read immediately or who read the title.

7. *Starting the timer when the student reads the title.* When students read the title, the correct procedure is to wait to start the timer until the student reads the first word in the passage.

8. *Selecting the score from the middle passage, not the median score.* We often see examiners record the score from the second passage, as opposed to recording the numerical middle score on the front of the booklet. An easy procedure to determine the middle score is to cross off the high score and cross off the low score. The middle score is the one remaining.

9. *Averaging the three scores, rather than selecting the middle score.* The average and middle (median) scores can be very different. The average score is not as robust as the median score for predicting reading skills.

FREQUENTLY ASKED QUESTIONS ABOUT ORF

1. Can we give only one ORF if the student is a very poor reader?

If the student reads fewer than 10 words correctly on the first passage, do not administer the second and third passages and do not administer Retell Fluency for the first passage. Record the ORF score from the first (and only) passage read on the Summary of Scores Page. If a student reads fewer than 10 words accurately in one minute, we know that he or she is struggling with the passage and we do not need further information. If a student reads 10 or more words correctly in the first passage, he or she should be asked to read the next two passages, even if the score on the second passage is lower than 10.

2. If the student reads 10 or more words correctly on the first passage and then reads fewer than 10 words correctly on the next passage, what do I do?

Ask the student to read all three passages if he or she reads 10 or more words correctly in the first passage, no matter what the score is on the second passage.

3. Why aren't there pictures with the passages?

Giving the student passages to read that do not have pictures is intentional so that the student must rely on reading the words and not using picture clues.

DIBELS measures the ability to decode words and to use context clues, not picture clues, to read and understand.

4. If I know a student reads below grade level, should I use an ORF passage from a lower grade for benchmark assessments?

No. Always use the ORF passage for the student's grade during benchmark assessments.

5. Can students use a ruler or other marker to track?

If the use of a marker such as a ruler or an index card is required in order to get the most accurate measure of what the student knows, a marker can be used. However, using a marker is an Approved Accommodation and generally should be allowed only after the student has taken the assessment without the Approved Accommodation and scored below benchmark. If this or any other Approved Accommodation is used, the "tested with an accommodation" box should be checked when submitting information to the DIBELS Data System.

6. If a child speaks in a dialect that drops suffixes, are those words with endings dropped counted as correct or incorrect? For example, the sentence "He *wants* to find help with his homework" is read "He *want* to find help with his homework."

Mark the word as incorrect. DIBELS scoring in this case requires taking the side of caution and marking questionable responses and answers as errors so that every child who needs intervention will receive it. If the student's DIBELS score suggests intervention and there is doubt that the student needs help with reading, then teacher observation and other assessments may be used to determine whether that student is placed in intervention.

The answer to this question is one of the most controversial among those who administer and use DIBELS. Some people believe that if the child's normal speech includes dropping suffixes, that child should not be penalized because he or she is reading what is grammatically correct in his or her dialect. The *DIBELS Administration and Scoring Guide* states that children should not be "penalized for imperfect pronunciation due to dialect, articulation, or second language interference." Dropping endings is not a case of different pronunciation. Dropping endings constitutes a misreading of the words. (In English, suffixes and prefixes carry important information about tense and number.) It is often the case that even when a child drops endings, the child's ORF score is at or above benchmark and he or she does not need intervention. When marking the dropped endings causes a student's score to be at a different risk level, the student most likely will benefit from intervention.

7. If a student is still trying to sound out a word after three seconds, do I still give a prompt or do I let the student keep trying to read the word?

Use the three-second hesitation prompt even if the student is still trying to sound out a word. It is important that the student not use more than three seconds to try to read any word. If the student is allowed to persevere at sounding out words and only two words are difficult, taking five extra seconds per word (10 seconds total) could materially lower his or her score.

8. **How do I score ORF when a student skips an entire line of words?**

The ORF score is the number of words read accurately. Because the words in the skipped line were not read, they are not counted as correct when totaling the student's score. Examiners can use the formula in *Figure 14-5* (page 191) to calculate the score, which includes skipped lines in the calculation

9. **What score do I record as the middle score if the student reads 10 or more words in the first ORF passage and then reads fewer than 10 words in the next two passages?**

You would select the middle (median) score to record on the front page. For example, if the student's scores on the three passages are 13, 8, and 9, the middle score would be 9.

10. **What do I do if a student goes back and reads a line of words that he or she missed?**

When a student reads a line previously missed, count the words read as correct. If you marked through the line when the student first missed it, you can put "sc" above words read correctly and slashes through words read incorrectly. You will need to make a note that the student read the line after skipping it so anyone looking at the Scoring Booklet understands what happened.

11. **Do you have to give the "official" directions for all three ORF measures?**

Yes, examiners need to read the directions for all three ORF passages during a benchmark assessment. (The *DIBELS Administration and Scoring Guide* is silent on this issue. We consulted the DIBELS creators on this, and they stated that the ORF directions must be read for all three passages.)

12. **Where in the *DIBELS Administration and Scoring Guide* does it say to give three ORF and RTF measures?**

This is an unintentional omission from the *DIBELS Administration and Scoring Guide*. The scoring rules for ORF in the *DIBELS Administration and Scoring Guide* include the following rules, which imply that three ORF and RTF measures are to be given:
- "If the student reads 3 passages, record his/her middle score on the front cover."
- "If the student reads fewer than 10 words correct on the first passage, record his/her score on the front cover and do not administer passages 2 and 3."

13. **Why are three ORF and RTF measures administered during the benchmark screening?**

The statistical reliability of ORF increases if three passages are read, as opposed to only one passage. The increase is significant enough that most schools elect to administer three passages rather than one. Another reason for administering three passages is that ORF scores are sensitive to differences in passage difficulty and differences in student interests. Administering three passages helps to control for variability in scores due to passage difficulty or interest.

14. **If I give three ORF passages during the benchmark assessment and make a mistake on one, can I use one of the two ORF scores that are valid, or do I have to give a retest?**

To be a purist, you should use a progress monitoring ORF passage to give a retest for the one ORF passage that was administered incorrectly. However, we know examiners are busy and often don't have time to go back and give retests. Our recommendation is to record the average of the two valid scores *if they both place the student in the same risk category*. If the two valid scores place the student in different risk categories, use an ORF progress monitoring passage to obtain a valid third score and record the middle (median) of the three scores.

15. **Do I score ORF before or after giving RTF? The *DIBELS Administration and Scoring Guide* and the Sopris West video say to score ORF "immediately after administering it," which implies that ORF should be scored before RTF is given.**

Do not score ORF before administering RTF. We believe that the *DIBELS Administration and Scoring Guide* and the video mean to imply that the examiner should be sure to mark the ORF passage accurately but not to count the score. (Marking the passage accurately includes placing a bracket after the last word read or attempted.)

16. **Why is the benchmark score for ORF lower at the beginning of third grade than at the end of second grade?**

DIBELS benchmarks are determined statistically by looking at scores for thousands of children who tested as reading at grade level at the end of third grade. The statistical analysis used yielded the numbers shown as benchmarks for each grade. The reason for the decrease in the benchmark score from 90 at the end of second grade to 77 at the beginning of third grade is attributed to the fact that the difficulty level of the passages increases from school end-of-second to end-of-third grade and, possibly, to a regression in skills over the summer.

17. **Why do DIBELS passages show the title when the student is not expected to read it?**

We are not certain why the title is included for ORF passages. It may be because the title helps the passage look like "real" text. Because the examiner points to the first word while reading the directions and saying, "Start here," most students do not read the title aloud.

18. Are the ORF passages written at grade level? Do the passages get more difficult from the beginning of the year to the end of the year?

Yes, all ORF passages in any grade are at the end-of-year grade level for that year. (The exception is first grade, with ORF passages at the beginning of second grade difficulty level.) The passages do not increase in difficulty from the beginning to the end of the year. DIBELS researchers took great care to determine the grade level of the passages and to reduce as much as possible the differences in passage difficulty at each grade level. The grade level for ORF passages was determined by using several readability formulas. Passages that were closest to the appropriate grade-level readability for the end of the year were selected for all benchmark periods. When minor differences based on one or more readability formulas were noted among the three passages in any benchmark assessments, the three passages were ordered from easiest to most difficult. (It is important to note that the readability-level differences among any ORF passages within a grade level are very minor, whether the passages are from benchmark assessments or progress monitoring.)

Retell Fluency (RTF)

Figure 15-1

RTF Student Booklet Page
Benchmark Assessment Sample Page, Second Grade, Beginning of Year

No Retell Student Materials / Student responds
to RTF directions immediately after reading ORF.

Benchmark 2.3
DIBELS® Oral Reading Fluency

Having a Checkup

I don't mind going to my doctor's office. There are lots of	12
things to do while we wait. My doctor has puzzles I like to put	26
together. There is a big fish tank in the waiting room. It has	39
yellow and black angel fish and a pretty blue fish. When I stare	52
at the fish they stare back at me.	60
Every door has an animal painted on it. Inside there are	71
chairs that look like zebras, tigers, or lions. Even the nurse wears	83
a jacket with animals on it. They must like animals.	93
Then I have my checkup. First I stand on the scale. Then the	106
nurse measures me. She looks in my ears. Then she asks	117
questions about how I feel. My mother helps me with the	128
answers if I'm not sure.	133
My doctor has taken care of me since I was a baby. She	146
comes in when the nurse is done. She asks more questions. She	158
says I look very healthy and won't need to come back until next	171
year.	172
I like having a checkup when I'm not sick. I didn't even have	185
to have a shot. And the nurse gave me some cool animal tickers.	198

Retell: _____ ORF Total: _____

⊗ • ✳	30
⊗ • ✳	60
⊗ • ✳	90
⊗ • ✳	120
⊗ • ✳	150
⊗ • ✳	180

Retell Total: _____

Page 16 © 2003 All Rights Reserved.

BASIC INFORMATION

Purpose	Measures the student's ability to tell about what was read in the ORF passage. Identifies the student who can read accurately and with speed but who does not comprehend or remember what was read.
Description	The student tells everything he or she can remember about the passage read. The examiner counts the total number of "on track" words the student uses in one minute.
Relationship to the NRP's five essential components	Measures student's reading comprehension.
Approximate time to administer per student	1.5 minutes (retelling three passages)
Additional information	Retell Fluency is an optional measure. The RTF risk level is indicated by a percentage. When RTF is lower than 25% of ORF, the student is At Risk for having difficulty with comprehension. There is no Some Risk level for RTF. The RTF measure is considered reliable and valid when the student's ORF score is 40 or higher. Do not administer RTF if the student reads fewer than 10 words.

RTF BENCHMARK ASSESSMENT SCHEDULE AND RISK LEVELS

RTF is given as a benchmark assessment along with ORF, beginning in the middle of first grade and continuing through the end of third grade. (RTF is also given in Grades 4–6.) Risk categories for RTF are as described in *Table 15–1*. Researchers also believe that children need to score at least 40 on ORF for RTF to be indicative of comprehension skills (Good & Kaminski, 2003).

Table 15-1											RTF Benchmark Scores
	Kindergarten			First Grade			Second Grade			Third Grade		
Retell Fluency	B	M	E	B	M	E	B	M	E	B	M	E
Low Risk				RTF score is 25% or higher than ORF score.								
At Risk				RTF score is less than 25% of ORF score.								

RETELL FLUENCY BENCHMARK SCORES

The benchmark cut point is when the RTF score is more than 25% of ORF. (This benchmark cannot be gleaned from the raw score but must be calculated.) RTF is the only measure with only two risk categories:

- Low Risk—RTF score is 25% of ORF score or higher
- At Risk—RTF score is lower than 25% of ORF score.

The ORF and RTF scores in combination provide a reliable and valid measure of comprehension. RTF was developed to be used in combination with ORF to measure the comprehension portion of the National Reading Panel's five essential components of reading. In general, Oral Reading Fluency, as measured by ORF, is one of the best measures of reading competence, including comprehension (Good & Kaminski, 2003). However, when the RTF score is included along with the ORF score, the RTF score provides a comprehension check for the ORF assessment. The RTF score also provides teachers with some comfort that the purpose of ORF is not simply to speed read, but that comprehension is also a factor. Furthermore, when children know they are expected to remember what they read, they are less likely to consider speed the sole purpose for reading.

DIRECTIONS FOR STUDENT

The examiner will read these directions to the student immediately after the student finishes reading the ORF passage.

Please tell me all about what you just read. Try to tell me everything you can. Begin.

Start your stopwatch. Use the same directions for the first, second, and third Retell Fluency measures.

RTF ADMINISTRATION RULES

Timing	1.5 minutes for three RTF measures. (Most students do not use the entire minute for retelling the story.)
Stopwatch	*Start stopwatch* immediately after examiner says "begin."
Hesitation time allotment	3 seconds, then 5 seconds (see prompt for explanation).
Hesitation prompt	First, wait *3 seconds* after the student stops retelling the story and then give the prompt, "Try to tell me everything you can." This prompt can be used only once. Wait *5 seconds* after giving the prompt above or after the student gets off track and then say "stop."
Discontinue rule	Discontinue administering RTF when the student hesitates or repeats his "retell" for 5 seconds after you have given the hesitation prompt *or* discontinue after 1 minute.
Additional rule	Do not administer RTF if student reads fewer than 10 words correctly.

RECORDING STUDENT RESPONSES

Count the number of words the student uses in one minute to get the score for RTF. The examiner counts every word the student uses that is related to the story. (Scoring rules are explained later in this chapter). The examiner does this by moving a pen or pencil through the numbers in the box at the bottom of the ORF scoring page, as illustrated in *Figure 15–3*.

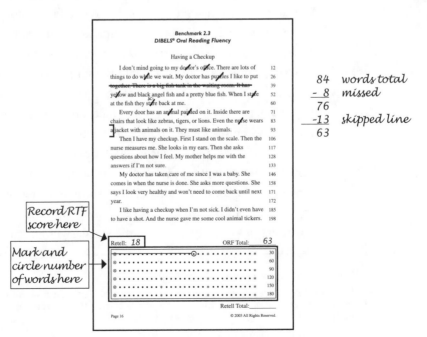

To count the student's words, the examiner begins with his or her pen or pencil on the number zero and moves it through the numbers as the student speaks. (Consider zero to be the starting place and move the pen or pencil through the number 1 as the student says the first word.) Continue moving the pen or pencil through the numbers until the student stops speaking.

The examiner circles the last number the pen or pencil is on at the end of one minute or when the student stops after hearing the prompt.[1] The score is the number circled and is recorded at the left side on the top of the RTF box, as shown in *Figure 15–3*.

The procedure for counting the words in RTF, as in WUF, only works if the examiner learns to count the words with a pen or pencil and not consciously count the words mentally or aloud. This skill takes some practice but is easily developed after administering a few RTF assessments.

Many examiners feel uncertainty about the accuracy of their scores when they begin administering RTF. One way to gain confidence when administering RTF is to team up with another examiner and "shadow score" while giving the DIBELS assessment. Shadow scoring means that both teachers score the same student. By comparing scores, examiners can talk about the differences in their scoring, and they can gain confidence that they are scoring RTF and all other measures correctly. Some examiners tape record their first few RTF practice sessions and check their word count to gain confidence in their ability to accurately score RTF.[2] (Tape recording students should occur only during practice. Tape recording students during benchmark assessment is not part of the allowable standardized procedures for administering DIBELS.) Other examiners practice with their spouses, children, friends, etc., until they feel comfortable with their ability to track the number of words spoken without conscious awareness of counting.

Description of Correct Responses

- Any sentences, phrases, or words that relate to the story count. A student does not have to give his retell in complete sentences. Individual words and phrases count as correct responses. If the student says only, "a big thing in the water," for a story about a whale, the student gets 6 points. If the student says only, "I think the story was about a whale," the student gets 8 points. If the student says only, "about a whale," the student gets 3 points. If the student says only, "whale," the student gets 1 point.

- Minor repetitions, redundancies, and irrelevancies should be counted as correct. If the student repeats something he or she said in the normal course of his retell, it counts. If the student starts a sentence and then changes the sentence, all the words he or she used count. If the student mentions something not directly stated in the story, such as "the mom was happy"

---

[1] Most children do not use the entire minute during RTF.

[2] Examiners who use a tape recorder during DIBELS practice sessions should be sensitive to whether students seem intimidated when they see that they are being recorded. If the student appears to be aware of or intimidated by the tape recorder, the examiner should not use it.

when the story was about a happy occasion for the mother, even though the passage didn't state the mom was happy, the words count (unless the student continues to talk about things not in the story).

- Minor inaccuracies count as correct. For example, if the student mixes up *brother* and *sister*, gets the events out of order, changes tenses, says *yesterday* instead of *tomorrow*, or gets the day of the week wrong, the answer is still counted as correct.

Description of Incorrect Responses

- Retelling events that don't relate to the passage is not counted. For example, the story is about a whale and the student talks about his own trip to the beach. Stop the student five seconds after you realize that he or she is off track and do not count any "off track" words.

- Songs are not counted. If the student reads about a baseball game and then starts singing "Take Me Out to the Ball Game," the song is not counted. Stop the student five seconds after you realize that he or she is singing, and do not count words the student sang.

- Recitations are not counted. If the student reads a story about animals and starts reciting "Mary Had a Little Lamb," the poem is not counted. Stop the student five seconds after you realize he or she is reciting a poem and do not count words recited from the poem.

- Rote repetition of phrases is not counted. If the student says, "there was a whale," "there was a whale," and "there was a whale," only the first time is counted. Stop the student if he or she continues a rote repetition for more than five seconds.

- Repeating the retell is not counted. This happens most often after the hesitation prompt is given. Stop the student five seconds after you realize he or she is repeating the retell and do not count the repeated words.

SELECTING THE MIDDLE SCORE

As with ORF, the middle score from the three passages is recorded on the Summary of Scores page in the Scoring Booklet. (The scores recorded on the Summary of Scores Page for ORF and RTF may be from different passages.) The *DIBELS Administration and Scoring Guide* gives no explanation as to how to determine the middle RTF score. However, Dr. Roland Good explains in workshops that the middle RTF score is recorded and not the RTF score that goes with the ORF passage that has the middle score. As an example, the scores for a student are:

Passage 1—ORF = 63, RTF = 22
Passage 2—ORF = 51, RTF = 35
Passage 3—ORF = 56, RTF = 21

Given these scores, the ORF score recorded on the Summary of Scores page would be 56 (passage 3), and the RTF score recorded would be 22 (passage 1).

PROGRESS MONITORING

Progress monitor RTF only if the student's benchmark score is lower than 25% of the ORF score *or* if the teacher thinks comprehension needs to be taught and assessed during intervention. RTF progress monitoring occurs along with ORF progress monitoring. (Only one ORF and one RTF need to be administered during progress monitoring.) The ORF progress monitoring booklets have space on the scoring pages to record RTF scores, but there is no chart on which to track RTF scores. To track RTF scores, teachers can note the RTF score and the percentage on the ORF progress monitoring page.

HELPING CHILDREN PREPARE FOR RETELL FLUENCY

The RTF directions are easily understood by most children, so there is little need to prepare the children for them. The skills measured in RTF are those that should be taught in a comprehensive language program. It is important that children learn how to retell the story as part of their comprehension instruction. Comprehension instruction also should include how to summarize a story and what the difference is. With this instruction as part of the core language arts curriculum, children who read words accurately would be learning the skills measured by RTF.

Some children who are taught to summarize as part of their core reading program may be giving summaries instead of retells, causing their RTF scores to be lower. If students have been taught to summarize, teachers should explain the difference between a retell and a summary and let students know that they are expected to give a retell during the DIBELS assessments.

It is important for teachers to understand that retelling is only one of a number of important comprehension skills that should be included as part of a core reading program. Children need to know how to retell, summarize, state the main idea, compare and contrast, etc.

INTERPRETATION OF RETELL SCORES

ORF scores alone provide some information about comprehension because students who read accurately and fluently generally have good comprehension skills. If children show risk with ORF, they also have risk for comprehension. However, some students read fluently and accurately and do not comprehend well. The *combination* of ORF and RTF scores provides the most accurate information about comprehension abilities because the combination will identify those students who read accurately and fluently but do not comprehend at a level on par with their fluency skills. In other words, a low RTF score will identify comprehension difficulties not otherwise represented by a student's ORF scores.

At Risk RTF scores are indicators that students need classroom and intervention instruction targeting comprehension skills broadly, including teaching how to retell, summarize, state the main idea, compare and contrast, etc. Because RTF scores measure a student's ability to use words to tell about what they read as well as their ability to remember what they read, some children will need intervention instruction that includes explicit strategies for helping them orally retell what they read. The oral expression instruction should also extend to other comprehension strategies.

The RTF score adds to the predictability of comprehension skills when children read more than 40 words per minute (Good & Kaminski, 2003). Children who read fewer than 40 words per minute may not have developed sufficient reading skills to comprehend well what they have read, even though their listening comprehension may be satisfactory. When children past first grade read fewer than 40 words per minute, difficulties with decoding or fluency may be the cause of their inability to recall what they read. Because children in first grade are learning to decode and are expected to devote attention to decoding and fluency, ORF scores at or lower than 40 may indicate that their decoding skills, fluency skills, or both are developing and that their slow reading may negatively affect their ability to retell a passage.

Most students who have pure comprehension issues have very low RTF scores, often using fewer than 10% of the words they read in ORF, in spite of reading the words accurately and rapidly enough to meet or exceed the DIBELS ORF benchmark scores. Students who have a ratio of RTF to ORF scores lower than 25% fall in the At Risk category and are likely to be demonstrating either poor comprehension or poor oral expressive skills. The At Risk category is one that needs special attention when developing targeted intervention instruction. Children in this category may need further diagnostic assessment for comprehension skills, especially if their RTF scores do not improve quickly in intervention lessons.

MISTAKES MADE WHEN ADMINISTERING RETELL

1. *Examiners try to verbally or mentally count the words, causing the examiner to lose his place or get behind when scoring.* The proper way to count the words is for the examiner to move a pen or pencil over the numbers as the student speaks. When examiners try to explicitly count the words, they inevitably lose track when the student's answer is more than a few words.

2. *Examiners are too strict on the interpretation of what is counted as a correct answer.* We have seen examiners expect perfection from the student's retell. RTF answers are acceptable when the student is generally on track when telling the story. This is because the student has been able to read the passage only once and is not allowed to look back at it during the retell. Therefore, DIBELS does not require a comprehensive and perfectly accurate retelling. The purpose of the retell is to determine whether the student understands

what he or she reads. If a student mixes up *brother* and *sister*, gets the name of the day wrong, relates events out of order, or misses retelling some of the story, we do not count that student's words wrong. The student has to be obviously off track before we do not count his or her answer.

3. *Examiners select the RTF score that goes with the middle ORF score, rather than the middle RTF score.* The middle (median) RTF score is recorded on the Summary of Scores Page, whether or not it matches the ORF score recorded on the page. The RTF score and the ORF score recorded may be from separate passages. No information is included about which RTF score to record in the *DIBELS Administration and Scoring Guide.* However, at his workshops, Dr. Roland Good is very clear that the middle RTF score is recorded, regardless of the ORF passage score.

FREQUENTLY ASKED QUESTIONS ABOUT RETELL FLUENCY

1. **Do you record the RTF that accompanies the middle ORF score or do you pick the middle RTF score?**

Select the middle (median) RTF score, regardless of the ORF score. This scoring rule is not included in the *DIBELS Administration and Scoring Guide.* However, Dr. Roland Good answers this question at many workshops.

2. **Why do we use the middle RTF score instead of the RTF score associated with the middle ORF score?**

The middle (median) RTF score is used so examiners can get a more reliable estimate of students' expressive comprehension skills. Just as with ORF, it is important to discard the high and low scores and report the middle score for a more accurate picture of students' retell skills.

3. **Do you have to give the "official" directions for all three ORF and RTF measures?**

You need to use the same official DIBELS directions all three times that you administer RTF.

4. **Where in the *DIBELS Administration and Scoring Guide* does it say to give three ORF and RTF measures?**

This is an unintentional omission from the *DIBELS Administration and Scoring Guide.* The scoring rules for ORF in the *DIBELS Administration and Scoring Guide* include the following rules, which imply that three ORF and RTF measures are to be given.

• If the student reads three passages, record his/her middle score on the front cover.

- If the student reads fewer than 10 words correctly on the first passage, record his/her score on the front cover and do not administer the second and third passages.

5. **Why are three ORF and RTF measures administered during the benchmark screening?**

   Taking the middle ORF and RTF scores from three passages gives a significantly stronger predictor of reading skills than when the student reads only one passage.

6. **Do I score ORF before or after giving RTF? The *DIBELS Administration and Scoring Guide* says to "score reading passages immediately after administration," and the Sopris West video says to score ORF "right away before moving onto Retell Fluency." I think scoring ORF immediately makes the student wait too long before being asked to retell what he or she read.**

   Do not score ORF before administering RTF. We believe that the *DIBELS Administration and Scoring Guide* and the video mean to imply that the examiner should be sure to mark the ORF passage accurately but not to count the score. (Marking the passage accurately includes placing a bracket after the last word read or attempted so that the examiner knows where the student stopped when counting the words read correctly.)

7. **Do you give credit for RTF responses that are given in single-word utterances or incomplete sentences?**

   If the single-word utterances or incomplete sentences are related to the story, they count toward the total score. A student does not have to use complete sentences to get credit for his retelling of the passage.

8. **How can I score RTF without counting the words in my head or on my fingers? This seems like an impossible task.**

   This task always looks harder than it really is. At first, the task of running your pen or pencil over the words as the student speaks is very difficult, but after practicing a few times it becomes automatic. Some examiners find shadow scoring makes it easier to gain confidence when they are learning to administer RTF. The Sopris West "Scoring and Administration" workshop designed by Linda Farrell has a practice session that helps most examiners develop confidence that they can track the words without consciously counting.

9. **Can I use a tape recorder for RTF and WUF so I can check my accuracy?**

   You may *not* use a tape recorder during benchmark or progress monitoring assessments. However, you may use a tape recorder for your practice sessions. Many examiners find this helps them check their accuracy when they practice administering DIBELS. Generally, examiners become very comfortable with their ability to record RTF and WUF scores after 5–10 assessments, and they find that they do not need to spend the extra time using a tape recorder. Many schools will require a parent's permission if an examiner uses a tape recorder, even for practice assessments. Occasionally, children will express either verbally or nonverbally that they do not want to be tape recorded. In this case, the examiner should not use a tape recorder, even during practice sessions.

10. How long do I let a student stay off track before I stop the student?

If you think the student has been off track for more than 5 seconds, say "stop," and record the score. Do not include the words that were off track in the Retell Fluency score.

11. I have a student whose RTF score is higher than his ORF score. Is this acceptable?

Yes. This happens occasionally, especially with poor readers when many of the words that contribute meaning to the passage are given to the student when he hesitates for 3 seconds. This scoring pattern can indicate good listening comprehension for a student who needs accuracy or fluency practice when reading passages orally.

16

Word Use Fluency (WUF)

Figure 16-1

WUF Student Booklet Page
Benchmark Assessment Sample Page, First Grade, Middle of Year

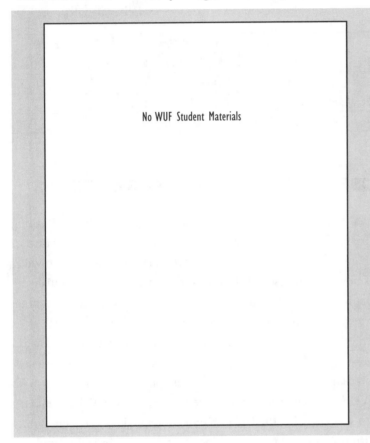

No WUF Student Materials

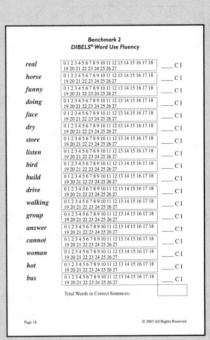

BASIC INFORMATION

Purpose	Provides an indicator of the student's vocabulary knowledge and expressive language skills.
Description	The student responds to a word given orally by the examiner by using the word accurately in an oral response or giving a definition or synonym.
Relationship to the NRP's five essential components	Measures student's vocabulary.
Approximate time to administer per student	1.5 minutes
Additional information	WUF is an optional measure. Validated national norms have not been established, and schools, districts, or states electing to use this measure will need to develop risk levels based on local norms. Schools and districts using the DIBELS Data System get local norms on their reports. Because WUF is optional and does not have validated national norms, some schools elect to use other assessment tools to screen for vocabulary.

WUF BENCHMARK ASSESSMENT SCHEDULE AND RISK LEVELS

WUF is given as a benchmark assessment in all grades at all benchmark assessment periods. The risk categories that DIBELS researchers recommend for WUF are as described in *Table 16–1*.

Table 16-1												WUF Benchmark Scores
WUF Fluency	**Kindergarten**			**First Grade**			**Second Grade**			**Third Grade**		
	B	M	E	B	M	E	B	M	E	B	M	E
Low Risk	Students above 40th percentile, based on local scores											
Some Risk	Students in 20th–40th percentile, based on local scores											
At Risk	Students below 20th percentile, based on local scores											

WORD USE FLUENCY BENCHMARK SCORES

WUF was developed to measure the vocabulary portion of the National Reading Panel's five essential components of reading instruction (National Institute of Child Health and Human Development, 2000). Benchmark scores are not provided for WUF because not enough research has been conducted yet to establish the linkage of the measure to a student's command of vocabulary as related to reading. However, there are indications in the current DIBELS research that WUF does provide some predictability with regard to the student's vocabulary and word usage skills.

The DIBELS researchers recommend that a school, district, or state use its own database of WUF scores to establish local benchmark scores. (The Summary Report, available to schools using the DIBELS data system, gives WUF cut points at the 20th and 40th percentiles.) Currently, the recommendation is that students in the lowest 20% of the database should be considered At Risk for poor language and reading outcomes. Those between the 20th and the 40th percentile should be considered as being at Some Risk. Students above the 40th percentile can be considered to be Low Risk.

DIRECTIONS FOR STUDENT

WUF directions require the student to respond by using the word *rabbit*. When giving the student directions for WUF, the examiner will read different responses, depending on whether the student uses the word correctly or incorrectly.

- If the student uses the word *rabbit* **correctly**, the examiner will respond with the words in the box on the left ("Very good.") and then say the words beneath the boxes ("OK. Here is your first word.") before giving the student the first word.

- If the student uses the word *rabbit* **incorrectly** or **does not respond** at all after three seconds have elapsed, the examiner will respond with the words in the box on the right

> ### Listen to me use the word "rabbit." (pause) "The rabbit is eating a carrot." Your turn. "Rabbit."

and then give the student a second chance to respond. Whether the student's second response is correct, incorrect, or to say nothing, the examiner continues by saying the words beneath the boxes

> ### OK. Here is your first word.

and then gives the student the first word on the scoring page.

Some examiners notice that there are two versions of directions for DIBELS WUF in different Scoring Booklets, depending on the edition. One version includes the words "in a sentence" in the next-to-last sentence, which reads "Your turn to use a word in a sentence." The other version excludes the words "in a sentence," and the next-to-last sentence reads, "Your turn to use a word." Currently, the DIBELS creators have not reached a decision about which version they recommend[1] although the most recent versions omit the words "in a sentence."

The reason for the two different versions of directions is that, when the first WUF directions included the words "in a sentence," some examiners and teachers noticed and believed that the directions were inaccurate. This is because technically an answer that is not a complete sentence is acceptable if it is a definition or gives an indication that the student understands the meaning of the word. (For example, both "hopping animal" and "hare" would be correct responses for the word *rabbit* even though neither answer is a complete sentence.)

However, when the directions were changed to exclude the words "in a sentence," many teachers believed that their students, especially in kindergarten and first grade, had understood the directions much better when the words "in a sentence" were included in the directions. Our recommendation is that the school, district, or state makes a decision about which version to use and that examiners consistently use that version.[2]

We have included the version with "in a sentence" below and on the "Directions for Seven DIBELS Measures" handout in the Appendix. Schools that elect to exclude the words may cross them out. The examiner will read these directions to the student.

---

[1] Based on comments by Dr. Roland Good at the DIBELS Summit held in February 2004 outside Albuquerque, New Mexico.

[2] Dr. Ruth Kaminski stated at the DIBELS Summit in February 2005 that using different versions does not impact scores.

Figure 16-2

WUF Directions

Listen to me use this word: "green." (pause) *"The grass is green." Here is another word: "jump"* (pause) *"I like to jump rope." Your turn to use a word in a sentence.* (pause) *"Rabbit."*

CORRECT RESPONSE: If student uses the word correctly, say	INCORRECT RESPONSE: If student gives any other response, say
Very good.	*Listen to me use the word "rabbit."* (pause) *"The rabbit is eating a carrot." Your turn. "Rabbit."*

OK. Here is your first word.

WUF ADMINISTRATION RULES

Timing	1 minute continuous.
Stopwatch	Start the stopwatch immediately after the examiner gives the first word.
Hesitation time allotment	5 seconds.
Hesitation prompt	No prompt. Give the next word.
Discontinue rule	Stop administering WUF when the student does not respond correctly to any of the first five words. (If the student gets even one of the first five words correct or misses any other five words in a row, continue for the entire minute.)

RECORDING STUDENT RESPONSES

Scores for WUF are obtained by counting the number of words that the student uses correctly in one minute in response to words presented orally by the examiner. The examiner counts the words for all responses (whether correct or incorrect) by moving a pen or pencil through the numbers in the box on the WUF scoring page. The examiner begins with his or her pen or pencil on the number zero and moves it through the numbers as the student speaks. The examiner circles the last number that the pen or pencil is on at the end of one minute.

If the student's response was correct as shown below, the examiner records the number of words read and circles the capital letter *C*, as illustrated below. (The *C* represents that the answer was *correct*.)

Student response to "nest" is "The nest is very high in a great big tree."

nest | 0 1 2 3 4 5 6 7 8 9 ⑩ 11 12 13 14 15 16 17 18 19 20 21 22 23 24 25 26 27 | <u>10</u> Ⓒ I

If the student's response was incorrect as shown below, the examiner circles the number of words used in the response, but records a score of zero and circles the capital letter *I*, as illustrated in the following example. (The *I* represents that the answer was *incorrect*.)

Student response to "nest" is "The nest is a big rabbit."

nest | 0 1 2 3 4 5 (6) 7 8 9 10 11 12 13 14 15 16 17 18 19 20 21 22 23 24 25 26 27 | _0_ C(I)

All examiners giving WUF need to learn to count the number of words automatically without conscious thought. This is accomplished by moving the pen or pencil through the numbers *without the examiner counting the words aloud or silently in his or her mind.* This takes some practice, but every examiner we know has mastered this skill with relative ease after practicing 5 to 10 times. The reason it is imperative not to count the words silently or aloud is that the examiner will use too much time counting and not be able to give the student the next word quickly enough. When this happens, the student's score may be lowered because he or she does not have the opportunity to respond to as many words as if the examiner had not taken the extra time to count the words.

WUF Scoring Booklet Page—Marked   Figure 16-3

Benchmark 2
DIBELS® Word Use Fluency

Word	Count	Score
real	0 1 2 3 (4) 5 6 7 8 9 10 11 12 13 14 15 16 17 18 19 20 21 22 23 24 25 26 27	_4_ C(I)
horse	0 1 2 3 4 5 6 (7) 8 9 10 11 12 13 14 15 16 17 18 19 20 21 22 23 24 25 26 27	_7_ C(I)
funny	0 1 2 3 4 5 6 (7) 8 9 10 11 12 13 14 15 16 17 18 19 20 21 22 23 24 25 26 27	_6_ C(I)
doing	0 1 2 3 4 5 6 7 8 9 10 11 12 13 14 15 16 17 18 19 20 21 22 23 24 25 26 27	_0_ c(I)
face	0 1 2 3 (4) 5 6 7 8 9 10 11 12 13 14 15 16 17 18 19 20 21 22 23 24 25 26 27	_4_ C(I)
dry	0 1 2 3 4 5 6 7 8 9 10 11 12 13 14 15 16 17 18 19 20 21 22 23 24 25 26 27	_0_ c(I)
store	0 1 2 3 4 (5) 6 7 8 9 10 11 12 13 14 15 16 17 18 19 20 21 22 23 24 25 26 27	_5_ C(I)
listen	0 1 2 3 4 5 6 7 8 9 10 11 12 13 14 15 16 17 18 19 20 21 22 23 24 25 26 27	_0_ c(I)
bird	0 1 2 3 (4) 5 6 7 8 9 10 11 12 13 14 15 16 17 18 19 20 21 22 23 24 25 26 27	_4_ C(I)
build	0 1 2 3 4 5 6 7 8 9 10 11 12 13 14 15 16 17 18 19 20 21 22 23 24 25 26 27	_0_ c(I)
drive	0 1 2 3 4 5 6 7 8 9 10 11 12 13 14 15 16 17 18 19 20 21 22 23 24 25 26 27	___ C I
walking	0 1 2 3 4 5 6 7 8 9 10 11 12 13 14 15 16 17 18 19 20 21 22 23 24 25 26 27	___ C I
group	0 1 2 3 4 5 6 7 8 9 10 11 12 13 14 15 16 17 18 19 20 21 22 23 24 25 26 27	___ C I
answer	0 1 2 3 4 5 6 7 8 9 10 11 12 13 14 15 16 17 18 19 20 21 22 23 24 25 26 27	___ C I
cannot	0 1 2 3 4 5 6 7 8 9 10 11 12 13 14 15 16 17 18 19 20 21 22 23 24 25 26 27	___ C I
woman	0 1 2 3 4 5 6 7 8 9 10 11 12 13 14 15 16 17 18 19 20 21 22 23 24 25 26 27	___ C I
hot	0 1 2 3 4 5 6 7 8 9 10 11 12 13 14 15 16 17 18 19 20 21 22 23 24 25 26 27	___ C I
bus	0 1 2 3 4 5 6 7 8 9 10 11 12 13 14 15 16 17 18 19 20 21 22 23 24 25 26 27	___ C I

Total Words in Correct Sentences: | *30* |

Description of Correct Responses

Correct responses include sentences in which the word is correctly used[2] and incomplete *sentences*, *phrases*, or *individual words* that demonstrate knowledge of the meaning of the presented word. Perfect grammar or syntax is not required in order for the students to receive credit for the response. In essence, either the response must include the word used correctly in a sentence or the student must provide an incomplete sentence, phrase, or word that indicates that the student knows the word's meaning.

A correct response includes correct use of the word in any of the following forms:

- Sentence in which the word is used correctly.

again	"I tried again even though it was difficult."	Word used correctly in a sentence.

again　　0 1 2 3 4 5 6 7 8 9 10 11 12 13 14 15 16 17 18 19 20 21 22 23 24 25 26 27　　_8_ ⓒI

- Question in which the word is used correctly.

ever	"Will you ever come home?"	Word used correctly in a question.

ever　　0 1 2 3 4 5 6 7 8 9 10 11 12 13 14 15 16 17 18 19 20 21 22 23 24 25 26 27　　_5_ ⓒI

- One-word response (utterance) in which the word is used correctly.

swan	"Bird."	Response shows knowledge of the word *swan* because a swan is a bird.

swan　　0 1 2 3 4 5 6 7 8 9 10 11 12 13 14 15 16 17 18 19 20 21 22 23 24 25 26 27　　_1_ ⓒI

- Phrase or incomplete sentence in which the word is used correctly.

wet	"In the water."	Phrase that shows knowledge of the word *wet*.

wet　　0 1 2 3 4 5 6 7 8 9 10 11 12 13 14 15 16 17 18 19 20 21 22 23 24 25 26 27　　_3_ ⓒI

telephone	"Talk into it."	Incomplete sentence shows knowledge of word *telephone*.

telephone　　0 1 2 3 4 5 6 7 8 9 10 11 12 13 14 15 16 17 18 19 20 21 22 23 24 25 26 27　　_3_ ⓒI

---

[2] A word used correctly in a sentence does not have to demonstrate knowledge of the word, only correct usage. For example, if the word is *happy*, the student would receive full credit for "I am *happy*." Even though this response does not indicate knowledge of the word, it is a correct response. A student who consistently says "I am…" will eventually misuse words that do not fit that particular sentence format. ("I am *ever*" and "I am *been*" would not be correct.)

- Description

turnip	"Something in soup."	Correct use of word in a phrase, although it is not a "pure" description.

turnip   0 1 2 ③ 4 5 6 7 8 9 10 11 12 13 14 15 16 17 18 19 20 21 22 23 24 25 26 27   _3_ ⓒ I

ant	"Small animal that bites."	Correct description or definition even though it is not a complete sentence.

ant   0 1 2 3 ④ 5 6 7 8 9 10 11 12 13 14 15 16 17 18 19 20 21 22 23 24 25 26 27   _4_ ⓒ I

- Definition

light	"Not heavy."	Correct definition.

light   0 1 ② 3 4 5 6 7 8 9 10 11 12 13 14 15 16 17 18 19 20 21 22 23 24 25 26 27   _2_ ⓒ I

buck	"Dollar."	Correct definition (slang).

buck   0 ① 2 3 4 5 6 7 8 9 10 11 12 13 14 15 16 17 18 19 20 21 22 23 24 25 26 27   _1_ ⓒ I

- Synonym

bug	"Insect."	Correct one-word synonym or definition.

bug   0 ① 2 3 4 5 6 7 8 9 10 11 12 13 14 15 16 17 18 19 20 21 22 23 24 25 26 27   _1_ ⓒ I

party	"Celebration."	Correct one-word synonym or definition.

party   0 ① 2 3 4 5 6 7 8 9 10 11 12 13 14 15 16 17 18 19 20 21 22 23 24 25 26 27   _1_ ⓒ I

Correct responses also may include any usage of a word that is a *homophone* for the word given. (This is because the student does not see the word and cannot know which word the examiner is reading just by hearing the word.)

per	"My cat will purr."	Correct use of a homophone in a sentence.
weight	"Wait for me."	Correct use of a homophone in a sentence.
ant	"My Aunt Vickie is fun."	Correct use of a homophone in a sentence.
bare	"A big brown animal."	Correct definition for a homophone.
real	"A fishing reel."	Correct use of a homophone in a phrase.

Correct responses also include correct use of a word, even if the student changes the *word tense, number,* or *part of speech.*

dragged	"I drag myself out of bed every morning."	Tense changed from past to present, and word is used correctly in a sentence.
friends	"My friend lives next door."	Number changed from plural to singular, and word is used correctly in a sentence.
fisher	"I was fishing yesterday."	Part of speech changed from a noun to a verb, and the word is used correctly in a sentence.
proud	"I proudly showed my report card to my parents."	Part of speech changed from an adjective to an adverb, and the word is used correctly in a sentence.

Students are given credit for a word that is inserted into a repetitive sentence format when the sentence makes sense. Examples from the end-of-year WUF list for second grade benchmark assessment for which students would be given credit because all the sentences make sense include the following:

- "I like the heat."
- "I like legs."
- "I like turnips."
- "I like signs."

However, when the student uses the same repetitive sentence format for other words in the same list, the sentences would include the following:

- "I like content."
- "I like likes."
- "I like salty."

None of these sentences makes sense, and the student would not receive credit.

When a student uses a run-on sentence, all the words are counted if the responses are correct. The examiner should give the student the next word if he or she uses more than 27 words, which is the highest number on the WUF scoring page.

| *box* | "I put my toys in a box and I do not like boxing much and my cat sleeps in boxes and I once stacked 18 boxes." | 27 points | All the words relate to the word. (This is an actual response from a very loquacious child!) |

Sentences that use incorrect grammar but demonstrate knowledge or correct usage of the word are counted as correct. This is because DIBELS is measuring the student's knowledge of the word's meaning, not his or her ability to use correct grammar.

| *happy* | "He be happy when he get new clothes." | 8 points | Correct use of the word with incorrect usage of verbs. |
| *wish* | "I wish for a new bike on my last birthday." | 10 points | Incorrect verb tense used in a sentence that demonstrates knowledge of the word's meaning. |

When a student pronounces the word differently but uses it correctly, the response is counted as correct.

| *everything* | "*Everthang* we try goes wrong." | 5 points | The word is mispronounced, but the sentence demonstrates knowledge of the word's meaning. |

When a student uses a word with a meaning applicable only regionally, the response is counted as correct.

| *fix* | "I was *fixin'* to go home." | 6 points | The word is pronounced with a regional dialect and used in a way that demonstrates an understanding of the regional usage for the word. |

When a student uses a word in a sentence with poor syntax, the response is counted as correct, even though the syntax is not accurate.

| *jump* | "The boy, she will jump a rope." | 7 points | The sentence indicates proper usage of the word, even though the student did not use conventional English syntax and the pronoun does not match the gender of its antecedent noun. |

Description of Incorrect Responses

Incorrect responses include:

- Responding with a description that does not demonstrate knowledge of the word.

  Few—"A place you sit in church."

  Ago—"Something I do when I walk somewhere."

- Sentences that do not make sense.

  Shoe—"I will ride a shoe to the store." (The usage of the word *shoe* is obviously incorrect because we don't ride shoes.)

  Spit—"I will split the orange in half and share it with you." (The student used a sentence in which the word *split*, not *spit*, would make sense. Although the child may have misheard the word, we do not know that and we count the response as incorrect.)

- Repeating the target word.—The student gets no credit for repeating the target word.

- No response.—The examiner does not move his or her pen or pencil through any numbers if the student has no response to a word within five seconds. A score of zero is recorded. Neither the *C* nor the *I* is circled, indicating that there is no response.

- The student responds, "I don't know" or "What's (target word)?"—The examiner moves his or her pen or pencil through any numbers and circles *I* to indicate an incorrect response.

Description of Words and Utterances Not Counted

Certain words and utterances are not counted in student responses. These include:

- Repeating the target word, even when the student gives a correct answer after repeating the target word. Count only the words in the correct answer, but do not count repeating the target word.

  Spin—"Spin. I like to spin around until I get dizzy." This equals 9 points (give no point for repeating the word).

- Repeating part of a sentence. When a student repeats part of a sentence, do not count the part of the sentence that is repeated.

  Doctor—"My doctor . . . My doctor is very nice." This equals 5 points (give no points for the first utterance of "my doctor . . . ," which is repeated).

- Incomplete answers. When a student starts with one answer, but then stops and begins another answer, count only the final answer.

  Wish—"I wish that . . . My wish is . . . I hope I get my wish when I blow out all the candles on my birthday cake." This equals 17 points (Give no points for the first two starts, "I wish that . . ." and "My wish is . . . .")

- Repetitions. When a student repeats a word, count only the first time the word was uttered.

  Happy—"Smile, smile, smile." This equals 1 point (give 1 point because *smile* indicates knowledge of the word *happy*, but count the word only once).

- Fillers. Fillers that are not counted include "um," "you know," "like," and other words that do not carry meaning in the response.

  Shadow—"You know, the groundhog . . . um . . . saw his . . . um . . . shadow . . . like . . . um . . . yesterday when he . . . um . . . um . . . you know . . . um . . . came out of his hole." This equals 13 points (the basic sentence, without fillers, is, "The groundhog saw his shadow yesterday when he came out of his hole").

- I don't know. "I don't know" or any variation of this, such as "I don't know the (target word)" or "I'm not sure," is counted as an incorrect answer.

PROGRESS MONITORING

DIBELS provides WUF progress monitoring Scoring Booklets for kindergarten and first grade combined and for second and third grades combined. The progress monitoring booklets have 20 alternate assessment forms for WUF.

HELPING CHILDREN PREPARE FOR WUF DIRECTIONS

Many kindergartners and some first graders are baffled by the WUF directions. Teachers can help their students prepare for the WUF assessment by teaching them during regular classroom instruction to use words in complete sentences or to give definitions or synonyms for words. This is a common language arts activity in all grades, from kindergarten on, and can be practiced in relationship to any subject being studied.

In no case should teachers use the DIBELS word lists from benchmark assessment booklets or from progress monitoring booklets to develop word lists for practicing in class. Words for practicing in class can be found in stories and other materials used in the classroom.

INTERPRETATION OF WUF SCORES

Good readers are able to do more than decode the words accurately. They are also able to understand the meaning of the words that they read in order to reach the ultimate goal of reading, which is comprehending written text. In order to understand the meaning of words, children need to have good working vocabularies. A low WUF score can indicate that a student: (1) does not have enough depth of understanding of vocabulary to achieve comprehension when reading; (2) has low expressive language skills; or (3) is weak in both areas. Especially in kindergarten, low WUF scores may mean that the students do not understand the directions for this measure. It is often the case that when teachers use the suggestions in the previous section on "Helping Children Prepare for WUF Directions," scores for many children improve. (Whether the purpose of intervention instruction is to improve vocabulary or to improve expressive language skills, it should focus on using words students are encountering or learning in their classroom instruction.)

Intervention instruction needs to be aimed at the skill that the student is missing, whether it is lack of vocabulary understanding, low expressive language skills, or both. In our experience, intervention instruction in WUF can be effective very quickly when the students are primarily having difficulty understanding how they are supposed to use the word during the DIBELS WUF measure. This is especially true for students in kindergarten and early first grade who may give antonyms, repeat the word, or otherwise respond incorrectly because they are not sure what to do. With explicit instruction on how to use words appropriately, these students often raise their scores considerably after just a few weeks of instruction and practice. (In this case, the improvement in scores may reflect better language usage skills instead of improved vocabulary.) It is exciting for teachers and students when weekly or every-other-week progress monitoring scores show immediate and rapid improvement.

Students who have poor vocabularies, whether they are native English speakers or English language learners, often demonstrate obvious difficulty with the WUF measure, and they may not respond quickly to intervention. Improving vocabulary and word usage skills for these students may take a long time, and teachers may not see improvement in the progress monitoring scores as quickly as in those for other skills being taught. However, it is always a wonderful accomplishment when students do improve their skills and raise their scores.

MISTAKES MADE WHEN ADMINISTERING WUF

1. *Examiners count the words after the student gives a response, causing the teacher to wait too long to give the student the next word.* The proper way to count the words is for the examiner to move his pen or pencil over the numbers as the student speaks, without consciously counting the words. This technique allows the examiner to give the next word immediately when the student finishes his response.

2. *Examiners forget to record incorrect answers by circling the* I *(for incorrect) at the end of the line.* When a student gives an incorrect response, the examiner must remember to immediately circle the *I* to indicate an incorrect response. If the examiner waits to circle the *I* until after the minute is up, there is a good chance the examiner will not remember that the response was incorrect and will record the answer as correct.

3. *Examiners mistakenly time WUF intermittently.* DIBELS WUF is to be timed continuously for one minute. The examiner starts the timer after he gives the first word and stops after one minute. Sometimes examiners confuse WUF with Initial Sound Fluency (ISF), which is the only DIBELS measure that is timed intermittently.

FREQUENTLY ASKED QUESTIONS ABOUT WUF

1. **Why does WUF use homophones and why does DIBELS sometimes include two homophones in one list (such as *by* and *buy*)?**

   Words in WUF lists are randomly selected from a master list of words from the *Educator's Word Frequency Guide* (Zeno, 1995). Some of the words in the master list are homophones. When DIBELS researchers discover that two homophones are included in the same list, they take one of the words out in later versions. (An example is that the homophones *buy* and *by* were included in one list, and the list was subsequently corrected in later versions of the book.)

2. **When the word is a homophone (such as *aunt* or *knows*), how should I respond when the student asks, "Which one do you mean?"**

   Say, "Use the word the best you can." If the student does not respond within five seconds, move to the next word.

3. **Does the student's answer have to be grammatically correct?**

   No. WUF is a measure of expressive language and vocabulary, not grammar. Answers that are grammatically incorrect are acceptable. For example, the target word is "written." The student's response is correct even if he says "I written a letter yesterday" because he demonstrates knowledge of the word even though his sentence is grammatically incorrect.

4. **I have had several students who "misheard" the word and used a very similar word in the response. One example is a student who used the word *once* in a sentence when I gave the word *ones*. How do I score this answer?**

   Score this answer as incorrect. We cannot know whether the student "misheard" the word or whether he or she heard the word correctly and thinks that it has a different meaning. If this happens only once, it should not materially affect the student's score. If this happens several times, count the responses as incorrect and note the pattern because a problem has been identified and further informal or formal diagnosis may be warranted. Examiners who have this experience with more than one student should check whether they are enunciating the words clearly and with sufficient volume so that the student can hear accurately.

5. **How do I score a vague response? Here are some examples from a kindergarten student:**
   - word, *doctor*; response, "I help you."
   - word, *dart*; response, "They can move."
   - word, *cut*; response, "paper"
   - word, *light*; response, "switch"

   All of these answers are incorrect. When there is doubt that the student understands the meaning of the word, score the response as incorrect.

6. **If a student goes on and on and on with a definition or sentence, can I tell him or her to stop?**

   If a student's answer exceeds 27 words, which is the highest number on the WUF scoring grid, interrupt the student by saying "stop" when he or she gets to 27 words and proceed to the next word. The student's score would be 27 points for the word with an interrupted response.

7. **Why are the words in WUF for kindergarten so hard, when the age is considered?**

   Having some difficult words allows scores to reflect the growth in children's language and vocabulary skills.

8. **If the student is in the middle of a response when the minute is up, do I let him finish?**

   If the minute is up when the student is in the middle of a response, circle the number of words used when the minute ends, let the student finish the response, and then decide whether the response was correct or incorrect, giving credit for the number of words circled when the minute ended if the response was correct.

9. **If the student is in the middle of a response when the minute is up and I don't know whether the student is going to give a correct answer because he or she hasn't gotten far enough in the sentence, how do I score the answer? For example, the word is *dozen* and the student responds, "My mother bought . . ." when the one minute time is up.**

   The student receives a score for the response only if the word is obviously used correctly in a response. Examiners should stop recording at the time the minute expires, but let the student continue if the response is incomplete so that the examiner knows whether the words used will count as correct. In the example above, the word *dozen* must be used in the response and the response must indicate that the student knows the meaning of the word *dozen* in order for the response to be counted as correct. However, only the three words said before the minute expired would be counted (or alternatively, the examiner could cut the student off after three words and not count the response. The *DIBELS Administration and Scoring Guide* is not clear about this procedure).

10. **If a child hears a word other than the word the examiner gives and provides a correct sentence for a word that is very similar, how would the response be scored? For example, the examiner gives the word *feeding*, and the student responds, "My grandmother is not feeling well."**

    The only correct answers are those that demonstrate understanding of the exact word given. A student gets no points for using a word that sounds similar to the word given but that has a different meaning (for example, *feel* instead of *fell*, *cross* instead of *across*, *ones* instead of *once*, *bit* instead of *bet*, and *fast* instead of *fist*). The examiner cannot know with certainty that the student misheard the word and did not elect to respond with a word that is in the student's vocabulary. If the student consistently uses a word similar to the one given, the examiner should note this and discuss with the teacher whether the student needs a hearing test or perhaps has another learning difficulty.

Some examiners are tempted to repeat a word when they think the student misheard it. This is not standardized procedure. Testers are responsible to clearly articulate the words with sufficient volume when saying the word. (Instead of repeating the word, the student's time is better spent moving on to another word.)

11. If the student asks me to repeat a word, what should I do?

Give the next word to the student.

12. Why do some editions of the Scoring Booklets and the *DIBELS Administration and Scoring Guide* have directions to students that are different from those of other editions?

The DIBELS researchers have tried different wording, in response to examiner comments, in order to make the directions more accurately understood by the children. Directions in older Scoring Booklets include the phrase "in a sentence" and more recent versions omit the phrase. The directions in this chapter and in the Appendix include the words "in a sentence." As of February 2005, the DIBELS creators had not determined which set of directions to recommend.

13. Is using a tape recorder for RTF and WUF allowed?

Using a tape recorder for benchmark or progress monitoring assessments for RTF or WUF is not allowed. You may use a tape recorder for practice sessions only. (Some schools require a parent's permission before tape recording a student, even for practice sessions.) A few examiners find tape recording during practice sessions helps them check their accuracy as they practice DIBELS assessments. Generally, examiners become very comfortable with their ability to record RTF and WUF scores after 5–10 assessments and find they do not need to spend the extra time that using a tape recorder requires. Occasionally, a practice student will express either verbally or nonverbally that he or she does not want to be tape recorded. In this case, the examiner should not use a tape recorder, even in a practice session.

Beyond Scoring and Administration

The primary purposes of this manual are to introduce DIBELS, to explain scoring and administration procedures, to help teachers and examiners interpret DIBELS scores, and to answer frequently asked questions about scoring and administering DIBELS.

Educators know that assessment without taking action based on the knowledge gained from the assessment scores is fruitless and a waste of time. The most important part of improving reading skills on an individual and a systemwide basis is not giving the assessment, but rather providing appropriate and effective instruction. An effective early reading assessment merely guides the instruction, and progress monitoring ensures that instruction is working as intended.

DIBELS benchmark assessment scores can provide guidance on whether a student needs additional instruction to achieve the goal of reading at or above grade level by the end of third grade. DIBELS progress monitoring scores can provide information about whether the intervention being provided is effective enough to enable the student to read at or above grade level by the end of third grade. However, to meet the early reading goals that DIBELS is designed to ensure, teachers who provide core and intervention instruction for reading need to learn and implement research-based strategies and techniques for teaching reading skills to their students.

We encourage all early grade educators and all teachers of struggling readers of any age to immerse themselves in learning all they can about effective reading instruction. They should get a heavy dose of professional development in effective and research-based early reading instruction and intervention techniques.

An important part of any early reading program is to adopt and use a core reading program that is based on scientific research. Another important part of an early reading or intervention program is grouping students appropriately so that they all have the same instructional needs. DIBELS scores and an error analysis can be the basis for placing students in effective intervention groups. Once students are grouped appropriately, they need intervention instruction that is focused on their needs. This requires teachers who have programs, tools, and teaching strategies and techniques that allow the highest-quality intervention.

We do not recommend core reading programs or intervention programs in this book. However, *I've DIBEL'd, Now What?* by Susan Hall (2006) covers the subjects of grouping students and providing intervention in depth and is recommended as a follow-up and companion to this manual.

A list of the core reading programs and intervention programs approved by Reading First states can be found on each state's Reading First Web site. Generally, core reading programs found on a state's Reading First Web site have passed rigorous review and meet the qualifications for scientifically based reading research. Therefore, these lists provide good sources for schools selecting core reading programs.

An excellent resource for information about comprehensive core programs and intervention programs is the Florida Center for Reading Research (FCRR) at http://www.FCRR.org. The Web site also covers pre-K programs, programs that may be implemented by tutors or mentors, intervention and remedial programs for students above third grade, and professional development.

When this book was written, reports from the FCRR site could be accessed as follows:

- To access the reports on core reading programs or supplemental and intervention programs:
  - Go to the home page http://www.FCRR.org
  - Click on "FCRR Reports"
  - Click on the first topic "FCRR reports"
  - Click on "Core Reading Programs" or "Supplemental and Intervention Programs"
  - Click on the name of the program for a review.
- To access a summary of all programs reviewed:
  - Go to the home page http://www.FCRR.org
  - Click on "FCRR Reports"
  - Click on the first topic "FCRR reports"
  - Go to the bottom of the page and click on "Summary Table for FCRR Reports"
  - To view the full report, click on the name of any report on the "Summary Table for FCRR Reports"
- To access a summary table of all programs reviewed:
  - Go to the home page http://www.FCRR.org
  - Click on "FCRR Reports"
  - Click on "Summary Table for FCRR Reports." In the first paragraph, click on "Summary Table."

Another Web-based resource that reviews core reading programs is the University of Oregon's Big Ideas in Beginning Reading Web site. The reports on core reading programs from the Big Ideas Web site can be accessed as follows:

- Go to http://reading.uoregon.edu/curricula/
- Click on "Oregon Reading First Center: Review of Comprehensive Programs"
- Click on "Oregon Reading First Center: Review of Supplemental and Intervention Programs.
- Click on 106 High Priority Supplemental and Intervention Programs for the list of programs, or
- Click "here" to go to a page with numerous reports reviewing the programs.
- Click the "next" icon twice to go to the third page of the document for a list of programs reviewed.
- Click the "DOWNLOAD" button next to the name of the program to get the report.

This Web site also lists and reviews supplemental and intervention programs.

Appendix

DIBELS Administration Rules

	Timing/ Stopwatch	Discontinue Rule	Hesitation Rule and Prompt	
			Seconds to Wait	Prompt after waiting
Letter Naming Fluency	**Continuous** Start stopwatch after saying, "Begin."	First 10 letters (one row) incorrect	3	Say name of letter. Point to next letter and ask, **"What letter?"**
				Note: Prompt allowed once if student says sound instead of letter name: **"Remember to tell me the letter name, not the sound it makes."**
Initial Sound Fluency	**Intermittent Cumulative** Start stopwatch after giving question and stop after student answers.	None of first 5 pounds is correct	5	None — move to next question.
				Note: Prompt allowed once if student has answered the examples correctly and does not answer a question correctly: **"Remember to tell me a picture that begins with the sound** (repeat stimulus sound)."
Phoneme Segmentation Fluency	**Continuous** Start stopwatch after giving the first word.	No correct sound segments in first 5 words	3	None — move to next word.
Nonsense Word Fluency	**Continuous** Start stopwatch after saying, "Begin."	No sounds correct in first 5 words	3	Provide sound or word. Point to next sound or word and say, "What sound?" or "What word?"
Oral Reading Fluency (Three passages for benchmark screening, unless student reads fewer than 10 words on first passage. 1 passage for progress monitoring.)	**Continuous** Start stopwatch after student reads first word in text. (Do not count title.)	No words in first row read correctly *If student reads fewer than 10 words correctly, (1) on the first passage only, score that passage and do not ask student to read more passages; (2) on any passage, do not give Retell Fluency.*	3	Tell the student the word. If necessary, indicate for student to continue with next word. (You may do this by pointing to the next word or saying **"next word,"** or both.)
Retell Fluency (Three retells, one for each ORF passage, unless student reads fewer than 10 words on first passage. 1 passage for progress monitoring.)	**Continuous** Start stopwatch after saying, "Begin."	(1) When the student first hesitates, wait **3 seconds** and say, **"Try to tell me everything you can."** Give this prompt only once. After you give the prompt, when the student doesn't say anything after **5 seconds**, say **"stop."** (2) If the student gets off track for **5 seconds**, say **"stop"** and do not give a prompt.		
Word Use Fluency	**Continuous** Start stopwatch after giving the first word.	First 5 words are not used correctly in a phrase, expression, or sentence	5	Give the next word.

DIBELS Benchmark Scores

	Beginning of Year		Middle of Year		End of Year	
	Score	Status	Score	Status	Score	Status

Kindergarten

	Score	Status	Score	Status	Score	Status
Initial Sound Fluency	0–3	At Risk	0–9	Deficit		
	4–7	Some Risk	10–24	Emerging		
	8+	Low Risk	25+	Established		
Letter Naming Fluency	0–1	At Risk	0–14	At Risk	0–28	At Risk
	2–7	Some Risk	15–26	Some Risk	29–39	Some Risk
	8+	Low Risk	27+	Low Risk	40+	Low Risk
Phoneme Segmentation Fluency			0–6	At Risk	0–9	Deficit
			7–17	Some Risk	10–34	Emerging
			18+	Low Risk	35+	Established
Nonsense Word Fluency			0–4	At Risk	0–14	At Risk
			5–12	Some Risk	15–24	Some Risk
			13+	Low Risk	25+	Low Risk
Word Use Fluency (optional)	No benchmark goals are established. The informal goal is for students in the lowest 20th percentile of a district to be considered At Risk; those between the 20th and the 40th percentile, Some Risk; and those above the 40th percentile, Low Risk.					

First Grade

	Score	Status	Score	Status	Score	Status
Letter Naming Fluency	0–24	At Risk				
	25–36	Some Risk				
	37+	Low Risk				
Phoneme Segmentation Fluency	0–9	Deficit	0–9	Deficit	0–9	Deficit
	10–34	Emerging	10–34	Emerging	10–34	Emerging
	35+	Established	35+	Established	35+	Established
Nonsense Word Fluency	0–12	At Risk	0–29	Deficit	0–29	Deficit
	13–23	Some Risk	30–49	Emerging	30–49	Emerging
	24+	Low Risk	50+ and reads 15 whole words accurately	Established	50+ and reads 15 whole words accurately	Established
Oral Reading Fluency			0–7	At Risk	0–19	At Risk
			8–19	Some Risk	20–39	Some Risk
			20+	Low Risk	40+	Low Risk
Retell Fluency (optional)			At Risk—RTF score lower than 25% of ORF Low Risk—RTF score 25% of ORF or higher			
Word Use Fluency (optional)	Word Use Fluency is the same as that for kindergarten.					

DIBELS Benchmark Scores

	Beginning of Year		Middle of Year		End of Year	
	Score	Status	Score	Status	Score	Status

Second Grade

Nonsense Word Fluency	0–29	Deficit				
	30–49	Emerging				
	50+ and reads 15+ whole words accurately	Established				
Phoneme Segmentation Fluency	0–25	At Risk	0–51	At Risk	0–69	At Risk
	26–43	Some Risk	52–67	Some Risk	70–89	Some Risk
	44+	Low Risk	68+	Low Risk	90+	Low Risk
Retell Fluency and Word Use Fluency (optional)	Retell Fluency is the same as that for first grade; Word Use Fluency is the same as that for kindergarten.					

Third Grade

Oral Reading Fluency	0–52	At Risk	0–66	At Risk	0–79	At Risk
	53–76	Some Risk	67–91	Some Risk	80–109	Some Risk
	77+	Low Risk	92+	Low Risk	110+	Low Risk
Retell Fluency and Word Use Fluency (optional)	Retell Fluency is the same as that for first grade; Word Use Fluency is the same as that for kindergarten.					

Fourth Grade

Oral Reading Fluency	0–70	At Risk	0–82	At Risk	0–95	At Risk
	71–92	Some Risk	83–104	Some Risk	96–117	Some Risk
	93+	Low Risk	105+	Low Risk	118+	Low Risk

Fifth Grade

Oral Reading Fluency	0–80	At Risk	0–93	At Risk	0–102	At Risk
	81–103	Some Risk	94–114	Some Risk	103–123	Some Risk
	104+	Low Risk	115+	Low Risk	124+	Low Risk

Sixth Grade

Oral Reading Fluency	0–82	At Risk	0–98	At Risk	0–103	At Risk
	83–108	Some Risk	99–119	Some Risk	104–124	Some Risk
	109+	Low Risk	120+	Low Risk	125+	Low Risk

Note: The categories of At Risk, Some Risk, and Low Risk are used when progress toward an established predicting benchmark is being measured. The score demarcating Low Risk is called the target score. The categories of Deficit, Emerging, and Established are used when the established final predicting benchmark for that task is being measured. The score demarcating Established is called the benchmark score.

Note: Goals and cut points for risk for grades 4–6 are based on CBM normative information from 4th and 5th grade students in the fall, winter, and spring from Hasbrouck and Tindal (1992) as well as the average slope of reading progress information from Fuchs, Fuchs, Hamlett, Walz, & Germann (1993). Empirical evidence of the percentage of achieving subsequent literacy goals is not yet available for these initial estimates. In addition to these preliminary estimates of goals and risk indicators, local normative information is available for each participating school district. A reasonable approximation of goals and cut scores for risk is also available from the local norms. The 40th percentile using local norms provides an approximate goal, and below the 20th percentile, using local norms provides an approximate at-risk indicator. System-wide norms will be available in fall of 2004 as schools begin using these measures. With additional research, these preliminary estimates will be refined based on the odds of achieving subsequent literacy goals. Each district can examine these odds by entering scores on a selected outcome for relevant grade levels. For example, in Oregon, a state assessment is given in fifth grade with a specific goal for meeting expectations. If a participating school district enters the fifth grade scores for all fifth grade students and the Oregon state assessment goal, the DIBELS Data System will provide the odds of achieving the goal for these initial estimates of goals and risk indicators.

Available from the DIBELS Web site, http://dibels.uoregon.edu. Used by permission of the Center on Teaching and Learning (CTL), Institute for the Development of Educational Achievement (IDEA), College of Education, University of Oregon. Preliminary estimates based on Fuchs et al. (1993) and Hasbrouck and Tindal (1992).

236

SCORING PAGES FOR DIBELS PRACTICE ASSESSMENTS

By using these pages for practice, you avoid using assessment materials for practice purposes.

Directions for Practicing DIBELS Benchmark Assessments

You will give all seven measures to five students, friends, relatives, etc., who are at least at the end of first grade or older.

Use the Student Materials packet to show students the pages they need to see for ISF, LNF, NWF, and ORF. There are no Student Materials pages for PSF, RTF, and WUF.

As you give each practice assessment, record the scores on the table to the right.

Copying requirements

You may use the Student Materials from this book, or you may want to copy one set to use for the practice assessments.

You will need to make one copy of practice scoring pages 2–8 for each person to whom you give a practice assessment.

We recommend giving at least five practice assessments.

DIBELS Practice Assessments

Examiner: _____

Student #1 _____   Student #4 _____

Student #2 _____   Student #5 _____

Student #3 _____

	Practice 1	Practice 2	Practice 3	Practice 4	Practice 5
Date					
Initial Sound Fluency					
Letter Naming Fluency					
Phoneme Segmentation Fluency					
Nonsense Word Fluency					
Oral Reading Fluency					
Retell Fluency (optional)	(Optional)	(Optional)	(Optional)	(Optional)	(Optional)
Word Use Fluency (optional)	(Optional)	(Optional)	(Optional)	(Optional)	(Optional)

Practice Scoring—Page 1 of 8

Benchmark K.1
DIBELS® Initial Sound Fluency

This is comb, chicken, book, radio (point to pictures).

1. **Which picture begins with /r/?**   0   1
2. **Which picture begins with /k/?**   0   1
3. **Which picture begins with /b/?**   0   1
4. **What sound does "chicken" begin with?**   0   1

This is dog, stairs, moon, bear (point to pictures).

5. **Which picture begins with /b/?**   0   1
6. **Which picture begins with /st/?**   0   1
7. **Which picture begins with /m/?**   0   1
8. **What sound does "dog" begin with?**   0   1

This is bed, house, fish, chair (point to pictures).

9. **Which picture begins with /ch/?**   0   1
10. **Which picture begins with /h/?**   0   1
11. **Which picture begins with /b/?**   0   1
12. **What sound does "fish" begin with?**   0   1

This is swing, grass, television, fork (point to pictures).

13. **Which picture begins with /t/?**   0   1
14. **Which picture begins with /sw/?**   0   1
15. **Which picture begins with /f/?**   0   1
16. **What sound does "grass" begin with?**   0   1

Time: _____ Seconds   Total Correct: _____

$$\frac{60 \times Total\ Correct}{Seconds} = \underline{\hspace{1cm}} \ Correct\ Initial\ Sounds\ per\ Minute$$

Practice Scoring—Page 2 of 8

Initial Sound Fluency

Short Form Directions

Make sure you have reviewed the long form of the directions and have them available. Say these specific directions to the student:

This is mouse, flowers, pillow, letters (point to each picture while saying its name). **Mouse** (point to mouse) **begins with the sound /m/. Listen, /m/, mouse. Which one begins with the sounds /fl/?**

CORRECT RESPONSE: Student points to flowers, you say	INCORRECT RESPONSE: If student gives any other response, you say
Good. Flowers begins with the sounds /fl/.	**Flowers** (point to flowers) **begins with the sounds /fl/. Listen, /fl/, flowers. Let's try it again. Which one begins with the sounds /fl/?**

Pillow (point to pillow) **begins with the sound /p/. Listen, /p/, pillow. What sound does letters** (point to letters) **begin with?**

CORRECT RESPONSE: Student says /l/, you say	INCORRECT RESPONSE: If student gives any other response, you say
Good. Letters begins with the sound /l/.	**Letters** (point to letters) **begins with the sound /l/. Listen, /l/, letters. Let's try it again. What sound does letters** (point to letters) **begin with?**

Here are some more pictures. Listen carefully to the words.

238

Letter Naming Fluency
Short Form Directions

Make sure you have reviewed the long form of the directions in the *Administration and Scoring Guide* and have them available. Say these specific directions to the students:

Here are some letters (point to the student probe). ***Tell me the names of as many letters as you can. When I say, "Begin,"*** *start here* (point to first letter), ***and go across the page*** (point). ***Point to each letter and tell me the name of that letter. If you come to a letter you don't know I'll tell it to you. Put your finger on the first letter. Ready, begin.***

Practice
Letter Naming Fluency

Q	c	u	N	P	O	y	A	p	i
T	G	r	E	a	s	W	d	L	T
B	S	f	z	F	R	V	g	D	h
X	j	K	l	z	H	q	S	x	J
c	W	v	P	n	B	Y	m	U	f
q	I	r	G	w	t	C	F	w	M
H	e	R	V	y	Q	u	X	k	t
i	L	o	p	D	k	I	a	E	s
T	A	e	K	f	N	g	J	d	l
Z	x	C	Y	b	v	M	n	d	O

Total: _____

Practice Scoring—Page 3 of 8

239

Practice
Phoneme Segmentation Fluency

shine	/sh/ /ie/ /n/	birth /b/ /ir/ /th/ ___/6
mix	/m/ /i/ /k/ /s/	tell /t/ /e/ /l/ ___/7
toes	/t/ /oe/ /z/	sticks /s/ /t/ /i/ /k/ /s/ ___/8
lake	/l/ /ae/ /k/	how /h/ /ow/ ___/5
shut	/sh/ /u/ /t/	type /t/ /ie/ /p/ ___/6
pull	/p/ /uu/ /l/	love /l/ /u/ /v/ ___/6
burn	/b/ /ir/ /n/	cook /k/ /uu/ /k/ ___/6
dodge	/d/ /o/ /j/	add /a/ /d/ ___/5
walk	/w/ /o/ /k/	marks /m/ /ar/ /k/ /s/ ___/7
paste	/p/ /ae/ /s/ /t/	lamb /l/ /a/ /m/ ___/7
mint	/m/ /i/ /n/ /t/	roast /r/ /oa/ /s/ /t/ ___/8
mind	/m/ /ie/ /n/ /d/	wreath /r/ /ee/ /th/ ___/7

Error Pattern: Total: ____

Practice Scoring—Page 4 of 8

Phoneme Segmentation Fluency
Short Form Directions

Make sure you have reviewed the long form of the directions and have them available. Say these specific directions to the student:

I am going to say a word. After I say it, you tell me all the sounds in the word. So, if I say, "sam," you would say /s/ /a/ /m/. Let's try one (one-second pause). *Tell me the sounds in "mop."*

CORRECT RESPONSE: If student says /m/ /o/ /p/, you say	INCORRECT RESPONSE: If student gives any other response, you say
Very good. The sounds in "mop" are /m/ /o/ /p/.	*The sounds in "mop" are /m/ /o/ /p/. Your turn. Tell me the sounds in "mop."*

OK. Here is your first word.

Practice
Nonsense Word Fluency

f a p	a p	z i b	j o p	v i d
v o p	t i z	b u p	i b	y o m
v a d	t u p	z u g	r o g	p o b
n u d	m a b	l e p	k i b	l u d
j a d	h i g	n o p	f u t	d a p
b e m	n u g	y a d	z o d	u g
v i t	t o z	b a b	s e m	l o d
d o d	p u d	r a d	t e t	f u g
t e p	v i p	y u g	v a p	d a g
p u m	r o g	s a n	r a b	n i n

Total: _____

Error Pattern:

Practice Scoring—Page 5 of 8

Nonsense Word Fluency
Short Form Directions

Make sure you have reviewed the long form of the directions and have them available. Say these specific directions to the students:

Look at this word (point to the first word on the practice probe). ***It's a make-believe word. Watch me read the word:*** /s/ /i/ /m/, *"sim"* (point to each letter, then run your finger fast beneath the whole word). ***I can say the sounds of the letters,*** /s/ /i/ /m/ (point to each letter), ***or I can read the whole word,*** *"sim"* (run your finger fast beneath the whole word).

Your turn to read a make-believe word. Read this word the best you can (point to the word "lut"). ***Make sure you say any sounds you know.***

CORRECT RESPONSE: If the child responds "lut" or with some or all of the sounds, say	INCORRECT OR NO RESPONSE: If the child does not respond within 3 <u>seconds</u> or responds incorrectly, say
That's right. The sounds are /l/ /u/ /t/ ***or "lut."***	***Remember, you can say the sounds or you can say the whole word. Watch me: The sounds are*** /l/ /u/ /t/ (point to each letter) ***or "lut"*** (run your finger fast beneath the whole word). ***Let's try again. Read this word the best you can*** (point to the word "lut").

Place the student copy of the probe in front of the child.

Here are some more make-believe words (point to the student probe). ***Start here*** (point to the first word) ***and go across the page*** (point across the page). ***When I say, "Begin," read the words the best you can. Point to each letter and tell me the sound or read the whole word. Read the words the best you can. Put your finger on the first word. Ready, begin.***

241

Shadow and Bob

Bob liked to fly kites. It was a breezy day in April and	13
Bob was walking home from school. He was thinking about	23
flying kites as he walked home. He was also thinking about his	35
dog, Shadow.	37
When Bob reached home, he got Shadow and his	46
best kite. Bob and Shadow walked to the park. Two of	57
Bob's friends and their dogs were at the park.	66
The wind was just right for flying kites. Bob flew	76
his kite with his friends while Shadow played with the two	87
other dogs. Everybody had fun until a big cloud covered	97
the sky and it began to rain. Bob and his friends sat under a	111
tree while it rained, but the dogs kept playing.	120
Finally, the rain stopped, but it was time to go home.	131
Bob and Shadow were both very wet when they walked	141
into the house. Bob was glad when his mom gave him a	153
big hug and found some dry clothes for him to wear.	164
Shadow was happy when Bob's dad got a big towel and	175
dried him off.	178
That night Bob dreamed about flying kites with his	187
friends. Shadow dreamed about playing in the mud with	196
the other dogs. They both slept very well.	204

ORF Total: _____

Retell: _____

Retell Total: _____

Oral Reading Fluency

Short Form Directions

Make sure you have reviewed the long form of the directions and have them available. Say these specific directions to the student:

Please read this (point) ***out loud. If you get stuck, I will tell you the word so you can keep reading. When I say "Stop," I may ask you to tell me about what you read, so do your best reading. Start here*** (point to the first word of the passage)**.** ***Begin.***

Start your stopwatch when the student says the first word of the passage.

At the end of **1 minute**, place a bracket ( ]) after the last word provided by the student, stop and reset the stopwatch, and say, ***"Stop."*** (remove the passage)

If the student reads more than 10 words correct, proceed with the retell part. Say,

Please tell me all about what you just read. Try to tell me everything you can. Begin. Start your stopwatch after you say "Begin."

The first time the student does not say anything for 3 seconds, say, ***"Try to tell me everything you can."*** This prompt can be used only once.

If the student does not say anything or gets off track for 5 seconds, circle the total number of words in the student's retell and say, ***"Stop."***

At the end of **1 minute**, circle the total number of words in the student's retell and say, ***"Stop."***

Linda Likes Books

Whenever Linda has spare time, she reads a book. She   10
loves to read. Everyone knows that Linda loves books, and very   21
often she gets books as gifts. That makes her very happy.   32

Linda's sister gave her the book, **Horse Stories**. It is her   43
favorite book and she has read it five times. She has also read   56
many other books about horses.   61

Last week Linda's teacher finished reading **Tom Takes a**   70
Trip to Linda's class. Everyone in the class liked the book. Linda   82
asked her mother if she could check the book out of the library so   96
she could read it again.   101

Yesterday, when Linda got home from school she was   110
expecting to go to the library. Instead of going to the library,   122
Linda's mother gave her a surprise. It was her own copy of **Tom**   135
Takes a Trip. Linda thanked her mother by giving her a big hug.   148

Sometimes Linda daydreams about what she will be when   157
she grows up. She is quite sure she will be an English teacher so   171
that she can spend every day sharing her love of books with her   184
students. She hopes all her students will want to read **Horse Stories**   195
and **Tom Takes a Trip**.   201

Retell: ___

ORF Total: ___

Retell Total: ___

	30
	60
	90
	120
	150
	180

Practice Scoring—Page 7 of 8

Bobcats

The bobcat has a short tail. It is named bobcat because   11
"bob" means cut off. The bobcat's tail looks like it has been   23
cut off or "bobbed." Sometimes a bobcat is also called a   34
wildcat because it likes to run free and is not a good pet.   47

Like most other cats, bobcats like to sleep in the day.   58
Bobcats are like other cats because they see very well at night.   70
They wander around at night to look for birds and small   81
animals to eat. Because they see so well, hunting at night gives   93
them an advantage over other animals.   99

Bobcats are not much larger than a common housecat.   108
Bobcats are 25 to 30 inches long, while common housecats are   119
15 to 20 inches long. Bobcats weigh from 15 to 35 pounds, while   132
common housecats weigh from 7 to 20 pounds.   140

Bobcats are brown with black spots and a white belly.   150
The bobcat's tail is black at the end. The bobcat's coloring   161
helps it hide from other animals because it can blend in with   173
dirt and trees.   176

We call the bobcat's home a "den." Bobcats make their   186
dens in hollow logs and caves. They love to sun themselves on   198
top of flat rocks. They often run along the top of hills.   210

Retell: ___

ORF Total: ___

Retell Total: ___

	30
	60
	90
	120
	150
	180

Word Use Fluency

Short Form Directions

Make sure you have reviewed the long form of the directions and have them available. Say these specific directions to the student:

Listen to me use this word: "green." (pause) *"The grass is green." Here is another word: "jump."* (pause) *"I like to jump rope." Your turn to use a word.** (pause) *"Rabbit."*

CORRECT RESPONSE: If student uses the word correctly in a phrase, say	INCORRECT RESPONSE: If student gives any other response, say
Very good.	*Listen to me use the word "rabbit."* (pause) *"The rabbit is eating a carrot." Your turn. "Rabbit."*

OK. Here is your first word.

*Adding the words "in a sentence" is optional.

Practice
Word Use Fluency

Word	Scale		
talk	0 1 2 3 4 5 6 7 8 9 10 11 12 13 14 15 16 17 18 19 20 21 22 23 24 25 26 27	___	C I
two	0 1 2 3 4 5 6 7 8 9 10 11 12 13 14 15 16 17 18 19 20 21 22 23 24 25 26 27	___	C I
cookie	0 1 2 3 4 5 6 7 8 9 10 11 12 13 14 15 16 17 18 19 20 21 22 23 24 25 26 27	___	C I
until	0 1 2 3 4 5 6 7 8 9 10 11 12 13 14 15 16 17 18 19 20 21 22 23 24 25 26 27	___	C I
nurse	0 1 2 3 4 5 6 7 8 9 10 11 12 13 14 15 16 17 18 19 20 21 22 23 24 25 26 27	___	C I
long	0 1 2 3 4 5 6 7 8 9 10 11 12 13 14 15 16 17 18 19 20 21 22 23 24 25 26 27	___	C I
happy	0 1 2 3 4 5 6 7 8 9 10 11 12 13 14 15 16 17 18 19 20 21 22 23 24 25 26 27	___	C I
play	0 1 2 3 4 5 6 7 8 9 10 11 12 13 14 15 16 17 18 19 20 21 22 23 24 25 26 27	___	C I
tomorrow	0 1 2 3 4 5 6 7 8 9 10 11 12 13 14 15 16 17 18 19 20 21 22 23 24 25 26 27	___	C I
truck	0 1 2 3 4 5 6 7 8 9 10 11 12 13 14 15 16 17 18 19 20 21 22 23 24 25 26 27	___	C I
that	0 1 2 3 4 5 6 7 8 9 10 11 12 13 14 15 16 17 18 19 20 21 22 23 24 25 26 27	___	C I
food	0 1 2 3 4 5 6 7 8 9 10 11 12 13 14 15 16 17 18 19 20 21 22 23 24 25 26 27	___	C I
her	0 1 2 3 4 5 6 7 8 9 10 11 12 13 14 15 16 17 18 19 20 21 22 23 24 25 26 27	___	C I
yellow	0 1 2 3 4 5 6 7 8 9 10 11 12 13 14 15 16 17 18 19 20 21 22 23 24 25 26 27	___	C I
safe	0 1 2 3 4 5 6 7 8 9 10 11 12 13 14 15 16 17 18 19 20 21 22 23 24 25 26 27	___	C I
face	0 1 2 3 4 5 6 7 8 9 10 11 12 13 14 15 16 17 18 19 20 21 22 23 24 25 26 27	___	C I
miss	0 1 2 3 4 5 6 7 8 9 10 11 12 13 14 15 16 17 18 19 20 21 22 23 24 25 26 27	___	C I
apple	0 1 2 3 4 5 6 7 8 9 10 11 12 13 14 15 16 17 18 19 20 21 22 23 24 25 26 27	___	C I

Total Words in Correct Sentences: _____

STUDENT MATERIALS FOR
DIBELS PRACTICE ASSESSMENTS

Dynamic Indicators of Basic Early Literacy Skills™ 6th Ed.

Kindergarten—Initial Sound Fluency

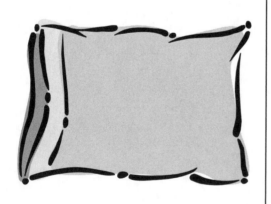

ISF Practice Pictures – 1

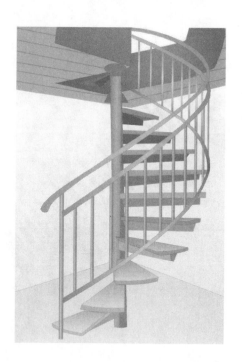

ISF Practice Pictures – 2

Student Materials for Practice

Page 3

ISF Practice Pictures – 3　　　　　　　　Student Materials for Practice

250

Q c u N P O y A p i

T G r E a s W d L T

B S f z F R V g D h

X j K l z H q S x J

c W v P n B Y m U f

q I r G w t C F w M

H e R V y Q u X k t

i L o p D k I a E s

T A e K f N g J d l

Z x C Y b v M n d O

PHONEME SEGMENTATION FLUENCY

No Student Materials are required for this measure.

sim   lut

fap	ap	zib	jop	vid
vop	tiz	bup	ib	yom
vad	tup	zug	rog	pob
nud	mab	lep	kib	lud
jad	hig	nop	fut	dap
bem	nug	yad	zod	ug
vit	toz	bab	sem	lod
dod	pud	rad	tet	fug
tep	vip	yug	vap	dag
pum	rog	san	rab	nin

NWF Practice   Student Materials for Practice

Shadow and Bob

Bob liked to fly kites. It was a breezy day in April and Bob was walking home from school. He was thinking about flying kites as he walked home. He was also thinking about his dog, Shadow.

When Bob reached home, he got Shadow and his best kite. Bob and Shadow walked to the park. Two of Bob's friends and their dogs were at the park.

The wind was just right for flying kites. Bob flew his kite with his friends while Shadow played with the two other dogs. Everybody had fun until a big cloud covered the sky and it began to rain. Bob and his friends sat under a tree while it rained, but the dogs kept playing.

Finally, the rain stopped, but it was time to go home. Bob and Shadow were both very wet when they walked into the house. Bob was glad when his mom gave him a big hug and found some dry clothes for him to wear. Shadow was happy when Bob's dad got a big towel and dried him off.

That night Bob dreamed about flying kites with his friends. Shadow dreamed about playing in the mud with the other dogs. They both slept very well.

Bobcats

The bobcat has a short tail. It is named bobcat because "bob" means cut off. The bobcat's tail looks like it has been cut off or "bobbed". Sometimes a bobcat is also called a wildcat because it likes to run free and is not a good pet.

Like most other cats, bobcats like to sleep in the day. Bobcats are like other cats because they see very well at night. They wander around at night to look for birds and small animals to eat. Because they see so well, hunting at night gives them an advantage over other animals.

Bobcats are not much larger than a common housecat. Bobcats are 25 to 30 inches long, while common housecats are 15 to 20 inches long. Bobcats weigh from 15 to 35 pounds, while common housecats weigh from 7 to 20 pounds.

Bobcats are brown with black spots and a white belly. The bobcat's tail is black at the end. The bobcat's coloring helps it hide from other animals because it can blend in with dirt and trees.

We call the bobcat's home a "den." Bobcats make their dens in hollow logs and caves. They love to sun themselves on top of flat rocks. They often run along the top of hills.

Linda Likes Books

Whenever Linda has spare time, she reads a book. She loves to read. Everyone knows that Linda loves books, and very often she gets books as gifts. That makes her very happy.

Linda's sister gave her the book, **Horse Stories**. It is her favorite book and she has read it five times. She has also read many other books about horses.

Last week Linda's teacher finished reading **Tom Takes a Trip** to Linda's class. Everyone in the class liked the book. Linda asked her mother if she could check the book out of the library so she could read it again.

Yesterday, when Linda got home from school she was expecting to go to the library. Instead of going to the library, Linda's mother gave her a surprise. It was her own copy of **Tom Takes a Trip**. Linda thanked her mother by giving her a big hug.

Sometimes Linda daydreams about what she will be when she grows up. She is quite sure she will be an English teacher so that she can spend every day sharing her love of books with her students. She hopes all her students will want to read **Horse Stories** and **Tom Takes a Trip**.

RETELL FLUENCY AND WORD USE FLUENCY

No Student Materials are required for these measures.

DIRECTIONS FOR SEVEN DIBELS MEASURES

Initial Sound Fluency

This is mouse, flowers, pillow, letters (point to each picture while saying its name). *Mouse* (point to mouse) *begins with the sound /m/. Listen, /m/, mouse. Which one begins with the sounds /fl/?*

CORRECT RESPONSE: Student points to flowers, you say	INCORRECT RESPONSE: If student gives any other response, you say
Good. Flowers begins with the sounds /fl/.	*Flowers* (point to flowers) *begins with the sounds /fl/. Listen, /fl/, flowers. Let's try it again. Which one begins with the sounds /fl/?*

Pillow (point to pillow) *begins with the sound /p/. Listen, /p/, pillow. What sound does letters* (point to letters) *begin with?*

CORRECT RESPONSE: Student says /l/, you say	INCORRECT RESPONSE: If student gives any other response, you say
Good. Letters begins with the sound /l/.	*Letters* (point to letters) *begins with the sound /l/. Listen, /l/, letters. Let's try it again. What sound does letters* (point to letters) *begin with?*

Here are some more pictures. Listen carefully to the words.

Show the student the first page of pictures. Ask the questions in the Scoring Booklet.

Timing is intermittent. After you finish asking the question, begin your stopwatch. Stop your stopwatch as soon as the child responds.

<u>Discontinue rule</u> – None of the first 5 responses is correct.

<u>Hesitation rule</u> – 5 seconds – No prompt. Move to next question.

Letter Naming Fluency

Here are some letters (point to the page with the letters). *Tell me the names of as many letters as you can. When I say "Begin," start here* (point to first letter), *and go across the page* (underline the first row with your finger). *Point to each letter and tell me the name of that letter. If you come to a letter you don't know, I'll tell it to you. Put your finger on the first letter. Ready, begin.* Start your stopwatch after you say "begin."

<u>Discontinue rule</u> – First 10 letters incorrect (first line).

<u>Hesitation rule</u> – 3 seconds – Say name of letter. Point to next letter and ask, "What letter?"

If student says sound instead of letter name: – One time only prompt – "Remember to tell me the letter name, not the sound it makes."

Phoneme Segmentation Fluency

I am going to say a word. After I say it, you tell me all the sounds in the word. So, if I say "sam," you would say /s/ /a/ /m/. Let's try one (one-second pause). *Tell me the sounds in "mop."*

CORRECT RESPONSE: If student says /m/ /o/ /p/, you say	INCORRECT OR NO RESPONSE: If student gives any other response, you say
Very good, the sounds in "mop" are /m/ /o/ /p/.	*The sounds in "mop" are /m/ /o/ /p/. Your turn. Tell me the sounds in "mop."*

OK. Here is your first word.

Give the student the first word and start your stopwatch.

After one minute, say "Stop."

<u>Discontinue rule</u> – No correct sound segments in the first 5 words.

<u>Hesitation rule</u> – 3 seconds – No prompt. Move to next word.

260

Nonsense Word Fluency

Look at this word (point to first word on practice page). *It's a make-believe word. Watch me read the word: /s/ /i/ /m/ "sim"* (point to each letter, then run your finger fast beneath the whole word). *I can say the sound of the letters, /s/ /i/ /m/* (point to each letter) *or I can read the whole word "sim"* (run your finger fast beneath the whole word).

Your turn to read a make-believe word. Read this word the best you can (point to the word "lut"). *Make sure you say any sounds you know.*

CORRECT RESPONSE: If student responds with "lut" or all the sounds, say	INCORRECT RESPONSE: If student does not respond within 3 seconds or responds incorrectly, say
That's right. The sounds are /l/ /u/ /t/ or "lut."	*Remember, you can say the sounds or you can say the whole word. Watch me: The sounds are /l/ /u/ /t/* (point to each letter) *or "lut"* (run your finger fast beneath the whole word). *Let's try again. Read this word the best you can* (point to the word "lut").

Note: Shortened version starts here.

Here are some more make-believe words (point to page the student will read). *Start here* (point to the first word) *and go across the page* (run your finger under the first row). *When I say "Begin," read the words the best you can. Point to each letter and tell me the sound or read the whole word. Read the words the best you can. Put your finger on the first word. Ready, begin.*

Start your stopwatch after saying "Begin."

After one minute, say "Stop," and put a bracket ([) after the last word read.

<u>Discontinue rule</u> – No correct sounds in the first 5 words.

<u>Hesitation rule</u> – 3 seconds – Provide sound or word. Point to next sound or word and say "What sound?" or "What word?"

Oral Reading Fluency

Read the following directions before each passage:

Please read this (point) *out loud. If you get stuck, I will tell you the word so you can keep reading. When I say "Stop," I may ask you to tell me about what you read, so do your best reading. Start here* (point to the first word of the passage)*. Begin.*

Start your stopwatch when the student says the first word of the passage.

After one minute, say *"Stop"* and put a bracket ( ]) after the last word read.

<u>Discontinue rule</u> – No words read correctly in the first row.

<u>Hesitation rule</u> – 3 seconds – Tell the student the word. If necessary, indicate for student to continue with next word.

If student reads fewer than 10 words correctly on the first passage, stop and record that score. Do not give passages #2 and #3 and do not administer Retell. (This applies to the first passage only.)

Retell Fluency

Please tell me all about what you just read. Try to tell me everything you can. Begin. Start your stopwatch.

<u>Discontinue rule</u> – Stop after 5 seconds if the student doesn't say anything after the first prompt, or if student gets off track.

<u>Hesitation rule</u> – 3 seconds – Say, *"Try to tell me everything you can."* Use this prompt only once.

IMPORTANT - Use the same directions for the first, second, and third Retell Fluency measures.

Word Use Fluency

Listen to me use this word: "green." (pause) *"The grass is green." Here is another word: "jump"* (pause) *"I like to jump rope." Your turn to use a word in a sentence.** (pause) *"Rabbit."*

CORRECT RESPONSE If student uses the word correctly, say	INCORRECT RESPONSE: If student gives any other response, say
Very good.	*Listen to me use the word "rabbit."* (pause) *"The rabbit is eating a carrot." Your turn. "Rabbit."*

OK. Here is your first word.

Start your stopwatch after you give the student the first word.

<u>Discontinue rule</u> – None of the first 5 words is used correctly in a phrase, expression, or sentence.

<u>Hesitation rule</u> – 5 seconds – No prompt. Give the next word.

---

* Some versions of DIBELS materials exclude the words "in a sentence" at the end of this sentence in the directions. Use of these words is optional because the measure is not yet normed and a decision has not been made about which version to use. If your school does not use the words, mark out the words on this page.

SUMMARY OF SCORING AND MARKING RULES

Initial Sound Fluency

1. **Scoring**
    *   Correct answers – Record the number of correct answers at the bottom right of the scoring page, just above the formula.
    *   Total time – Record the total time it takes student to give all 16 answers, both correct and incorrect, at the bottom left of the scoring page, just above the formula.
        *   Do this by starting the stopwatch after you finish giving the question and stopping the stopwatch after the student finishes giving the answer.
    *   Calculating DIBELS score – Use the formula at the bottom of the scoring page to determine the DIBELS score, which is recorded on the first page of the Scoring Booklet.

2. **Marking conventions**
    *   Give all 16 questions – Always give every student all 16 questions, unless the student misses the first 5 questions (which is the discontinue rule).
    *   Correct answer – Circle 1.
        Example:
        Which picture begins with /t/?   0
    *   Incorrect answer – Circle 0.
        Example:
        Which picture begins with /t/?   1

Letter Naming Fluency

1. **Scoring**
    *   Count the number of letters correctly named. (Each line has 10 letters, to make counting easy.)

2. **Marking conventions**
    *   Correct responses – No mark.
    *   Incorrect responses – Put a slash (/) through the letter. (Optional: Record what the student said when he/she gives an incorrect answer.)
    *   Omissions – Put a slash (/) through the letter.
    *   Skipped row of letters – Draw a line through the row. (Do not count these letters when scoring because the student did not read them accurately.)
    *   Self-corrections – Write "sc" above the corrected letter.
    *   Indicate last letter read – Put a bracket ( ]) after the final letter.
    *   Exception:
        *   If the student mistakes uppercase *I* (*eye*) for lowercase *l* (*el*), or vice versa, count as correct. Any other mistakes (such as "b" for "d" or "p" for "q") are marked as incorrect responses.

Phoneme Segmentation Fluency

1. **Scoring**
   - Count the number of underlines.
     - Exception: Do not count underlines that are exactly the same, which indicates the student repeated the same segment more than once.
   - This gives you the number of *different* and *correct* segments named.

2. **Marking conventions**
   - Correct responses - Underline each segment of the word the student says.
     - Individual phonemes: /t/ /a/ /s/ /k/ – 4 points
     - Word segments: /t/ /a/ /s/ /k/ – 2 points
     - Overlapping word segments: /t/ /a/ /s/ /k/ – 3 points

   - Incorrect responses – Put a slash through the entire segment. Even if only one part of the segment is incorrect, the student does not get any credit for the segment. The entire segment must be said correctly to get credit. (Optional: Record what the student said when he or she gives an incorrect answer.)
     - /t/ /a/ /s/ /k/   est – 1 point   (Student said /t/ /est/. The entire second segment is incorrect, even though the student got one sound correct when articulating the segment.)

   - Omissions – Do not mark under any parts the student does not attempt.
     - /t/ /a/ /s/ /k/   – 3 points   (Student said /t/ /ă/ /k/. The student did not say the /s/ phoneme.)

     - /t/ /a/ /s/ /k/   g – 1 point   (Student said initial phoneme correctly and misread final phoneme as /g/.)

   - Repeats word – Circle the word. Give no credit.
     - /t/ /a/ /s/ /k/   – 0 points

   - Self-corrections – Write "sc" above the corrected segment.
   - Indicate last word read – Put a bracket ( ]) after the final word given.

Nonsense Word Fluency

1. **Scoring**
   - Count the number of letters underlined that do not have a slash through them.

2. **Marking conventions – student reads word by word**
   - <u>Correct responses</u> – Underline the word:

     – <u>j   u   p</u>   – 3 points

   - <u>Incorrect responses / student reads part of word incorrectly</u> – Underline that entire word and put a slash (/) through the letter(s) read incorrectly. (Optional: Record what the student said when he or she gives an incorrect answer.)

     – <u>j   ǒ̷   p</u>   – 2 points   (Student reads entire word, but read short *o* for middle letter.)

     – <u>j   u̷   ǒb̷</u>   – 1 point   (Student reads "job," reading first letter–sound correspondence correctly and missing the last two letter–sound correspondences.)

     – <u>j   ǒ̷   t</u>   – 2 points   (Student reads "jot," missing only the vowel.)

   - <u>Incorrect responses / student reads entire word incorrectly</u> – Put a slash (/) through the entire word; no need to underline. (Optional: Record what the student said when he or she gives an incorrect answer.)

     – j̷   u̷   p̷ chob   – 0 points   (Student reads "chob.")

3. **Marking conventions – student reads sound by sound or in segments**
   - <u>Correct responses</u> – Underline any segment of the word the student reads correctly.

     – <u>j</u>   <u>u</u>   <u>p</u>   – 3 points   (Student reads sound by sound.)

     – <u>j</u>   <u>u   p</u>   – 3 points   (Student reads first sound, then remaining part of word.)

- Incorrect responses – Put a slash (/) through the letter(s) read incorrectly; no need to underline if entire spoken segment is incorrect. (Optional: Record what the student said when he or she gives an incorrect answer.)

– <u>j</u>   ŏ/   <u>p</u>   – 2 points

(Student reads sound by sound, getting first and last letter–sound correspondences correct, but reading short *o* for middle letter.)

– j̸ ⟋ yŏ/u   <u>p</u>   – 2 points

(Student reads word in two parts, getting first two letter–sound correspondences incorrect by saying /yŏ/ and getting the last one correct.)

- Omissions – Do not underline any part of the word the student does not attempt to read.

– <u>j</u>   u   <u>p</u>   – 2 points

(Student reads sound by sound, omitting middle letter.)

– <u>j</u>   u   b/p̸   – 1 point

(Student reads sound by sound, omitting middle letter and reading incorrect sound for final letter.)

4. **Marking conventions – other**
   - Skipped row of words – Draw a line through the row. (Do not count these words because the student did not read them accurately.)
   - Self-corrections – Write "sc" above the corrected letter or word.
   - Indicate final word or letter read – Put a bracket (**]**) after the final word or letter–sound correspondence attempted.

Oral Reading Fluency

1. **Scoring**
   - Count the number of words correctly read.

2. **Marking conventions**
   - <u>Words read correctly</u> – No mark.
   - <u>Words read incorrectly</u> – Put a slash (/) through the word. (Optional: Record what the student said when he or she gives an incorrect answer.)
   - <u>Omissions</u> – Put a slash (/) through the word.
   - <u>Skipped row</u> – Draw a line through the row. (Do not count these words when scoring because the student did not read them accurately.)
   - <u>Self-corrections</u> – Write "sc" above the corrected word.
   - <u>Indicate final word read</u> – Put a bracket ( ]) after the final word.

Retell Fluency

1. **Scoring**
    - Count the number of words used to retell the passage.
      – To do this:
        ▪ Put your pen or pencil on the 0 in the box to get ready to start.
        ▪ Move your pencil across the numbers as the student talks.
        ▪ Circle the last number your pen or pencil is on when the student stops.
        ▪ Record the number at the top left side of the box.

Retell: 22

| 1 2 3 4 5 6 7 8 9 10 11 12 13 14 15 16 17 18 19 20 21 ㉒ 23 24 25 26 27 28 29 30 |
| 32 33 34 35 36 37 38 39 40 41 42 43 44 45 46 47 48 49 50 51 52 53 54 55 56 57 58 |

2. **These words are counted:**
    - Sentences, phrases, and single words that relate to the passage.
    - Minor repetitions, redundancies, and irrelevancies.
      – The crucial judgment is whether the student has gotten off track and is on another story or topic.
    - Minor inaccuracies.
      – Events can be out of order.
      – Tenses can change ("is" to "was").
      – Person can change ("I" to "they").
      – Similar words can be used ("like" instead of "love" / "sister" instead of "brother" / "mommy" instead of "parents").

3. **These words are not counted:**
    - Stories or irrelevancies that are off track.
    - Songs or recitations.
    - Obvious repetition of phrases.
    - Obviously repeating what has been said previously.
    - Filler words and sounds such as "you know" or "um."
    - Repetition of words ("The mom . . . the mom went to the store." = 6 words).

Word Use Fluency

1. **Scoring**
   - Count the number of words correctly used in a:
     - Sentence
     - Phrase
     - Definition
     - Utterance (one word).
   - To do this:
     - Put your pen or pencil on the 0 by the word to get ready to start.
     - Move your pencil across the numbers as the student talks.
     - Circle the last number your pen or pencil is on when the student stops.
     - Circle C if the answer is correct.
     - Circle I if the answer is incorrect.
   - Correct answer: ("The ant bit me.")

   ant      4 ©I

   - Incorrect answer: ("Ants are furry pink animals that bark.")

   ant   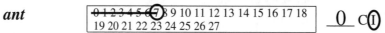   0 c①

2. **These words are counted:**
   - <u>Sentences</u> that correctly use the word, even if it isn't clear the student knows the meaning:
     - If the word is *rabbit*, "I like the rabbit." would count as 4 words.
     - If the word is *rabbit*, "animal" would count as 1 word.
   - <u>Phrases</u> that correctly use or define the word:
     - If the word is *rabbit*, "big, hopping rabbit" or "soft and furry" would each count as 3 words.
   - <u>Single words</u> that correctly define or relate to the word:
     - If the word is *rabbit*, "animal" would count as 1 word.
   - <u>Homophones</u>:
     - If the word is *ant*, "My Aunt Patty is pretty" would count as 5 words.
   - <u>Changes in word tense, number, or part of speech</u> are counted as correct:
     - If the word is *space*, correct uses include:
       - I want to go to outer space. (7 points)
       - Mom found two empty parking spaces. (6 points)
       - I spaced out when the teacher called on me. (9 points)
       - The room is spacious. (4 points)

3. **These words are not counted:**
   - <u>Incorrect usage</u> of any type.
   - <u>Repeating the target word</u>.
   - <u>Repetition of any word or part of the sentence</u>.
   - <u>Fillers</u> such as "um" or "you know."

Observer's Checklist
Initial Sound Fluency (ISF)

Check one box for each category. Provide comments when "no" box is checked.

CLIPBOARD

Held <u>clipboard</u> so child could not see scoring.

❑ yes   ❑ no — comments:

DIRECTIONS

Gave <u>directions</u> exactly as written.

❑ yes   ❑ no — comments:

This is mouse, flowers, pillow, letters (point to each picture while saying its name). *Mouse* (point to mouse) *begins with the sound /m/. Listen, /m/, mouse. Which one begins with the sounds /fl/?*

CORRECT RESPONSE If student points to or says flowers, you say	INCORRECT RESPONSE: If student gives any other response, you say
Good. Flowers begins with the sounds /fl/.	*Flowers* (point to flowers) *begins with the sounds /fl/. Listen, /fl/, flowers. Let's try it again. Which one begins with the sounds /fl/?*

Pillow (point to pillow) *begins with the sound /p/. Listen, /p/, pillow. What sound does letters* (point to letters) *begin with?*

CORRECT RESPONSE If student says /l/, you say	INCORRECT RESPONSE: If student gives any other response, you say
Good. Letters begins with the sound /l/.	*Letters* (point to letters) *begins with the sound /l/. Listen, /l/, letters. Let's try it again. What sound does letters* (point to letters) *begin with?*

Here are some more pictures. Listen carefully to the words.

TIMING

Started timer immediately after asking each question.

❑ yes   ❑ no — comments:

Stopped timer immediately after student answered each question.

❑ yes   ❑ no — comments:

ASKS QUESTIONS EXACTLY AS WRITTEN

Asked questions exactly as written in Scoring Booklet.

❑ yes   ❑ no — comments:

DISCONTINUE RULE

Stopped assessment if student did not get any of the first 5 answers correct and recorded score of 0 (zero).

❑ not applicable   ❑ yes   ❑ no — comments:

SCORING

Asked all 16 questions, unless discontinue rule was used.

❑ yes   ❑ no — comments:

Circled 1 for correct answers and 0 for incorrect answers.

❑ not applicable   ❑ yes   ❑ no — comments:

Accurately recorded time.

❑ yes   ❑ no — comments:

Accurately added correct answers.

❑ yes   ❑ no — comments:

Accurately used formula to calculate answer.

❑ yes   ❑ no — comments:

HESITATION RULE AND PROMPT

Gave next question after student did not respond or struggled with response for 5 seconds.

❑ not applicable   ❑ yes   ❑ no — comments:

Gave additional prompt once if student gave letter name instead of sound: *"Remember to point to or tell me a word that begins with the sound (name stimulus sound)."*

❑ not applicable   ❑ yes   ❑ no — comments:

SHADOW SCORING

Number of correct answers is within 1 point of total recorded by other examiner.

❑ not applicable   ❑ yes   ❑ no — comments:

Time recorded is within 2 seconds of other examiner.

❑ not applicable   ❑ yes   ❑ no — comments:

CHECK ANY OF THESE FREQUENTLY OBSERVED MISTAKES MADE BY EXAMINER:

❑ Named letter instead of sound when reading questions.

❑ Inserted the words "a," "the," or "and" when reading questions.

❑ Cleared timer before recording time in student booklet

Observer's Checklist
Letter Naming Fluency (LNF)

Check one box for each category. Provide comments when "no" box is checked.

CLIPBOARD
Held <u>clipboard</u> so child could not see scoring.

❑ yes   ❑ no — comments:

DIRECTIONS
Gave <u>directions</u> exactly as written.

❑ yes   ❑ no — comments:

Here are some letters (point to the page with the letters).
*Tell me the names of as many letters as you can.
When I say "Begin," start here* (point to first letter),
and go across the page (underline the first row with your
finger). *Point to each letter and tell me the name of
that letter. If you come to a letter you don't know,
I'll tell it to you. Put your finger on the first letter.
Ready, begin.*

TIMING
Started timer after saying "Begin."

❑ yes   ❑ no — comments:

Stopped timer after 1 minute (or applied discontinue rule below).

❑ yes   ❑ no — comments:

Used bracket ( ]) after final letter attempted.

❑ yes   ❑ no — comments:

DISCONTINUE RULE
Stopped assessment if student did not read any letters in the first
line correctly.

❑ not applicable   ❑ yes   ❑ no — comments:

SCORING
Put a slash through any incorrectly named letters.

❑ not applicable   ❑ yes   ❑ no — comments:

Made no mark for letters named correctly.

❑ yes   ❑ no — comments:

Allowed student to name lowercase L as I and vice-versa.

❑ not applicable   ❑ yes   ❑ no — comments:

HESITATION RULE AND PROMPT
Gave hesitation prompt after student did not respond or struggled
with response for 3 seconds.

❑ not applicable   ❑ yes   ❑ no — comments:

Used correct hesitation prompt: Pointed to next letter and said,
"What letter?"

❑ not applicable   ❑ yes   ❑ no — comments:

ADDITIONAL PROMPT IF STUDENT GIVES SOUNDS INSTEAD OF LETTER NAMES:
Gave additional prompt **once** if student gave sound instead of letter
name: **"Remember to tell me the letter name, not
the sound it makes."**

❑ not applicable   ❑ yes   ❑ no — comments:

SHADOW SCORING
Score is within 2 points of other examiner.

❑ not applicable   ❑ yes   ❑ no — comments:

Observer's Checklist
Nonsense Word Fluency (NWF)

Check one box for each category. Provide comments when "no" box is checked.

CLIPBOARD
Held <u>clipboard</u> so child could not see scoring.

❏ yes   ❏ no — comments:

DIRECTIONS
Gave <u>directions</u> exactly as written.

❏ yes   ❏ no — comments:

Look at this word (point to first word on practice page). *It's a make-believe word. Watch me read the word: /s/ /i/ /m/ "sim"* (point to each letter, then run your finger fast beneath the whole word). *I can say the sound of the letters, /s/ /i/ /m/* (point to each letter) *or I can read the whole word "sim"* (run your finger fast beneath the whole word).

Your turn to read a make-believe word. Read this word the best you can (point to the word "lut"). *Make sure you say any sounds you know.*

CORRECT RESPONSE If student responds with "lut" or all the sounds, say	INCORRECT RESPONSE: If student does not respond within 3 seconds or responds incorrectly, say
That's right. The sounds are /l/ /u/ /t/ or "lut."	*Remember, you can say the sounds or you can say the whole word. Watch me: The sounds are /l/ /u/ /t/* (point to each letter) *or "lut"* (run your finger fast beneath the whole word). *Let's try again. Read this word the best you can* (point to the word "lut").

Here are some more make-believe words (point to page the student will read). *Start here* (point to the first word) *and go across the page* (run your finger under the first row). *When I say "Begin," read the words the best you can. Point to each letter and tell me the sound or read the whole word. Read the words the best you can. Put your finger on the first word. Ready, begin.*

TIMING
Started timer after saying "Begin."

❏ yes   ❏ no — comments:

Stopped timer after 1 minute (or applied discontinue rule below).

❏ yes   ❏ no — comments:

Used bracket (**]**) after last letter or word attempted.

❏ yes   ❏ no — comments:

DISCONTINUE RULE
Stopped assessment if student did not read any of the sounds correctly in the first 5 words.

❏ not applicable   ❏ yes   ❏ no — comments:

SCORING
Put a slash through incorrectly read letters and words.

❏ yes   ❏ no — comments:

Underlined correctly read letters and words.

❏ yes   ❏ no — comments:

Made no mark on letters not attempted.

❏ yes   ❏ no — comments:

Accurately counted underlines to obtain score.

❏ yes   ❏ no — comments:

HESITATION RULE AND PROMPT
After student hesitated or struggled for 3 seconds, pointed to next sound or word and said, **"What sound?"** or **"What word?"**

❏ not applicable   ❏ yes   ❏ no — comments:

SHADOW SCORING
Scored within 2 points of other examiner.

❏ not applicable   ❏ yes   ❏ no — comments:

273

Observer's Checklist
Oral Reading Fluency (ORF)

Check one box for each category. Provide comments when "no" box is checked.

CLIPBOARD

Held <u>clipboard</u> so child could not see scoring.

❑ yes   ❑ no — comments:

DIRECTIONS

Gave <u>directions</u> exactly as written.

❑ yes   ❑ no — comments:

Please read this (point) *out loud. If you get stuck, I will tell you the word so you can keep reading. When I say "Stop," I may ask you to tell me about what you read, so do your best reading. Start here* (point to the first word of the passage). *Begin.*

TIMING

Started timer after student said first word of the passage.

❑ yes   ❑ no — comments:

Stopped timer after 1 minute (or applied discontinue rule below).

❑ yes   ❑ no — comments:

Used bracket (**]**) after last word read.

❑ yes   ❑ no — comments:

DISCONTINUE RULE

Stopped assessment if student did not read any words in the first line correctly.

❑ not applicable   ❑ yes   ❑ no — comments:

SCORING

Put a slash through any incorrectly read words.

❑ not applicable   ❑ yes   ❑ no — comments:

Did not mark correctly read words.

❑ yes   ❑ no — comments:

HESITATION RULE AND PROMPT

If student hesitated or struggled for 3 seconds, told the student the word. If necessary, indicated for student to continue with next word. (For example, pointed to the next word or said, **"Keep reading,"** or both.)

❑ not applicable   ❑ yes   ❑ no — comments:

Did not correct student when student read a word incorrectly.

❑ yes   ❑ no — comments:

FEWER THAN 10 WORDS READ

If student read fewer than 10 words in the first passage, scored that passage; did not give Retell Fluency and did not ask student to read more passages.

❑ not applicable   ❑ yes   ❑ no — comments:

If student read 10 or fewer words in the second or third passage, did not give Retell Fluency.

❑ not applicable   ❑ yes   ❑ no — comments:

SHADOW SCORING

Scored within 2 points of other examiner.

❑ not applicable   ❑ yes   ❑ no — comments:

Observer's Checklist
Phoneme Segmentation Fluency (PSF)

Check one box for each category. Provide comments when "no" box is checked.

CLIPBOARD

Held <u>clipboard</u> so child could not see scoring.

❏ yes   ❏ no — comments:

DIRECTIONS

Gave <u>directions</u> exactly as written.

❏ yes   ❏ no — comments:

I am going to say a word. After I say it, you tell me all the sounds in the word. So, if I say "sam," you would say /s/ /a/ /m/. Let's try one (one-second pause). *Tell me the sounds in "mop."*

CORRECT RESPONSE: If student says /m/ /o/ /p/, you say	INCORRECT RESPONSE: If student gives any other response, you say
Very good, the sounds in "mop" are /m/ /o/ /p/.	***The sounds in "mop" are /m/ /o/ /p/. Your turn. Tell me the sounds in "mop."***

OK. Here is your first word.

TIMING

Started timer immediately after giving first word.

❏ yes   ❏ no — comments:

Stopped timer after 1 minute (or applied discontinue rule below).

❏ yes   ❏ no — comments:

Put bracket (❳) after last segment attempted.

❏ yes   ❏ no — comments:

DISCONTINUE RULE

Stopped assessment if student did not get any correct sound segments in the first 5 words and recorded score of 0 (zero).

❏ not applicable   ❏ yes   ❏ no — comments:

SCORING

Read words left to right (not down the columns).

❏ yes   ❏ no — comments:

Underlined entire sound segment student named correctly.

❏ not applicable   ❏ yes   ❏ no — comments:

Put slash through entire sound segment student named incorrectly.

❏ not applicable   ❏ yes   ❏ no — comments:

Made no mark on sound segments not attempted.

❏ not applicable   ❏ yes   ❏ no — comments:

Circled repeated words.

❏ not applicable   ❏ yes   ❏ no — comments:

Accurately counted underlines to obtain score.

❏ yes   ❏ no — comments:

HESITATION RULE AND PROMPT

Gave next word if student did not respond after 3 seconds.

❏ not applicable   ❏ yes   ❏ no — comments:

SHADOW SCORING

Scored within 2 points of other examiner.

❏ not applicable   ❏ yes   ❏ no — comments:

Observer's Checklist
Retell Fluency (Retell)

Check one box for each category. Provide comments when "no" box is checked.

CLIPBOARD

Held <u>clipboard</u> so child could not see scoring.

❑ yes   ❑ no — comments:

SCORING

Correctly ran pencil or pen through numbers to count words as student responded.

❑ yes   ❑ no — comments:

Circled last number to indicate number of words in score.

❑ yes   ❑ no — comments:

DIRECTIONS

Gave <u>directions</u> exactly as written.

❑ yes   ❑ no — comments:

Please tell me all about what you just read. Try to tell me everything you can. Begin.

Counted only words related to the story.

❑ yes   ❑ no — comments:

TIMING

Started timer after saying "Begin."

❑ yes   ❑ no — comments:

HESITATION RULE AND PROMPT

Gave hesitation prompt once after student hesitated 3 seconds: "Try to tell me everything you can."

❑ yes   ❑ no — comments:

Stopped timer after 1 minute or after hesitation or discontinue prompt.

❑ yes   ❑ no — comments:

SHADOW SCORING

Scored within 2 points of other examiner:

❑ not applicable   ❑ yes   ❑ no — comments:

DISCONTINUE RULE

Stopped assessment after student heard hesitation prompt once and hesitated again for 5 seconds or after student was off track for 5 seconds. (Stopped immediately after student was off track 5 seconds and did not give a hesitation prompt.)

❑ yes   ❑ no — comments:

Observer's Checklist
Word Use Fluency (WUF)

Check one box for each category. Provide comments when "no" box is checked.

CLIPBOARD

Held <u>clipboard</u> so child could not see scoring.

❑ yes   ❑ no — comments:

DISCONTINUE RULE

Stopped assessment if student had no correct responses for the first 5 words.

❑ not applicable   ❑ yes   ❑ no — comments:

DIRECTIONS

Gave <u>directions</u> exactly as written.

❑ yes   ❑ no — comments:

HESITATION RULE AND PROMPT

Gave next word after student hesitated 5 seconds.

❑ not applicable   ❑ yes   ❑ no — comments:

Listen to me use this word: "green." (pause) *"The grass is green." Here is another word: "jump"* (pause) *"I like to jump rope." Your turn to use a word in a sentence.* (pause) *"Rabbit."*

CORRECT RESPONSE If student uses the word correctly, say	INCORRECT RESPONSE: If student gives any other response, say
Very good.	*Listen to me use the word "rabbit."* (pause) *"The rabbit is eating a carrot." Your turn. "Rabbit."*

OK. Here is your first word.

SCORING

Correctly ran pencil or pen through numbers to count words as student responded.

❑ yes   ❑ no — comments:

Circled last number to indicate number of words in response.

❑ yes   ❑ no — comments:

Appropriately categorized responses as correct or incorrect by circling C for each correct response and I for each incorrect response.

❑ yes   ❑ no — comments:

TIMING

Started after giving the first word.

❑ yes   ❑ no — comments:

Stopped after 1 minute (or applied discontinue rule below).

❑ yes   ❑ no — comments:

Pace was fast enough so that time was not wasted while examiner scored each response.

❑ yes   ❑ no — comments:

SHADOW SCORING

Scored within 2 points of other examiner.

❑ yes   ❑ no — comments:

PSF PROGRESS MONITORING CHART

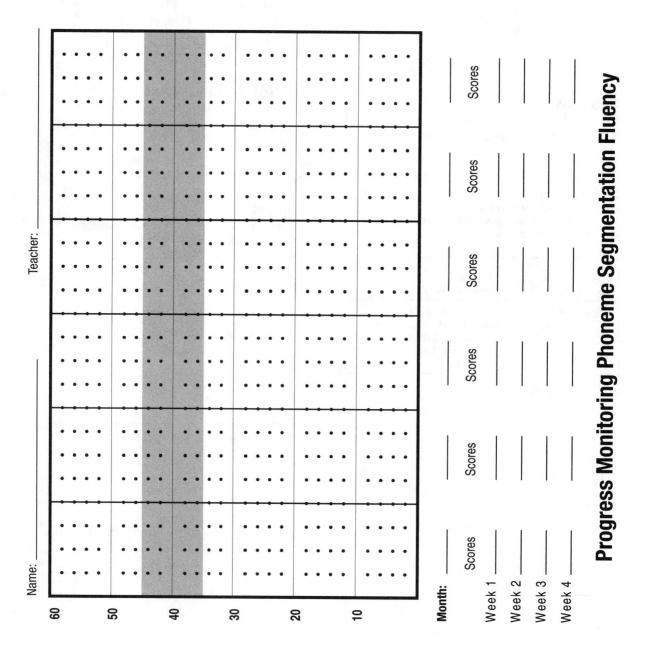

Name:

Teacher:

Month: _____

	Scores
Week 1	_____
Week 2	_____
Week 3	_____
Week 4	_____

Progress Monitoring Phoneme Segmentation Fluency

NWF PROGRESS MONITORING CHART

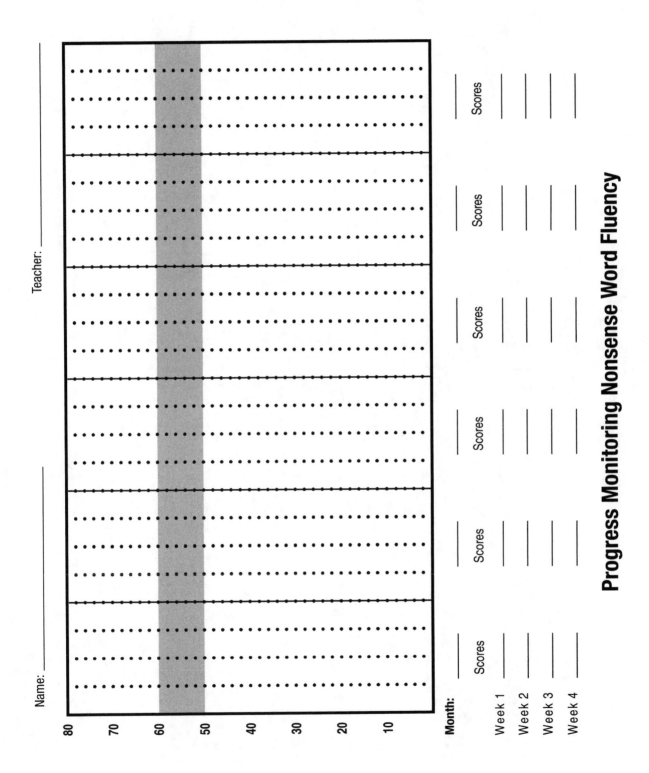

Glossary

Accommodations—Special procedures or steps taken outside normal educational procedures for students who are not likely to succeed without the special steps or procedures. One of the most common accommodations in schools is to provide extra time for tests and assignments. DIBELS has its own approved list of accommodations, and extra time is not on that list because *extra time is never granted for DIBELS assessments.*

Alphabetic Principle—The concept that in an alphabetic language letters represent sounds. Some definitions also include the concept that sounds are combined to form words.

Alternate Forms—Another term for certain progress monitoring materials. Progress monitoring materials can be used as alternate forms for giving the benchmark assessment or when a retest is needed. An important feature of alternate forms is that they are equivalent in difficulty and interchangeable with one another and with benchmark assessment forms.

Approved Accommodations—DIBELS' list of accommodations that are approved for use. No other accommodations are allowed.

Articulation Differences—Articulation differences occur when a student ordinarily articulates a speech sound differently from what is expected. For example, younger students often pronounce the /r/ phonemes as a /w/ or /s/ as a /th/. Some students have speech impediments that cause articulation differences. DIBELS does not penalize students for these differences when scoring any measure.

Benchmark Assessment—A specific set of DIBELS assessments given three times a year to screen students for reading difficulties. The specific set of DIBELS assessments is not the same for each benchmark assessment period.

Benchmark Score—The lowest score for any measure that indicates a student has achieved satisfactory proficiency in the skill being measured at the time the benchmark assessment is administered.

Big Ideas in Beginning Reading—The University of Oregon's Web site at reading.uoregon.edu defines the Big Ideas in Beginning Reading as phonemic awareness, phonics, fluency with text, vocabulary, and comprehension. These are the same areas identified by the National Reading Panel as being esssential components of reading instruction.

Comprehension—The ability to understand what has been read. Comprehension is one of the five essential components of reading instruction identified in the *Report of the National Reading Panel*. The National Reading Panel concluded that a teacher's ability to demonstrate and teach an intentional, thoughtful interaction between the reader and the text improves comprehension (National Institute of Child Health and Human Development, 2000).

Continuant—A speech sound (phoneme) that can be spoken uninterruptedly until the speaker runs out of breath. Continuant phonemes are all of the vowels and /f/, /m/, /n/, /r/, /s/, /v/, /z/, /sh/, /zh/, and /ng/. (The phonemes /y/, /w/, and /h/ are considered glides because they "glide" into the vowel that follows them. Linguists who do not classify these phonemes as glides differ as to whether these should be categorized as stop or continuant phonemes.)

Criterion-Referenced Assessment—A formal assessment that establishes standards of performance for students that indicate the student is making adequate progress toward developing a skill. These are different from norm-referenced assessments, which are percentile rankings used to establish a student's score in relationship to the performance of other students. DIBELS provides both norm-referenced and criterion-referenced information. For DIBELS, the research-based criterion-referenced information is more important than percentile rankings.

Cut Point—Score that delineates a DIBELS risk level for a measure. Cut points are shown on the Benchmark Scores Table in the Appendix.

CVC—A consonant–vowel–consonant letter pattern in a word. A CVC word has a consonant, a vowel, and a consonant, in that order. Examples of CVC words are *bat*, *yes*, *him*, *cop*, and *run*.

Data—When the word *data* is used with regard to DIBELS, it refers to student scores.

Dialectical Differences—Dialectical differences occur when students have a regional or other type of accent and do not pronounce words in accordance with standard English. For example, in Boston, many students omit the /r/ phoneme from the words *car* and *park* and say *"cah"* or *"pahk."* In some southern states, students pronounce the word *oil* as *all*. Dialectical differences are not penalized in any DIBELS measure.

DIBELS—Dynamic Indicators of Basic Early Literacy Skills. Screening and progress monitoring assessments for literacy skills in kindergarten through Grade 6.

DIBELS Web Site—A Web site (http://dibels.uoregon.edu) maintained at the University of Oregon that offers DIBELS materials for downloading, DIBELS benchmark scores and risk levels, technical reports about DIBELS, and other DIBELS-related information.

Five Essential Components of Reading Instruction—The National Reading Panel concluded that scientific research shows the most effective reading instruction includes explicit and systematic instruction in five areas: phonemic awareness, phonics, fluency, vocabulary, and comprehension (National Institute of Child Health and Human Development, 2000).

Fluency—One of the five essential components of reading instruction, according to the National Reading Panel. The National Reading Panel concluded that guided oral reading is an effective method for improving fluency. The National Reading Panel found no evidence that independent silent reading improves achievement in any area of reading, including fluency (National Institute of Child Health and Human Development, 2000). Fluency is measured as a reading rate, most often as the words read correctly in one minute. Oral Reading Fluency is measured by DIBELS. Some assessments measure silent reading fluency.

Formal Assessment—Assessments that have been given to a large number of people in order to obtain a range of expected scores (the norm). Formal assessments use standardized directions that must be given the same way every time, and they use standardized scoring procedures and conventions. Formal assessments can be reliably used for comparison of scores.

Grapheme—A letter or letters that represents a phoneme in a word. The word *dough* has two phonemes, /d/ and /ō/, and two graphemes, *d* and *ough*.

High-Stakes Assessment—Any assessment given that determines future educational decisions about students or is the basis for decisions about school funding, accreditation, etc.

Informal Assessment—Any procedure that gathers information for planning and delivering instruction. Informal assessment instruments do not have standardized directions, and the scores are not "normed." Informal assessments are used for gathering information but cannot be reliably used to compare scores.

Instructional Recommendations—Every student in the DIBELS Data System receives an instructional recommendation based on the combined DIBELS scores for a benchmark period. The instructional recommendations are Benchmark support for students who need no instruction beyond the core reading program, Strategic support for students who need additional support in targeted areas, and Intensive support for students who need immediate intensive intervention.

National Reading Panel—Fourteen educators and educational scholars who assessed the status of research-based knowledge about the effectiveness of various approaches to teaching reading. They published the results of their meta-analysis in the *Report of the National Reading Panel* in 2000, which can be found at http://www.nationalreadingpanel.org (National Institute of Child Health and Human Development, 2000).

No Child Left Behind Act—An act of law signed on January 8, 2002, by President Bush that is designed to ensure that each child in America is able to meet the high learning standards of the state in which he or she lives. Goals related to reading are: (1) By 2013–2014, all students will attain proficiency or better in reading and mathematics. (2) All limited-English students will become proficient in English. (3) By 2005–2006, all students will be taught by highly qualified teachers. For more information, go to the No Child Left Behind Web site: http://www.ed.gov/nclb.

Nonsense Word—A word that does not have meaning in the English language. Nonsense words are called "make-believe words" in the Nonsense Word Fluency directions. All DIBELS nonsense words are spelled with two or three letters and each letter represents its most frequently occurring sound. All DIBELS nonsense words have the VC or CVC pattern, the vowels are pronounced with short vowel sounds, and words with the letters *c* and *g* use the hard *c* (/ k /) and hard *g* (/g /) sounds.

Norm-Referenced Assessment—A formal assessment used to establish a student's score in relationship to those of other students. These assessments are different from criterion-referenced assessments, which use data to establish standards of performance for students. DIBELS provides both norm-referenced and criterion-referenced information. For DIBELS, the research-based criterion-referenced information is the most important.

Onset—The part of a syllable before the vowel. In the word *shrimp*, *shr* is the onset. Not all words have onsets. For example, the words *I*, *oak*, and *ice* do not have onsets.

Outcome-Based Assessment—An assessment used to evaluate the overall effectiveness of an educational program or to determine whether instruction for a student has been successful.

Phoneme—The smallest unit of sound in a word. Phonemes are combined in a language system to make words.

Phonemic Awareness—The conscious awareness that words are made of phonemes that can be segmented, blended, and manipulated. The National Reading Panel found that instruction in "manipulating phonemes in words was highly effective under a variety of teaching conditions with a variety of learners across a variety of grade and age levels and that teaching phonemic awareness to children significantly improves their reading more than instruction that lacks any attention to PA" (National Institute of Child Health and Human Development, 2000).

Phonics—Study of the relationship between sounds and letters. Also, the system of instruction that teaches the relationship between sounds and letters. The National Reading Panel concluded that "systematic phonics instruction produces significant benefits for students in kindergarten through sixth grade and for students having difficulty learning to read" (National Institute of Child Health and Human Development, 2000).

Phonological Awareness—Conscious awareness of all levels of the speech sound system, including pronouncing words, remembering names and lists, identifying syllables, blending and segmenting syllables into words, creating rhymes, detecting syllable stress, and blending and segmenting phonemes into words.

Probe—The materials used to show to the student or a list of words to use when administering a measure. Specifically, probes include pictures and questions for ISF, a page of letters for LNF, a list of words to be given orally for PSF, a page of nonsense words for NWF, a page with a written passage for ORF, a question for RTF, and a list of words to be given orally for WUF.

Progress Monitoring Assessment—DIBELS progress monitoring assessments provide information about the child's progress in intervention. Progress monitoring assessments are given for one measure only, as opposed to benchmark assessments, which are screening assessments and include several measures. (Note: ORF progress monitoring requires the student to read only 1 passage, as opposed to benchmark assessment which requires 3 passages.)

Reading First—The No Child Left Behind Act, which became law on January 8, 2002, established Reading First as a new, high-quality evidence-based program for students in the United States. Under Reading First, funds are dedicated to help states and local school districts eliminate the reading deficit by establishing high-quality, comprehensive reading instruction in kindergarten through Grade 3. Reading First is designed to ensure that more children receive effective reading instruction in the early grades. Schools receiving Reading First funds are required to use scientifically based reading programs, to provide research-based professional development for teachers, and to ensure accountability through ongoing, valid, and reliable screening, diagnostic, and classroom-based assessment. For more information, go to the Reading First Web site: http://www.ed.gov/programs/readingfirst.

Rime—The part of a syllable that includes the vowel and everything after it. In the word *shrimp, imp* is the rime. A rime may include only the vowel. For example, in the word *toe,* the rime is *oe.*

Scoring Booklet—The booklet in which the DIBELS examiner marks student responses and records the scores for each measure.

Screening Assessment—An assessment given to provide information about an individual student's skills with regard to a particular subject. DIBELS benchmark assessments are screening assessments.

Shadow Scoring—This occurs when two examiners score the same student. One examiner gives the directions and both examiners score, allowing them to compare scores. This is an especially effective way for new examiners to ensure the integrity of their scores.

Short Vowel—A term used by educators to denote a vowel sound that is spoken with lax vocal cords. The short vowel sounds used in DIBELS Nonsense Word Fluency assessments are /ă/ as in *apple*, /ĕ/ as in *echo*, /ĭ/ as in *itch*, /ŏ/ as in *opera*, and /ŭ/ as in *up*.

Sopris West—A publishing company that sells DIBELS print materials, including this manual, and offers DIBELS scoring and administration training. Sopris West also publishes many other educational materials.

Sound Segment—A part of a syllable that is not the complete word. A sound segment can be a phoneme or a part of the syllable that is not the whole syllable. In Phoneme Segmentation Fluency, a student gets a point for each sound segment that the student names correctly. All the sounds in a sound segment must be accurate in order for the student to get credit.

Standardized Assessment—Also called a formal assessment. Standardized assessments have been given to a large number of people in order to obtain a range of expected scores (the norm). They have standardized directions that must be given the same way every time, as well as standardized scoring procedures and conventions.

Stop—Consonant speech sound that is articulated with a complete obstruction of the air stream creating the sound. Stop phonemes are /p/, /b/, /t/, /d/, /ch/, /j/, /k/, and /g/. (The phonemes /y/, /w/, and /h/ are considered glides because they "glide" into the vowel that follows them. Linguists who do not classify these phonemes as glides differ as to whether these should be categorized as stop or continuant phonemes.)

Strategic Support—The label given by the DIBELS Data System to an instructional recommendation for students who need additional support in targeted areas. These students are in the group that has an approximately 50–50 chance of achieving the next benchmark score without some intervention.

Student Materials—The booklets that contain the pictures, letters, words, or stories that students look at when responding to ISF, LNF, NWF, and ORF measures for DIBELS. Student Materials for benchmark assessments contain the pages for all measures that are used for every benchmark assessment in one year. Student Materials for progress monitoring have pages only for one measure. (There are no Student Materials for PSF, WUF, and RTF.)

Summary of Scores Page—The first page in a Benchmark Assessment Student Booklet. The benchmark assessment scores for each measure are recorded on this page.

Syntax—The rule system governing sentence formation. Also, the study of sentence structure.

VC—Vowel–consonant letter pattern in a word. A VC word has one vowel followed by one consonant. Examples of VC words are *on*, *at*, *it*, and *up*.

Vocabulary—One of the five essential components of reading, according to the National Reading Panel. The National Reading Panel found many ways to effectively improve a student's vocabulary (National Institute of Child Health and Human Development, 2000).

Wireless Generation, Inc.—The company that developed and sells *mCLASS: DIBELS* software, which is used to administer and score DIBELS with a handheld computer. Wireless Generation also maintains the database of DIBELS scores and the Web site used to access reports and other information related to DIBELS data. The Web site address is http://www.wirelessgeneration.com.

References

Adams, M. J. (1990). *Beginning to read: Thinking and learning about print.* Cambridge, MA: MIT Press.

Barger, J. (2003). *Comparing the DIBELS oral reading fluency indicator and the North Carolina end of grade level reading assessment* (Technical Report). Ashville, NC: North Carolina Teacher Academy.

Buck, J., & Torgesen, J. (2003). *The relationship between performance on a measure of oral reading fluency and performance on the Florida Comprehensive Assessment Test.* Tallahassee, FL: Florida Center for Reading Research.

Deno, S. L., Mirkin, P. K., & Chiang, B. (1982). Identifying a valid measure of reading. *Exceptional Children, 49,* 36–45.

Ehri, L. C., & Sweet, J. (1991) Fingerpoint-reading of memorized text: What enables beginners to process the print? *Reading Research Quarterly, 26,* 442–462.

Fuchs, L. S., Fuchs, D., Hamlett, C. L., Walz, L. E., Germann, G. (1993). Formative evaluation of academic progress: How much can we expect? *School Psychology Review, 22,* 27–48.

Gillon, G. T. (2004). *Phonological awareness: From research to practice.* New York: Guilford Press.

Good, R. H., Gruba, J., & Kaminski, R. A. (2001). Best practices in using dynamic indicators of basic early literacy skills (DIBELS) in an outcomes-driven model. In A. Thomas & J. Grimes (Eds.), *Best practices in school psychology IV* (pp. 679–700). Washington, DC: National Association of School Psychologists.

Good, R. H., & Kaminski, R. A. (2002). *DIBELS oral reading fluency passages for first through third grades* (Technical Report No. 10). Eugene: University of Oregon Press.

Good, R. H., & Kaminski, R. A. (2003). *DIBELS administration and scoring guide.* Longmont, CO: Sopris West Educational Services.

Good, R. H., Simmons, D. C., & Kame'enui, E. J. (2001). The importance and decision-making utility of a continuum of fluency-based indicators of foundational reading skills for third grade high stakes outcomes. *Scientific Studies of Reading, 5,* 257–288.

Good, R. H., Simmons, D. S., Kame'enui, E. J., Kaminski, R. A., & Wallin, J. (2002). *Summary of decision rules for intensive, strategic, and benchmark instructional recommendations in kindergarten through third grade* (Technical Report No. 11). Eugene: University of Oregon Press.

Hall, S. (2006). *I've DIBEL'd, now what?: Designing interventions with DIBELS data.* Longmont, CO: Sopris West Educational Services.

Harn, B. (2000). Approaches and considerations of collecting schoolwide early literacy and reading performance data. Available from http://dibels.uoregon.edu/logistics/data_collection.pdf

Hasbrouck, J. E., & Tindal, G. (1992, Spring). Curriculum-based oral reading fluency norms in grades 2 through 5. *Teaching Exceptional Children*, 41–44.

Henry, M. K. (2003). *Unlocking literacy: Effective decoding and spelling instruction.* Baltimore: Paul H. Brookes.

Johns, J. L. (2001). *Basic reading inventory.* Dubuque, IA: Kendall/Hunt.

Leslie, L., & Caldwell, J. (2001). *Qualitative reading inventory—3.* New York: Longman.

National Institute of Child Health and Human Development. (2000). *Report of the National Reading Panel. Teaching children to read: An evidence-based assessment of the scientific research literature on reading and its implications for reading instruction* (NIH Publication No. 00-4769). Washington, DC: U.S. Government Printing Office.

Shaw, R., & Shaw, D. (2002). *DIBELS oral reading fluency-based indicators of third grade reading skills for Colorado state assessment program (CSAP).* (Technical Report). Eugene: University of Oregon Press.

Shaywitz, S. (2003). *Overcoming dyslexia: A new and complete science-based program for reading problems at any level.* New York: Alfred A. Knopf.

Torgesen, J. K., & Bryant, B. R. (2004). *Test of phonological awareness* (2nd ed. +). Austin, TX: Pro-Ed.

United States Department of Education. (2002). *No child left behind* (Title I: Paraprofessionals draft non-regulatory guidance, Part B: Student reading skills, Subpart 1: Reading first). (Electronic version). Washington, DC: U.S. Government Printing Office.

University of Texas Center for Reading and Language Arts (2003). *Three-tier reading model: Reducing reading difficulties for kindergarten through third grade students.* Austin: Texas Education Agency.

Wagner, R. K., & Torgesen, J. K. (1999). *Comprehensive test of phonological processing.* Austin, TX: Pro-Ed.

Wiederholt, J. L., & Bryant, B. R. (2001). *Gray oral reading tests* (4th ed.). Austin, TX: Pro-Ed.

Wolf, M. (1991). Naming speed and reading: The contribution of the cognitive neurosciences. *Reading Research Quarterly, 26,* 123–141.

Wolf, M. (2001). *Dyslexia, fluency, and the brain.* Timonium, MD: York Press.

Wolf, M., & Bowers, P. (1999). The "double-deficit hypothesis" for the developmental dyslexias. *Journal of Educational Psychology, 91,* 1–24.

Woodcock, R. W., McGrew, K. S., & Mather, N. (2001). *Woodcock-Johnson psycho-educational battery* (3rd ed.). Itasca, IL: Riverside.

Zeno, S. (1995). The *educator's word frequency guide.* Brewster, NY: Touchstone Applied Science Associates.